PHILIP'S

LONDON

ARCHITECTURE · HISTORY · ART

PHILIP'S

LONDON

ARCHITECTURE · HISTORY · ART

RICHARD TRENCH

PHOTOGRAPHY BY JOHN HESELTINE

GEORGE
PHILIP

TITLE PAGE Wren's dome of St Paul's Cathedral is never overwhelmed by the high-rise buildings which surround it.

Text © Richard French 1991
Photographs © John Heseltine 1991
Maps © George Philip Limited 1991

Reproduced from Ordnance Survey mapping with the permission of the Controller of Her Majesty's Stationery Office © Crown Copyright.

British Library Cataloguing in Publication Data

Trench, Richard
London.
1. London (England)
I. Title
914.2104859

ISBN 0-540-01242-4

Maps John Gilkes
Page design Gwyn Lewis
Typeset by Keyspools Limited, Golborne, Lancashire
Printed in Hong Kong

Contents

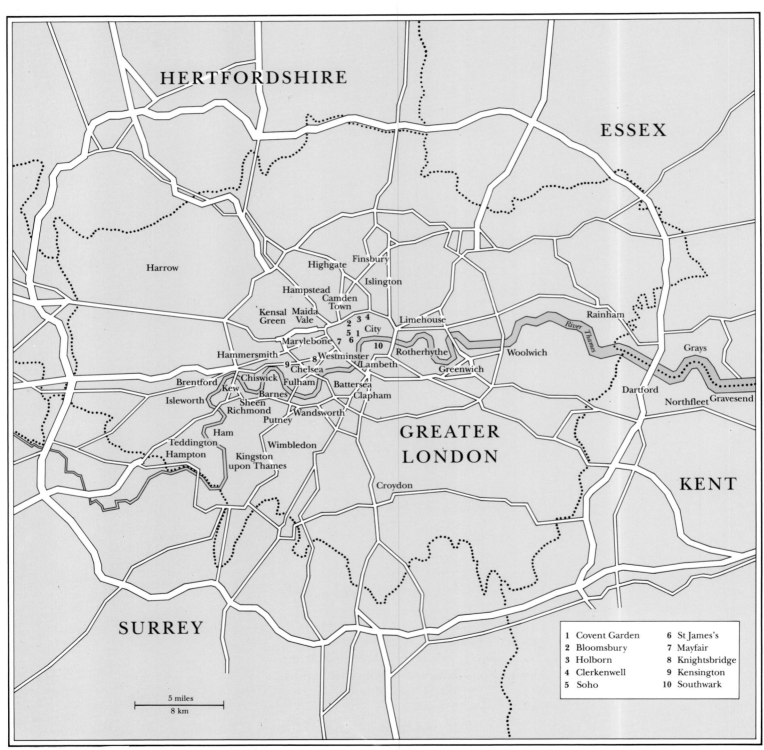

HERTFORDSHIRE

ESSEX

Harrow

Highgate   Finsbury
            Islington
Hampstead
Camden
Town
Kensal Maida
Green   Vale   City
                         Limehouse
Marylebone
                Rotherhythe
Hammersmith Westminster   Woolwich   Rainham
            Chelsea Lambeth
Brentford Chiswick Fulham Greenwich
Kew   Barnes   Battersea
Isleworth Sheen   Clapham   Dartford   Grays
          Richmond Wandsworth   Northfleet Gravesend
          Putney
      Ham
Teddington   Wimbledon   GREATER
Hampton   Kingston   LONDON
          upon Thames
                    Croydon   KENT

SURREY

5 miles
8 km

1 Covent Garden	6 St James's
2 Bloomsbury	7 Mayfair
3 Holborn	8 Knightsbridge
4 Clerkenwell	9 Kensington
5 Soho	10 Southwark

Preface

....

'City lives by remembering.'
Emerson

L
ondon is too big to take in in one breath, and this book makes no claim to encompass all of it. Rather, it takes seven themes and seven routes; along the river Thames, through the City, past the Inns of Court, across the royal parks, to the Georgian and Victorian squares, alongside the Regent's Canal, and over the northern suburbs. It is not necessary to follow the routes step by step (they can be taken in parts and deviations along your particular areas of interest are recommended), or even the themes, although keeping them vaguely in mind may help to bring some order to the chaos of a 2000-year-old city with seven-and-a-half million inhabitants, at least until you have built up your own personal map of the city.

There is nothing chronological in the book, and those who can see London only through its past will find fragments, which even put together will leave wide gaps. This is a topographical book, about a living city, whose charms are hidden by layers of alleys and passages, streets and gardens which need time to peel away.

OPPOSITE LONDON

Introduction

....

Every great city has its best entrance. Coming into New York it is by air, the plane descending to Kennedy Airport, the Statue of Liberty, the Hudson River and Manhattan revealing themselves below. Coming into Bombay it is by rail, steaming through the glare and dust into the imperial gothic railway terminal. Coming into London it is by ship, sailing into the Thames Estuary, the sky huge and overcast, merging with marsh and sea across a belt of haze. As Joseph Conrad wrote in *The Mirror of the Sea*:

> The estuary of the Thames is not beautiful, it has no noble features, no romantic grandeur of aspect, no smiling geniality; but it is wide open, spacious, inviting, hospitable at the first glance, with a strange air of mysteriousness which lingers about it to this very day.

You go on. The marshes are no longer empty, and the horizon is broken by garbage mountains, oil-tanks, paper mills, cement works, gravel pits and grain silos; interspersed with the ghosts of isolation hospitals, explosives factories, power stations and fortresses: the crumbling suburbs of a great port.

Between Tilbury and Gravesend, the estuary narrows to the width of two cannon shots, and for the first time the outlines on the shore become clearly defined. At Tilbury you see the new container docks which killed off the Port of London, and the pentagonal baroque fort, completed in 1683 after the Dutch burned the British fleet in the River Medway, which has never fired a shot in anger in its life. Beyond Tilbury the estuary meanders between the Essex and Kent marshes, where hulks rust and cormorants hover and dive in search of fish. On the north bank the giant neon Ford sign at Dagenham rises up over the car factory's generating station. On the south bank the ruins of Beckton Gas Works loom over Gallion's Reach.

Just around the corner Woolwich comes into view on the south side of the river. Woolwich has been an arsenal since Tudor times, and the nation's main

OPPOSITE *Inigo Jones's Queen's House, Greenwich, was one of the first renaissance Palladian buildings to be erected in Britain, 'solid, proportional according to the rules, masculine and unaffected,' as he put it. Commissioned by James I in 1605 for his wife, Anne of Denmark, it was completed by Queen Henrietta Maria between 1629 and 1640.*

The Thames Barrier became necessary for three reasons: the rising level of the sea, due to the melting of the polar ice caps; the tilting of Britain to the south-east at the rate of a foot every century; and the gradual sinking of London into its clay bed. The idea of a barrier to save London from flooding was first propounded by the philosoper Herbert Spencer in the 1850's, but it was not built until 1982.

artillery foundry since 1717. It was known as the Warren, a name it didn't justify until World War I, when most of its workshops were underground and it had its own subterranean railway. Its tunnels now lie empty. A few Queen Anne and early Georgian remnants by the playwright and architect Sir John Vanbrugh (1664–1726) survive on Warren Lane, Dail Square and the Royal Military Academy; and the delightful Rotunda survives, designed as a campaign tent by John Nash (1752–1835) and now used for gun displays. Woolwich was the Royal Dockyard before it was the Royal Arsenal. Here Henry VIII (1509–47) launched the *Great Harry*, at 1500 tons the largest ship afloat; Sir Francis Drake (1540–96) returned after circumnavigating the globe; and Sir Walter Ralegh (1552–1618), Sir Martin Frobisher (1535–94), Sir John Franklin (1786–1847) and James Cook (1728–79) left on their voyages. The Gatehouse and Clockhouse, built when Horatio Nelson (1758–1805) was still a midshipman, are the only dockyard memories left.

As you continue up the estuary, a plane takes off from the London City Airport, its engines straining as it gains height. The Royal Victoria, Royal

Albert and the George V Docks, 245 acres of water and the largest sheet of impounded water in the world, stretch along the north bank. In the 1930s they could accommodate the largest liners afloat, and their nine miles of quays landed grain, meat and vegetables for half the country. Now the quays have been turned into the London City Airport' runway. Sail on, and see before you, stretching across the river, the ten enormous flood gates of the Thames Barrier. From the river the central gates, weighing 3700 tons each and rising higher than a five-storey building, look like cut-out sections of an aluminium whale.

Beyond the Barrier the river swings north-west at Bugsby's Reach, where the River Lea sluggishly enters it at Bow Creek. Then the Thames turns south at Blackwall Point, and curves around the three sides of the Isle of Dogs on the north bank; while on the south bank you see what Sir Charles Reilly called 'one of the most sublime sights of English architecture – the most stately procession of buildings we possess', Greenwich.

The vista stretches back, from the four baroque blocks of the Royal Naval College on the riverside, past Inigo Jones's (1573–1652) classical renaissance Queen's House (now the National Maritime Museum) and its flanking colonnades, to Christopher Wren's (1632–1723) Royal Observatory on the crest of Greenwich Park in the distance. To the west the masts of the *Cutty Sark* and the baroque tower and cupola of Nicholas Hawksmoor's (1661–1736) St Alfege, Greenwich, ride the flanking skyline.

Originally there had been only one baroque block on the river, the Charles II Block, which was to be his riverside palace, but was never completed. William and Mary (1689–1702 and 1689–94) used it as a starting block for the Royal Naval Hospital, a home for wounded and elderly seamen. Only by walking through it do you become aware of the massive proportions, the pillars, pediments, colonnades and cupolas, ebbing and flowing like the tide. It synthesized the talents of Wren, Hawksmoor and Vanbrugh. The Painted Hall – depicting William and Mary, attended by sundry Virtues offering the cap of Liberty to Europe – boasts of one of the finest painted ceilings in England. Doctor Johnson (1709–84) disapproved. He thought it 'too magnificent for charity'.

On the opposite bank, on the Isle of Dogs in Dockland, the ambience is also too magnificent for charity. The Isle of Dogs has only been an island since 1805, when the West India Docks were excavated and a ship canal cut across the neck of the peninsula. The docks were closed in 1980, a derelict waste of sheets of corrugated iron and of water. Then the stilled dock cranes were joined by builder's cranes and the nineteenth-century warehouses were demolished and replaced by a post-Modern jostle of steel-framed office blocks reaching their climax at Canary Wharf, 800 feet high, and the tallest office block in Europe.

The traveller continues on, past the anorexic spire of St Paul's, Deptford, Thomas Archer's (1668–1743) baroque masterpiece, towards the Pool of

The Royal Observatory, Greenwich, designed by Wren and 200 years later the target of the anarchist Mr Verloc's bomb in Joseph Conrad's novel, The Secret Agent. *Since 1884, the north–south meridian line running through it has marked the prime meridian, or zero, from which all longitudes are measured.*

The Royal Naval College, Greenwich, built by Charles II as a naval hospital on the insistence of his wife Mary who had been shocked at the sight of the wounded after the victory at La Hogue. The building was split into two parts on Queen Mary's orders to enable Inigo Jones's Queen's House to be seen from the river. Wren gave his services free, Vanbrugh completed the west façade and Thornhill worked on the Painted Hall.

London. The skyscrapers of the City, London's traditional business quarter, stand out in the distance. A mile on you turn again, at Cuckold's Point on the south bank, its peninsula enclosing the sixteen different expanses of water that make up Surrey Docks. The ships that came here were from the north, unloading furs, whale blubber, sealskins and soft wood at Greenland Dock, Russia Dock, Quebec Dock and Canada Dock. Ships don't come here any more, and the new low-cost houses set besides the water have an intimacy that reminds you more of Amsterdam than of the Arctic fur trade.

Upstream from the Surrey Docks is Rotherhythe. St Mary's church, its octagonal obelisk protruding above the waterfront buildings and attendant trees, is homely, built in 1715 by the parishioners, 'chiefly seamen and watermen', which explains why its gallery looks like a ship's bridge, the piers made of cut-down masts. Its jewels, two Grinling Gibbons carvings on either side of the altarpiece, are set so discreetly that you hardly notice them. The churchyard, where the captain of the *Mayflower*, Christopher Jones, is buried, is equally discreet, guarded by an early Georgian watchhouse.

St Mary's Rotherhythe. The parishioners had petitioned the Church Commissioners to build them a church, and, if the Commissioners had accepted, it would have been one of the 50 Queen Anne churches, and probably have been built by Hawksmoor. The church that was built is more modest, by unknown hands, and more moving.

From St Mary's the bank is lined with warehouses, still recognizable as warehouses from the river, but gutted, hardened with steel, and then softened with office plants. The converted warehouses go on, past Terence Conran's Dockland Museum of Design, to Butler's Wharf, while ahead of you Tower Bridge frames St Paul's amid the gently rising skyscrapers, like a mosque in the foothills of a petrified forest. On the north bank, where the river straightens out after the Isle of Dogs, Dockland dies away at a single giant gasholder; while the tower of Hawksmoor's St Anne, Limehouse, not so much a tower as a bulwark, with the highest church clock in London, ignores the shining clutter of Dockland, proclaiming older values (see p. 147).

Upstream, the Prospect of Whitby, built in 1520, an olde English pub where the barmen are all Australian, sits squashed in by the late twentieth century. A quarter of a mile on, after a line of offices and luxury flats that had once been warehouses with names like Metropolitan Wharf, New Cranes Wharf and Gun Wharf, and beyond the little riverside garden lined by Georgian houses that greets you after another pub, the Town of Ramsgate, lie

the three intimate and interconnecting basins of St Katherine's Dock. In the middle of the dock, between three sheets of water, is the old Ivory House warehouse built in 1828 with its Italianate arches and iron pillars, an immovable object amongst the masts of a hundred sailing craft.

Behind St Katherine's Dock rears Tower Bridge, the gigantic gateway into the Pool of London. A steel-framed drawbridge clad in gothic to match the Tower of London, Tower Bridge was opened in 1894, and is as much a symbol of London as the Eiffel Tower is a symbol of Paris. Until the 1960s, when London ceased to be a great port, it was raised at least a dozen times a day. It still opens, but rarely. You sail beneath the drawbridge of Tower Bridge and come into the Upper Pool. To your right the Tower of London, the late Georgian Custom House, old Billingsgate Market and Wren's St Magnus Martyr line the waterfront. To your left is moored the naval cruiser HMS *Belfast*, a symbol of Britain's past maritime greatness and now a museum. The Pool is quiet now that London's docks are dead, and there are few vessels save the odd barge, water bus or police launch to disturb the simple lines of London Bridge. It is not the famous London Bridge of 1208 with nineteen arches, the one with the houses on it; nor even the romantic Regency replacement by Sir John Rennie (1794–1874). The best that can be said for the present three spans of pre-stressed concrete cantilevers is that they have no pretentions to competing with their more illustrious ancestors.

There, at London Bridge, the Pool comes to an end, and the traveller, whether coming on sailing ship, ocean liner or river bus from London City Airport, disembarks and sets foot in the City of London. All around, in Lower Thames Street, Great Tower Street, Fenchurch Street and Leadenhall Street, are the grain markets, shippers, insurers and mercantile offices that made the City rich, a reminder of London's origin as a great port.

Standing over the Pool is the Tower of London, which has had more history concentrated in it than any other building in Britain. It has witnessed half of London's 2000-year history and has been a fortress, arsenal, prison, palace, menagerie, mint, treasury and records office. In its cells Henry VI (1421–71), the Princes in the Tower (d. c.1483), Archbishop Fisher (1469–1535), the saintly Thomas More (1478–1535), Queen Ann Boleyn (1504–36), Queen Catherine Howard (d.1542), Lady Jane Grey (1537–54), Mary Queen of Scots (1542–87), Edward Seymour, Duke of Somerset (1506–52), John Dudley, Duke of Northumberland (d.1553), Lord Guildford Dudley (d.1553) and Sir Walter Ralegh have awaited death.

Unlike the Bastille, its Parisian counterpart, the Tower is treated with some affection by Londoners. The Tower and Bastille performed the same function, yet the Bastille is regarded as a symbol of tyranny, while the Tower is regarded as a symbol of ... tourism. It seems odd considering that executions were still taking place in the Tower in World War II. I blame the ice-cream sellers – for creating a false sense of security. The heart of the Tower is the White Tower, the original Norman keep, commissioned by William the

OPPOSITE *Tower Bridge, the gateway into the heart of London, built by Sir Horace Jones and opened by the Prince of Wales in 1894.*

Conqueror (1066–87) and built by Gundulf (1024–1108), the master builder from the Abbey of Bec who became Bishop of Rochester. Within it Gundulf built a chapel, St John's, which is one of the most solid examples of the pure Norman style in England. Henry III (1207–72) whitewashed the walls and gave the keep its name; today it houses the Royal Armouries.

South-west of the White Tower stands the Tudor-built Queen's House. Here Guy Fawkes (1570–1606) was tortured and Rudolf Hess (1894–1988) interrogated; and Anne Boleyn, Catherine Howard and Lady Jane Grey looked out of the window at the execution block in Tower Green that they would soon kneel to. North of the Green is the Church of St Peter ad Vincula where, wrote the London antiquarian John Stow (1525–1605), lie 'two dukes between two queens, to wit, the Duke of Somerset and Duke of Northumberland, between Queen Anne and Queen Catherine, all four beheaded'.

Around the White Tower and its precincts, the Inner Ward, are thirteen towers: among them Bell Tower, where More and Fisher were kept before their executions, and the future Queen Elizabeth (1558–1603) was imprisoned by her sister Queen Mary (1553–58); Beauchamp Tower where amongst the names carved in the stone wall is 'IANE', written by Lady Jane Grey; Devereux Tower, where Robert Devereux, Earl of Essex (1566–1601) was held before his execution; Bowyer Tower, where the Duke of Clarence was drowned in a butt of malmsey wine in 1478; Wakefield Tower, where Henry VI was stabbed to death; and Bloody Tower, where Ralegh wrote *The Historie of the World*, and the Princes in the Tower were murdered.

The Tower of London missed the first millennium of London's history. In its first 500 years *Londinium* had been founded by the Romans, burned by Queen Boadicea, and abandoned by its inhabitants after the Romans left. The Anglo-Saxons built a new *Lundunwick* upstream from the Roman city, straddling what is now the Strand. The chronicler Bede (673–735) called it 'the mart of all nations by land and sea'. The old City became a ghost town, empty except for the Saxon king's palace and the Court of the Aldermen at Aldermanbury, and the Cathedral of St Paul's on Ludgate Hill. The Danish invasions drove the inhabitants of the Strand back behind the old Roman walls, which Alfred the Great (871–99) repaired and refortified after driving the Danes from London in 886. By 1066, the city had become well-established again, the port was bringing in goods from all over Christendom, and a royal palace and abbey had been built at Westminster.

As the Middle Ages progressed London grew rich from trade, her tradesmen forming guilds – part trade monopolies, part trade unions – and building sumptuous company halls. A bridge was built across the Thames in 1176. As the generations passed by and the population increased, the suburbs, or 'Liberties', around the old city were built up, the lawyers taking over vast areas as Inns of Court and the feudal aristocracy taking over more tracts for their houses and gardens. A half-circle of monasteries stretched across the north of London, one of them, St Bartholomew's, dedicated to relieving the suffering of the poor. The monasteries were dissolved at the Reformation, and in 1551 the Venetian ambassador, Soranzo, wrote of 'many large palaces making a very fine show, but ... disfigured by the ruins of a multitude of churches and monasteries'. Humbler houses were demolished and bigger houses, with wider overhangs, replaced them. The timber-framed houses became more solid but the ambience and texture of London, which by 1605 had a population of 225,000, did not change in 600 years.

It changed on 2 September 1666. At 2 a.m., a fire broke out at a bakery in Pudding Lane. The baker and his family escaped, but the maid was left behind and died in the flames. The fire grew. The Lord Mayor, Sir Thomas Bloodworthy, hearing reports of its size, went to see it and was unimpressed. 'Pish! A woman might piss it out.' By nightfall 300 houses and half the houses on London Bridge had disappeared in the flames. Next day the Royal Exchange succumbed to the fire, and by evening half the City was burning. On the fifth St Paul's was engulfed, but by evening the worst was over. Next day three-quarters of the City, 400 acres, including the Guildhall, the Inner Temple Hall, 87 churches and 13,200 houses lay in smouldering ruins.

The City that was rebuilt – so much of it by Wren – was a baroque city on a medieval street plan; which is why so much of it looks like a fat man in a jacket two sizes too small for him. Wren's genius was in making the suit and the man look perfectly fitted. The speed of the rebuilding was remarkable. In 1668 1200 houses were being built, in 1669 the number was 1600.

By the reign of Queen Anne (1702–14) the cheaply-built post-Fire houses of Nicholas Barebone were already old-fashioned. Houses were becoming more elegant, clad in rich red brick. There were now 700,000 people living in London. Gradually the heart of fashionable London moved westwards from the City, first to Westminster and then to Mayfair, while Huguenot refugees moved into the empty houses in the east, starting a process of immigrants arriving in the East End and moving westwards that continues to this day. Georgian terraces and squares made their appearance, and a distinctive London house emerged, built of brick with a narrow front, and a front room and back room on each floor, uniform but not monotonous. There is a change of colour too. The new squares were built with brown, grey and yellow bricks rather than red. Most of these squares were named after the nobleman who owned the land they stood on: Berkeley, Portman, Grosvenor, Cavendish and Russell. One, Hanover, was named after the new dynasty.

The eighteenth century was the great age of London building, and it was served in those years by some of its finest architects, including Hawksmoor, Vanbrugh, Archer, James Gibbs (1682–1754), William Kent (1685–1748), Sir William Chambers (1723–96), Robert Adam (1728–92), Sir John Soane (1753–1837) and John Nash.

Once the empty spaces of Mayfair had been filled in, Georgian London colonized the fields of Marylebone and Bloomsbury. The squares needed space, space signified grandeur. The royal hunting grounds metamorphosed

The Tower of London, built for William the Conqueror by Gundulf, a monk who doubled up as a military engineer and rose to become Bishop of Rochester. His fortress has more of Britain's history concentrated in it than any other building, and has witnessed nearly a thousand years of London's history.

into the royal parks: St James's Park, Green Park, Hyde Park and Regent's Park. In 1801 London had its first census. Its population was over one million. By then the developers had reached Knightsbridge. Belgravia, an unhealthy swamp, was raised on spoil taken from the excavation of St Katherine's Dock and turned into one of the most stately areas of London.

The Victorians continued to build their middle-class developments around squares. They also threw their energies into giving the Thames a new grandeur: building gothic parliament houses on the water's edge, embanking, bridging, disciplining and glorifying the river – an act of gratitude from a city to the river that had brought it wealth. Ever-anxious to improve themselves, they built museums, some of the largest and grandest in the world. The Victorians' zeal for building was relentless, and they joined the villages around London – Chelsea, Pimlico, Paddington, Bayswater, Hampstead, Highgate and Hackney – into one vast brick conurbation.

World War II and the boom in office building in the late twentieth century have left ugly scars over central London, but have not destroyed its past. The inner city we know today is still essentially that eighteenth- and nineteenth-century city, with a Georgian centre and a Victorian periphery.

Until recently a London building had an average life of 120 years, so theoretically half the city changed every lifetime. Conservation has now given Georgian and early Victorian London a far longer span of life. Structures stay, although their uses change, so although Inner London will continue changing – changing its role, its seven-and-a-half million population and its perception of itself – its texture and its ambience will remain Georgian and Victorian for a long time to come. The emphasis on conservation also means that London will not lose its sense of being a collection of villages. Hampstead, Highgate, Chelsea and Paddington were villages before they were suburbs, and the old village street patterns can still be found in their centres.

What remains worth preserving is probably safe, although preservation can be so precious that it becomes meaningless, as has happened in parts of the City. But the seas of concrete are not all quite as awful as popular prejudice suggests. The tall towers of the 1970s and 1980s have enhanced, not damaged, the skyline of London. There must always be such intruders onto the landscape. The past can never be entirely safe. Nor should it be. London is a living city, not a museum. But like all living cities, she cannot abandon her past. She contains it:

> like the lines of a hand, written in the corners of the streets, the gratings of the windows, the banisters of the steps, the antennae of the lightning rods, the poles of the flags, every segment marked in turn with scratches, indentations, scrolls. (Italo Calvino: *Invisible Cities*, 1974)

OPPOSITE *Old and new: Billingsgate Market on Lower Thames Street, dwarfed by a gigantic office block, and doubled by its sheets of reflective glass.*

1
The River

....

The approach to London from the west along the River Thames is a total contrast to the Estuary approach. Instead of the great open spaces of sky and sea that characterize the estuary, here the river is bordered by parkland and suburbia. Upstream the Thames was as much a working river as downstream. There was constant traffic, carrying goods down to the city for export, which was injured but never killed off by the nineteenth-century railways and twentieth-century motorways, and the old rust-sailed Thames barges plied the river right up until the 1960s.

Daniel Defoe (1660–1731) regarded the way into London along the river – past Hampton Court; the grand houses at Twickenham; the palaces of Richmond and Kew; the fishing village of Strand-on-the-Green; the banks at Chelsea; medieval Westminster and the new post-Fire City of Christopher Wren – as the most beautiful road in the kingdom:

> Here is a plain and pleasant country, a rich fertile soil, cultivated and enclosed to the utmost perfection of husbandry, then bespangled with villages; those villages filled with these houses, and the houses surrounded with gardens, walks, vistas, avenues, representing all the beauties of building, and all the pleasures of planting. (Daniel Defoe: *A Tour Through the Whole Island of Great Britain*, 3 volumes, 1724–6)

The fashion for palatial riverside living west of London (where the river was still relatively clean) was started by Cardinal Thomas Wolsey (*c.*1475–1530), who was Henry VIII's Lord Chancellor and the last of England's great prelate–statesmen. He made his palace, **HAMPTON COURT**, one of the most magnificent in Europe. It was ostentatious, which was understandable coming from the son of an Ipswich butcher who had risen to become cardinal, papal legate and Lord Chancellor of England, and far more luxurious than anything Henry VIII owned, which may be one of the reasons why Wolsey

OPPOSITE *Decimus Burton's Palm House in the Royal Botanic Gardens, Kew, built between 1844 and 1848 and containing 3000 botanical species, including a giant Chilian wine palm, the second oldest plant in Kew.*

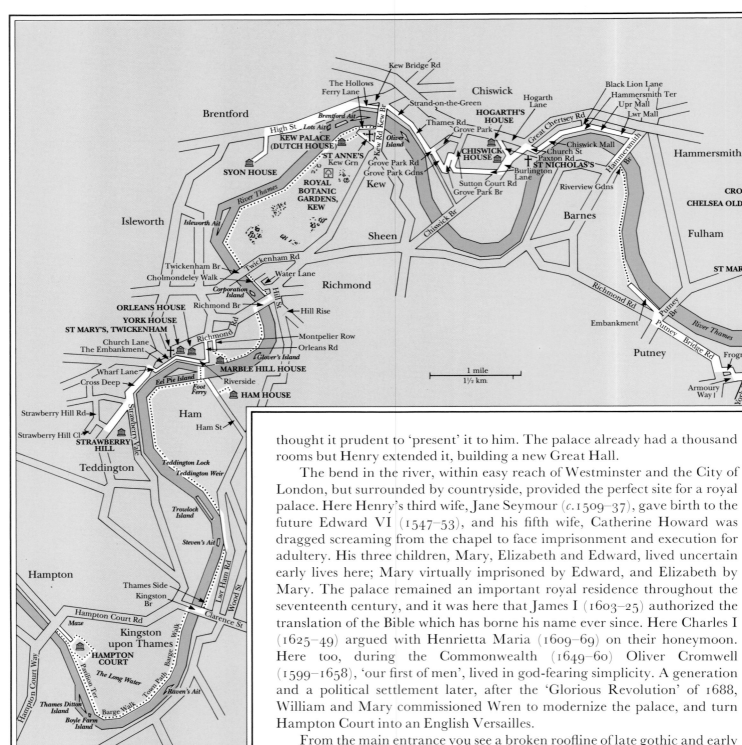

© Crown Copyright

thought it prudent to 'present' it to him. The palace already had a thousand rooms but Henry extended it, building a new Great Hall.

The bend in the river, within easy reach of Westminster and the City of London, but surrounded by countryside, provided the perfect site for a royal palace. Here Henry's third wife, Jane Seymour (*c.*1509–37), gave birth to the future Edward VI (1547–53), and his fifth wife, Catherine Howard was dragged screaming from the chapel to face imprisonment and execution for adultery. His three children, Mary, Elizabeth and Edward, lived uncertain early lives here; Mary virtually imprisoned by Edward, and Elizabeth by Mary. The palace remained an important royal residence throughout the seventeenth century, and it was here that James I (1603–25) authorized the translation of the Bible which has borne his name ever since. Here Charles I (1625–49) argued with Henrietta Maria (1609–69) on their honeymoon. Here too, during the Commonwealth (1649–60) Oliver Cromwell (1599–1658), 'our first of men', lived in god-fearing simplicity. A generation and a political settlement later, after the 'Glorious Revolution' of 1688, William and Mary commissioned Wren to modernize the palace, and turn Hampton Court into an English Versailles.

From the main entrance you see a broken roofline of late gothic and early renaissance turrets, pinnacles, cupolas and chimneys. Beyond the gatehouse the red brick Base Court presents you with a perfect Tudor court, untouched by any other architectural era. It leads to Clock Court, a complete contrast,

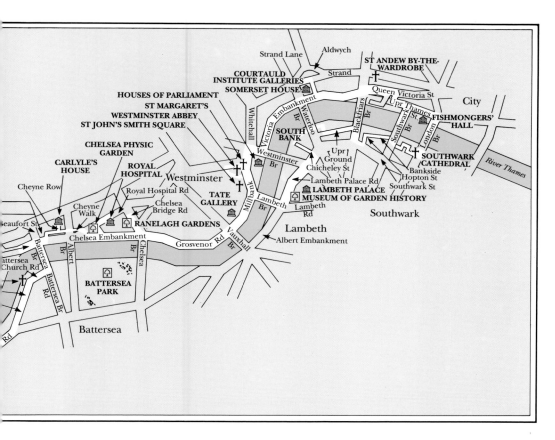

KEY TO MAP SYMBOLS

Monuments

Churches

Columns and statues

Houses, palaces and museums

with each of its ranges built in a different style. Along the south range, to the right, is a colonnade by Wren; looming over the south range, to the left, is Henry VIII's Great Hall, its splendours including an early Tudor hammer-beam roof, and the gigantic tapestries telling the Story of Abraham.

Beyond Clock Court, Wolsey's palace comes to an end and Wren's begins, at the baroque cloisters of Fountain Court, overlooked by the great chambers of state. You reach these chambers from the Queen's Grand Staircase, with an elaborate wrought iron balustrade by Jean Tijou. At the top of the stairs a corridor leads to the Chapel Royal, with its delicate fan vaulted ceiling and wreaths of cherubs dropping down both sides of the reredos carved by Grinling Gibbons (1648–1721). Another set of doors leads into the Queen's Guard Chamber, where the *Hampton Court Beauties*, painted by Sir Godfrey Kneller (1646–1723), a dozen Queen Anne lookalikes, gaze across at the windows over Fountain Court. Beyond, the rooms lead one off the other to the private suite of Frederick, Prince of Wales (1707–51), estranged son of George II, where the decor is by Sir John Vanbrugh, and there are paintings by Pieter Breughel the Elder, Pieter de Hooch, Daniel Mytens and Jacob van Ruysdael. The Communications Gallery in the west range is occupied by Peter Lely's (1618–80) *Windsor Beauties*, from the court of Charles II (1660–85). In the Public Dining Room is Mytens's portrait of Charles I, Henrietta Maria and Jeffrey Hudson, their dwarf. James Thornhill's (1675–1734) ceiling painting of Leucothoe restraining Apollo from getting

Hampton Court. The Great Fountain Garden, formal, mathematical and Dutch, with Wren's late renaissance east front behind it. William III had thirteen such fountains built. Now there is only one left.

into his chariot, spreads across the Queen's Bedroom. Grinling Gibbons's garlands of limewood fruit and veg, Sir Godfrey Kneller's painting of William III on horseback, and William's Chair of State grace the King's First Presence Chamber. Finally, through the King's Guard Chamber there is the King's Grand Staircase, with an iron balustrade by Jean Tijou, and dissipated baroque gods and *putti* on its Verrio ceiling.

The gardens, like the baroque interiors, are formal. North from the Gatehouse a disciplined 'Wilderness' (which includes that most unlikely 'Wilderness' of all, the Maze) leads round the outbuildings and Charles I's indoor Real Tennis court, to the Great Fountain Garden east of the palace, where Wren's late renaissance east range of red brick with stone pediment and dressings, presents its formal baroque face. This garden is one of the largest and most perfect late seventeenth-century 'Dutch' gardens in Britain, with gorgeous herbaceous borders lasting from May until September. It was designed by William III, himself a Dutchman and a 'great delighter' in gardens. To the south is a charming group of three smaller gardens: the tiny Tudor Knot Garden, with ribbons of box and thyme all knotted together against a background of flowers; the Privy Garden, dotted with unexpected statuary, which goes down to the elaborately and beautifully wrought Tijou

Ham House, from the recently restored late seventeenth-century garden: the Restoration rebuilding was completed by the Earl of Lauderdale in 1677.

gates and the Thames; and a pond garden. The pond garden leads to the Orangery which holds the nine enormous paintings depicting *The Triumph of Caesar*, painted by Andrea Mantegna (1431–1506). In a glass house beside it, a vine planted by Lancelot 'Capability' Brown (1716–83) 200 years ago, now seven feet thick at the stem and 100 feet long, still produces grapes.

From Hampton Court the riverbank takes you along the edge of Hampton Court Park. You can see deer grazing. The parkland stays almost all the way to the eminently Georgian Kingston Bridge, set amid clusters of cedar, willow and horse-chestnut trees. At Kingston the towpath crosses to the south bank and you walk through a mixture of country, suburbia and boatyards, as far as Teddington Weir, where the freshwater Thames pours down into the tidal Thames, through a complicated system of weirs, and you can stand on the island and watch the whole river foaming at the mouth.

Half-an-hour's walk downstream, the river makes a sharp right bend. Beyond, just out of sight from the towpath, is **HAM HOUSE**. It stands by itself, seemingly ignoring the river, with its back to it. If it wasn't for the Coade stone Father Thames cavorting on the front lawn in view of a semi-circle of expressionless Roman emperors, you would hardly know that there was a river nearby. Built in 1610 by Sir Thomas Vavasour as a Jacobean palace, with rich red brick and stone dressings, it was substantially altered by Elizabeth Murray, Countess of Dysart, who, with her second husband, John Maitland, Duke of Lauderdale – a Parliamentarian general turned Royalist politician and one of Charles II's Cabal of ministers – converted it into a sumptuous Restoration mansion in the 1670s, 'furnished like a great prince', according to John Evelyn (1620–1706), the London diarist.

Then Ham House was left, unchanged by less pretentious Dysart generations who followed Elizabeth, making it almost unique as a complete Restoration House. One of those less pretentious Dysarts was Charlotte Walpole (1738–89), who married a Dysart, and whose portrait by Sir Joshua Reynolds (1723–92) hangs in the Great Hall. Her uncle, Horace Walpole (1717–97), lived across the river at Strawberry Hill (see below), and was a frequent visitor at Ham House while it lived out its cobwebbed existence.

> There is an old brown gallery full of Van Dycks and Lelys, charming miniatures, delightful Wouvermans and Polennurghs, china, japan, bronzes, ivory cabinets, and silver dogs, pokers, billows, etc., without end. One pair of billows is a filigree. In this state of pomp and tatters my nephew intends it shall remain. (Horace Walpole: *Letters*)

Most of it remains: the Lely portraits lining the Long Gallery; the ceiling by Franz Cleyn in the Green Closet; the first flowering of English Chinoiserie in the antechamber to the Queen's Bedchamber; the Spitalfields silk in the withdrawing room; the miniatures by Nicholas Hilliard (1537–1619) of Elizabeth I and Robert Dudley, Earl of Leicester, off the Round Gallery; the sea scenes by Willem van de Velde the Younger (1633–1707) in the duchess's bedchamber, and the innumerable Verrio bedroom ceilings.

The gardens, unlike the house, did not survive changing fashions, and have only recently been restored by the National Trust to their earlier state of 'parterres, flower gardens, orangeries, groves, avenues, courts, statues, perspectives, fountains and aviaries', as John Evelyn put it.

Horace Walpole was not the only person to regard the failure of Ham House to keep up with changing fashions as a tragedy. It was the best-sited mansion on the river, the river on which most of the early eighteenth century's great and good, bad and beautiful, lived: Edward Hyde, Lord Clarendon (1609–74); George II's mistress Henrietta Howard (1688–1767); the poet Alexander Pope (1688–1744); Sir Godfrey Kneller, Lady Mary Wortley Montagu (1689–1762), Walpole himself; the actress Kitty Clive (1711–85); and the uncouth John Gay (1685–1732), who wrote *The Beggar's Opera*.

The most upstream of the surviving mansions on the north bank is Horace Walpole's unique gothic fantasy at **STRAWBERRY HILL**, his 'romance in lath and plaster . . . so pretty and so small that I am inclined to wrap it up and send it to you in a letter'. Now hidden from the river by the trees, in the eighteenth century it must have been one of the most striking sights on the Thames. It stood in a line of Restoration, baroque and Palladian villas, and was deliberately out of step with the prevailing conventions. Walpole would have nothing to do with his neighbours' classical 'good taste'. 'Columns and all their beautiful ornaments look ridiculous when crowded into a closet or a cheesecake house.'

He was 30 years old in 1747 when he leased 'a little plaything house, the prettiest bauble you ever saw', and began to convert it, displaying pinnacles, turrets and lancets like icing sugar. The interior is so gothic that it is almost rococo. The designs are all taken from elsewhere: the chimneypiece in the Holbein Room is modelled on an archbishop's tomb in Canterbury Cathedral; the *papier mâché* fan vaulting in the Long Gallery is copied from the Henry VII Chapel in Westminster Abbey; and in the Round Room the designs of Edward the Confessor's tomb, 'improved by Mr Robert Adam', made a fireplace. Even the Chapel is not real, having 'all the air of a Catholic chapel – bar consecration'. Some 200 years later the house was taken over by a Catholic teacher-training college. The chapel is now consecrated.

Sir Ratan Tata's beaux arts water nymphs, in the gardens of York House. He intended to use the pool to swim in, but the marble made the water too cold.

Alexander Pope is buried a little downstream from Strawberry Hill, under the chancel in **ST MARY'S, TWICKENHAM**. The early Georgian church, where the warm red brick of the nave makes a perfect contrast with the cold grey of the Early English ragstone tower, stands serenely amongst the willows and Georgian houses, looking out at the bungalows and boatyards of Eel Pie Island. The nave was built between 1713 and 1715 by John James (1672–1746). The nave and gallery walls are lined with monuments, including works by Michael Rysbrack (1693–1770) and John Bacon (1740–99). In the north gallery is Pope's memorial to his parents, and outside, on the church wall, is his memorial to his nanny, Mary Beach:

> Alex Pope, whom she nursed in his infancy, and constantly attended for thirty-eight years, in gratitude to a faithful servant erected this stone.

In the surrounding churchyard are buried Kneller (who was a churchwarden here); the actresses Hannah Pritchard and Kitty Clive (whom Dr Johnson called 'a better romp than I ever saw in nature'); William Tryon, Governor of North Carolina and New York; Sir William Berkeley, Governor of Virginia; and Thomas Twining, the tea merchant.

From St Mary's church the procession of great houses continues: York House, followed by Orleans House, followed by Marble Hill House. **YORK HOUSE** was the home of Edward Hyde, the Earl of Clarendon, father-in-law to James II (1685–88), and grandfather of queens Mary II and Anne. Its interior has been converted into local government offices, but the exterior and the garden give an idea of a grand Restoration house. The best part is in the gardens, across a hump-backed footbridge over a lane, and has nothing to do with the Restoration. It is a fountain built by the house's last owner before it went municipal, the Indian merchant prince Sir Ratan Tata.

A couple of minutes' walk away, hidden in an overgrown garden is **ORLEANS HOUSE**, once the home of Louis Philippe (1773–1850), deposed king of

France and Duc d'Orléans, hence the name of the house. There is not much of the original house left, save James Gibbs's Octagon Room, built onto the original (and now demolished) house by Caroline of Anspach (1683–1737), George II's extravagant consort, and now used as a gallery for changing exhibitions. The ceiling is exquisitely decorated in stucco by Giuseppe Artari and Giovanni Bagutti, and the gardens are a pleasure to lose yourself in.

The Georgian houses in Montpelier Row lead to **MARBLE HILL HOUSE**, clad in white, chaste, petite and Palladian, built between 1724 and 1729 for Henrietta Howard, Countess of Suffolk. Pope, who 'dangled here' (Jonathan Swift), admired her, and even helped plan the garden.

The entrance hall is low, with four columns forming a square in the centre. A magnificent mahogany staircase leads up to the main hall on the first floor, a perfect cube, and in the rooms around it, amongst the Knellers, Reynolds and Kuyls, is Richard Wilson's (1714–82) idyllic painting, *The Thames at Twickenham*.

From the grounds of Marble Hill the towpath continues along the north bank until you come to the five Georgian arches of Richmond Bridge, one of the prettiest bridges spanning the Thames with Richmond on the other side of it. Richmond was created by the river, a fishing village that became a suburb, but managed to retain its village characteristics. There was a palace here in the Middle Ages. Edward III (1327–77) died here and Richard II (1377–99) ordered the palace to be demolished after the death of his adored wife, Anne of Bohemia (1366–94). Henry V (1413–22) built a new palace, but it was outshone by Hampton Court and steadily crumbled over the following two centuries. You can still see the remains of it in Maids of Honour Row and Old Palace Yard, which lie between the river and Richmond Green. The green itself is quintessentially English, open and irregular, with a church, and surrounded by seventeenth-, eighteenth- and nineteenth-century houses.

Downstream from Richmond the land opens up in the Old Deer Park and you almost feel that you are in the country again as you follow the towpath to Kew Bridge. Kew Green is as quintessentially English as Richmond Green. There's even a church on it, **ST ANNE'S**, built in the reign of Queen Anne in yellow brick and topped by an octagonal cupola. Inside are Tuscan columns, a vaulted ceiling, and a gallery added by George III to accommodate his fifteen children. In the churchyard two artists, Thomas Gainsborough (1727–88) and John Zoffany (1733–1810), are buried.

At the far, south-west end, the green narrows into almost a triangle, at Decimus Burton's (1800–81) grand entrance to the **ROYAL BOTANIC GARDENS**. Augusta (d.1772), wife of Frederick, Prince of Wales, started the gardens and her son, George III (1760–1820), extended them. Capability Brown landscaped them and Sir William Chambers designed the orangery, pagoda and such classical conceits as the Temple of Bellona. George's wife, Queen Charlotte, built the delightful and unpretentious doll's house called Queen Charlotte's Cottage, which looks as if it comes straight out of a Jane Austen

ABOVE *Charles Fowler's Great Conservatory at Syon Park, all glass, gun-metal and warm Bath stone. Its cacti, tropical plants and exotic flowers are an unexpected delight.*

OPPOSITE *The Thames at dusk, looking upstream, with the Royal Botanic Gardens on the left and Syon Park on the right.*

The Earl of Burlington's Chiswick House and its surrounding gardens, dotted with neo-classical statuary. The building of Chiswick House between 1725 and 1729 marked the beginning of the Palladian revival in Britain. The gardens, designed by William Kent and Charles Bridgman, were the first to make a break from the stiff Dutch tradition.

novel, in 1773. The two Victorian glass houses – Decimus Burton's Palm House and Temperate House – temples of glass and wrought iron built in the 1840s and 1860s, dominate the grounds.

To the north stands the original **KEW PALACE**, an unassuming house in the Dutch style built in 1631 for a prosperous merchant and known as the Dutch House. It is the smallest royal residence and its simple domesticity, with the muslin hangings in the bedroom, the needlework pictures on the walls and the unpretentious bedrooms, is a delight. In front of the house, in a formal seventeenth-century garden, many kitchen herbs are grown.

South of Kew Palace the gardens and glass houses spread out like a fan, forming 300 acres (about 120 hectares) of flora from all over the world. Everyone has their favourite spots, and favourite times of year. For me they are the stretches to the north of Queen Charlotte's Cottage, carpeted in bluebells each spring; the Waterlily House in August when the giant water lily flowers; and the view west across the river to **SYON HOUSE**, a castellated square and four towers, alone in a water meadow, all year round.

Syon House is best approached across Kew Bridge and along Brentford High Street. Originally it was a Brigettine convent, founded by Henry V. Inevitably, with the Reformation, it passed to the Crown. Catherine Howard was imprisoned here by Henry VIII before her execution in 1542. Five years later, when his bloated corpse lay at Syon on its journey to Windsor, it burst, and the royal mourners arrived in the morning to find dogs licking up the innards. Syon passed on in turn as 'expenses' to the boy king Edward VI's two protectors, first Edward Seymour, Duke of Somerset, then John Dudley, Duke of Northumberland. Robert Adam gutted the interior and rebuilt it, from 1776. Capability Brown did much the same to the grounds.

Inside the great hall, all is pomp and circumstance: its aim was, according to Adam, to 'parade the convenience and the social pleasures of life'. The chequerboard floor is solid marble and the Adam ceiling is delicate plasterwork. The sculptures match the floor, the white *Apollo Belvedere* stands in an apse in the north end, the black *Dying Gaul* remains frozen in his death throes in the south apse. He guards the Ante Room, a piece of Adam blue and gilt theatre with just a suggestion of a screen in the marble pillars, and a scagliola floor that tricks the eye into thinking the room is a perfect cube. The white and gold dining room, with a beautiful relief of the Three Graces, leads to the Red Drawing Room, its coved ceiling painted by Angelica Kauffmann (1741–1807), and its walls lined in faded Spitalfields silk, and hung with equally silky Stuart monarchs and their hangers-on. Around the corner you step into the Long Gallery. Mauve and green, stretching the length of the house and facing the river, it is Adam's Jacobean fantasy. The ceiling is spectacular, verging on rococo. From there a corridor lined with portraits takes you past Adam's grand staircase, and back to the entrance hall again.

The grounds are as spectacular as the house. The first garden was created by Protector Somerset, and planted by his physician, Dr William Turner (1520–68), author of *Names of Herbs*, which he wrote at Syon in 1548 and dedicated to Somerset. A small portion of his garden remains, and two of his mulberry trees still bear fruit. The rest was swept away between 1767 and 1773 by Capability Brown, who carved out lakes, planted cedars, limes, oaks and chestnuts, added a Doric column topped by Flora, goddess of flowers, and staked out the stretches of shrub, meadow and woodland. The domed conservatory, built of glass and gun metal, which inspired Sir Joseph Paxton's (1801–65) Crystal Palace, came a couple of generations later.

Downstream from Syon is Strand-on-the-Green: a ribbon of Georgian houses and cottages. It still retains its village atmosphere with no two houses alike. Only the high steps to the doors, to protect the ground floors from flood tides, are common to every house. The novelist Nancy Mitford (1904–73) and the poet Dylan Thomas (1914–53) lived here. So did John Zoffany, who used the local fishermen as models for his *Last Supper*.

The river makes a wide loop to the south here, and in the middle of the loop lies **CHISWICK HOUSE**, one of the earliest Palladian houses in Britain, though not so much a house as an imaginary piece of classical Italy at a bend on a river. The pseudo-classical villas and their gardens, lined with statuary and built for Italian renaissance princes and merchants according to the strict

The steps of Chiswick House follow almost exactly their Palladian prototypes.

classical principles of ancient Rome, were the inspiration for Richard Boyle (1695–1753), Third Earl of Burlington. He saw them on his two Grand Tours, in 1714 and 1719, and was struck by their simplicity and purity in contrast to the sensuality of contemporary European baroque. Burlington was one of the richest men of his age, a friend and patron of Alexander Pope, George Frederick Handel (1685–1759), Jonathan Swift (1667–1745), John Gay and William Kent, and who 'possessed every quality of an artist except envy', according to Horace Walpole. He spent fortunes on his tours, buying up statues, paintings and columns; and even more building Chiswick House, and Burlington House in Piccadilly (see p. 130), with a little help from his friends, Colen Campbell (1676–1729) and Kent.

He designed the villa according to the rules of Palladio's (1508–80) *Four Books of Architecture* and Colen Campbell's *Vitruvius Britannicus*, and modelled it on Palladio's Villa Capra near Vicenza. The result is a series of perfectly proportioned boxes around an octagon. But what gives it its beauty is not only its proportions but its size. It is tiny, less than 70 feet square.

From your first view, from the gates of Burlington Lane, you are in renaissance Italy. In front of you, past an avenue of classical plinths enclosed by box hedges, stands the villa, with a low ground floor, and a single upper floor, which is reached up a staircase that flows in tight and disciplined classical lines down either side of the giant portico. Palladio stands at the bottom of one staircase, Inigo Jones at the other, both sculpted by Rysbrack. Above the portico of six Corinthian columns rises the dome, serene and grand, more like a mosque than a Venetian villa. You expect to hear a *muezzin*. Inside, the ground floor is simple and silent; the upper floor loud, ornamented and crowded with pictures and statues, and the ceiling beneath the dome is gilded like filigree lace.

The surrounding garden, landscaped by William Kent and Charles Bridgeman, and breaking completely with the formality of Tudor and Jacobean knot gardens and parterres, presents twists and turns, arbours and wildernesses, unexpected vistas and a serpentine lake, occasional temples and picturesque statuary, like a painting by Claude Lorraine (1600–82).

Immediately to the north of the gardens, with its elbows up against the Great West Road, is Hogarth's House, the 'little country box beside the Thames' where William Hogarth (1697–1764) lived from 1749 until his death, with his wife, Jane, his sister and his widowed mother-in-law. He detested his neighbours, Burlington and Kent, which may account for the high wall around his garden. If Burlington's garden is classical, Hogarth's is unpretentiously English, a triangle enclosed by a brick wall and shaded by a mulberry tree. The house is early Georgian, full of his prints and paintings; and in addition to the obvious satirical pictures – *Marriage à la Mode*, *The Election*, *The Harlot's Progress* and *London Scenes* – are many of his lesser-known works, including *The Inhabitants of the Moon*, a surrealist work from 150 years before the term was invented.

OPPOSITE *The Mall, Hammersmith, a charming stretch along the river's edge, divided into the Upper Mall and the Lower Mall at The Dove. Although its origins go back to the mid seventeenth century, most of the houses were built in the eighteenth and nineteenth centuries.*

Across Chertsey Road, Chiswick village begins, and you return to the river at **ST NICHOLAS'S CHURCH**, with a simple urn in an overgrown churchyard in memory of Hogarth, amid the graves of Lord Burlington, William Kent, Colen Campbell, the painter J. A. M. Whistler (1834–1903), two of Cromwell's daughters and Barbara Villiers (1640–1709), Duchess of Cleveland and Charles II's mistress, 'the fairest and the lewdest of the Royal concubines', who lived at Walpole House on Chiswick Mall. Chiswick used to be a fishing village. It still was when Pope was born there, and even now traces of it remain: in the Perpendicular tower of St Nicholas's, the weatherboarded cottages in the narrow lanes, and the Georgian houses on Chiswick Mall, bedecked in wistaria, and overlooking Chiswick Eyot where herons still nest.

You lose the river at Hammersmith Terrace, but are more than compensated by the lovely wrought iron balconies on the row of almost identical mid-Georgian houses, and you return to the river at Upper Mall. According to William Morris (1834–96), who lived at Kelmscott House, 'the situation is certainly the most pleasant in London'. Upper Mall turns into Lower Mall at the Dove pub, where the poet James Thomson (1700–48) wrote *Rule Britannia* one night in 1727. From the Dove, the Lower Mall leads to Hammersmith Bridge of 1887, hung by Sir Joseph Bazelgette (1819–90), its iron-boned towers with little pavilion tops, the whole effort so ridiculous that it is endearing. Here the north bank towpath disappears, and you cross Hammersmith Bridge to the south bank where Harrod's Depository, a twin-towered ochre fantasia in an architectural style that could only be Harrod's, looms up around the bend. The towpath continues, in its semi-rural, semi-urban way, and you walk on, past boathouses, breweries and blackberry bushes, to Putney Bridge, with the early fifteenth-century tower of St Mary the Virgin on its south side, and Fulham Palace, homely and Tudor and the summer residence of the Bishop of London until 1973, on its north side.

Downstream from Putney Bridge you leave the river bank until Battersea Reach where the church of **ST MARY'S, BATTERSEA** stands alone on the riverside, looking out at a panorama of power station, skyscrapers and moorings. St Mary's simple Georgian brick body, and square tower topped by a green copper spire, make it one of the most beautiful landmarks on the river. William Blake (1757–1827) was married in it, and J. M. W. Turner (1775–1851) painted the clouds and sunsets of Chelsea Reach from the vestry.

The present Battersea Bridge, by Sir Joseph Bazelgette, built in 1886, is not the same Battersea Bridge – the old wooden one – that Whistler painted in 1872 (which hangs in the Tate Gallery (see p. 38)), but the houses where Whistler and the other Chelsea artists lived still stand on the north bank in Cheyne Walk, just downstream from the village of houseboats and the remains of Cremorne Gardens. In the nineteenth century these were London's largest pleasure gardens, from where Charles Green (1785–1870) made his famous ascent in a gas balloon, accompanied by a lady in a leotard and a leopard, and a certain Madame Geneviève crossed the Thames on a tightrope in 1861. Cheyne Walk's list of one-time residents reads like a *Who's Who* of British artists: Turner lived at Number 19; Philip Wilson Steer (1860–1942) at 109; Walter Greaves (1846–1930) at 104 and Whistler at 96. Whistler loved the river and its buildings: 'They lose themselves in the dim sky and the tall chimneys become *campanili*, and the warehouses are palaces in the night, and the whole city hangs in the heavens.'

Downstream from Battersea Bridge stands **CROSBY HALL**, too grand to be a mere mansion and too modest to be a proper palace. It was moved brick by brick to Chelsea from Bishopsgate in the City in 1910. The hall, in which Richard III (1483–85) is supposed to have heard of the murder of the Princes in the Tower in 1483, was built in about 1470 and has a wonderfully delicate hammerbeam roof, a minstrels' gallery and a beautiful oriel window. At the far end of the hall hangs Hans Holbein's (1497–1543) painting of Thomas More and his family. This seems fitting since More once owned Crosby Hall, and it now stands on part of his old garden.

More, Wolsey's successor as the Lord Chancellor of England, and executed in 1535 because he refused to acknowledge Henry VIII as the head of the Church of England, was Chelsea's most illustrious resident. His statue stands on the Embankment, serene, stubborn, a little smug and intensely ordinary. Desiderius Erasmus (1466–1536), the Dutch scholar, spoke of his 'deeply set eyes which have specks in them – indications of a happy disposition'. His house stood in Beaufort Street, a Tudor mansion surrounded by courtyards and orchards. Evelyn called it that 'sweet place in Chelsea'.

More's church, All Saints, is only a few yards away, on the corner of Cheyne Walk and Old Church Street. It is known as **CHELSEA OLD CHURCH**, although it was rebuilt after the War. The inside is a beautiful example of sensitive restoration. The walls are bemedalled with Tudor, Jacobean and baroque memorials, while the chapel More raised for his first wife, one of the first renaissance chapels in England, survives to the right of the altar.

Running off Cheyne Walk, in a little street of Queen Anne and Georgian houses called Cheyne Row, is **CARLYLE'S HOUSE**. Thomas Carlyle (1795–1881), the eminent writer and historian, first saw it in 1834 and described it in a letter to his wife as 'on the whole a most massive, roomy, sufficient old house; with places, for example, to hang say three dozen hats or cloaks on'. As for the street, it 'runs out upon a beautiful "Parade" . . . huge shady trees; boats lying moored and the smell of shipping and tar . . . the broad River with white-trousered white-shirted Cockneys dashing by like arrows in their long canoes of boats'. To enter the house is to go back 150 years. It is preserved by the National Trust, and hardly a chair has been moved since the old man died. Here is a screen covered with postcards and prints, there a card table beside an ugly but comfortable chair, and a hat rack by the garden door, and everything a different shade of lacquered brown. Some 35 years after his death another writer, Henry James (1843–1916), died a few yards away, in Carlyle Mansions, named after the great man.

Beyond Albert Bridge and David Wynne's sculpture, *Boy with a Dolphin*, the Georgian houses on Cheyne Walk become larger and grander, with wrought iron balconies and cast iron railings. Dante Gabriel Rossetti (1828–82) lived at number 16 after his wife, Elizabeth Siddal, died of a laudanum overdose in 1862, and at the suitably numbered number 10, the Liberal Prime Minister David Lloyd George (1863–1945) lived. My favourite Cheyne Walk resident is the millionaire John Camden Neild, who lived at number 5. He was so disgusted by his ingratiating family that he left all his money to Queen Victoria (1837–1901). George Eliot (1819–80), the novelist, who died next door at number 4, never knew him, which is a pity. She could have made good use out of a character like that.

A little further on, across Royal Hospital Road and hidden by a high brick wall, is a secret garden where the smells of herbs blend and separate as you walk along its paths – the **CHELSEA PHYSIC GARDEN**. It was established by the Society of Apothecaries in 1673, for growing medicinal herbs and 'the manifestation of the glory, power and wisdom of God and in the works of creation'. In 1683 the first cedar tree to be grown in Britain was planted here and in 1732 the Society sent the first cotton seeds from the South Seas to Georgia. Its hothouse was famous, and in 1684 John Evelyn wrote of 'the subterraneous heat conveyed by a stove under the conservatory all vaulted with brick'. Overseeing it all, in the middle of the garden, is J. M. Rysbrack's statue of Sir Hans Sloane (1660–1753), who bought the lease of the garden, and gave it to the Apothecaries 'in perpetuity'.

A few minutes' walk along Chelsea Embankment, the Edwardian apartment blocks – and the extraordinary Swan House by Richard Norman Shaw (1831–1912) which seems to contain the complete history of British architecture in it – end and Wren's red bricked **ROYAL HOSPITAL** comes into view. It is not as spectacular as his Royal Naval College in Greenwich, but is more homely; 'quiet and dignified and the work of a gentleman' (Carlyle).

It was founded by Charles II for soldiers. In 1682 he laid the foundation stone, and the building took ten years to complete. It is stately without being ostentatious. The main building – dignified by Tuscan columns, entablature, pediment and colonnades – and its two wings, form an open court, Figure Court, with Grinling Gibbons's statue of Charles II in the centre. College Court and Light Horse Court guard its flanks. In the centre of the main range, on either side of the domed vestibule, stand the hall and chapel: the former is graced by a wall painting of Charles II on horseback; the latter is panelled, with a chequered marble floor, and has a painting inside the dome of the Resurrection by Sebastiano Ricci (1659–1734).

The small gardens that follow the Chelsea Hospital are all that is now left of **RANELAGH GARDENS**, the great pleasure haunt of Georgian London, painted by Canaletto (1697–1768) and as much a part of the eighteenth-century London landscape as Cremorne Gardens was part of the nineteenth. They were opened in 1742, and the centrepiece was a rococo rotunda where Mozart

ABOVE *Figure Court, Chelsea Hospital, built by Christopher Wren between 1682 and 1692 for veteran soldiers, to complement the Royal Naval Hospital at Greenwich. The statue in the foreground, of Charles II, the hospital's founder, dressed in Roman garb, is by Grinling Gibbons. The hall and chapel range stands sedately beyond.*

OPPOSITE *George Eliot's house, 4 Cheyne Walk: a Queen Anne house built in 1718 with early eighteenth-century wrought-iron railings leading to one of the most beautiful domestic doorways in London.*

Turner's Moonlight – a study at Millbank *is one of the hundreds of paintings, sketches and studies bequeathed by him to the nation on the understanding that they be kept and displayed together. It is now in the Clore Gallery of the Tate.*

played at the age of eight. They were famous for the paradings of the two sexes, and Edward Gibbon (1737–94) called them 'the best market we have in England'. At Chelsea Bridge, the heavy early Victorian iron towers built in 1858 (and rebuilt in 1937) hold up the iron span like puppeteers. Behind, on the other side of the water, stretches **BATTERSEA PARK**, marked by its Peace Pagoda, a piece of municipal chinoiserie, in front of the big brick towers of Battersea Power Station.

Here the river makes a slight turn to the north, and just beyond the turn, after Vauxhall Bridge Road, the **TATE GALLERY** comes into view, a little place of neo-classical grandeur by the Thames. Its glories are its English paintings, its modern works, and the Turner Bequest. A central corridor, roughly separating the English collection on the left from the modern collection on the right, leads to Auguste Rodin's (1840–1917) eternal *The Kiss*, and on to Room 1, which displays the earliest English paintings. The finest works in Room 2 are the Hogarth paintings, Thomas Gainsborough and George Stubbs (1724–1806) preserve the English eighteenth century in Room 3, and in Room 4 are Richard Wilson's *View of the Thames at Twickenham*, Samuel

Scott's (c.1702–72) *An Arch of Westminster Bridge* and his view of *Nine Elms from the River*. Three of the four walls in Room 6 are given to William Blake, and include his watercolour illustrations for the *Divine Comedy*. The biblical theme is repeated in a slightly more obvious way next door in Room 7 where an entire wall is devoted to three epics by John Martin (1789–1854), painted on a scale worthy of Cecil B. deMille. Beyond the pre-Raphaelite Room – its walls weeping Rossettis, Burne-Joneses, Holman Hunts and Millaises – Whistler's *Old Battersea Bridge* and Walter Greaves's *Battersea Reach* hang in Room 11. In Room 12, taking you completely by surprise is Pablo Picasso's (1881–1973) sad and beautiful *Girl in a Chemise*, and next door in Room 13 André Derain's (1880–1954) *Pool of London*. Most of the modern collection hangs on the other side of the main corridor. It changes more often than the English collection (some of it on a three-month cycle), but some works, like Salvador Dali's (1904–1989) surreally ridiculous *Mountain Lake*, Picasso's *Three Dancers* and his agonizing *Woman Weeping* will always be there. In the Clore extension, which comes off it, is the Turner Bequest, the largest and finest group of Turner's paintings under one roof, the different rooms devoted to Venice, the Classical Ideal, the Sublime, and England (including his two views of the Thames, from Richmond Hill and Greenwich).

On the South Bank you lose the river after Battersea Park and it does not return until Vauxhall, where you walk downstream, to Lambeth Bridge, and first catch sight of the early Tudor brickwork on the gatehouse of **LAMBETH PALACE**. Built on the river like all the great palaces, Lambeth Palace has been the London residence of the Archbishop of Canterbury since 1209. Inside the palace walls are a series of medieval domestic buildings unique in the country, and the oldest library in England, founded by Archbishop Richard Bancroft (1544–1610). The Palace is still in use, and very private, but from the small park behind you can catch glimpses of Archbishop Juxon's (1582–1663) mid seventeenth-century pinnacled hall (which Pepys called 'a new old-fashioned hall' when it was built), Archbishop Laud's (1573–1645) early seventeenth-century tower, and the fifteenth-century Water Tower.

Beside the gatehouse stands **ST MARY'S CHURCH**, all of which but the fourteenth-century tower was rebuilt in the nineteenth century by Philip Hardwick (1792–1870). In it lie Bishop Bancroft himself, close to his beloved library, Elias Ashmole (1617–92), whose collection forms the base of the Ashmolean Museum in Oxford, Admiral William Bligh (1753–1817) of the HMS *Bounty*, and the two John Tradescants, father (c.1580–1638) and son (1608–62), the leading gardeners in England in the first half of the seventeenth century, employed by Henrietta Maria as 'gardeners to the rose and lily queen'. They travelled as far as Russia and Virginia in search of new plants and fruits, introducing the pineapple, among other things, to England. They established a museum of rare plants in Lambeth, called The Ark. The churchyard has become another ark, a home of rare and beautiful plants in the centre of London, while the church is now a museum of garden history.

Downstream from the Tate, Lambeth Bridge, flanked by obelisks, stretches across the Thames. A short walk downstream and a few yards up Dean Stanley Street, is Thomas Archer's ST JOHN'S SMITH SQUARE, a baroque extravaganza with an enormous tower on each corner making it look like an upside-down chair, and surrounded by beautiful and unexpected Queen Anne and early Georgian houses. The road leaves the river bank here, and a delicate triangle of grass, Victoria Tower Gardens, separates Millbank from the Thames, the triangle gently opening up to Rodin's *Burghers of Calais*, with Charles Barry's (1795–1860) HOUSES OF PARLIAMENT behind.

Jutting out from the Houses of Parliament, just after Old Palace Yard, is the GREAT HALL, its lines merging so closely with the neo-gothic Houses of Parliament you hardly notice it. It is all that is left of the old Palace of Westminster, built by William II, William Rufus (1087–1100), and given a new hammerbeam roof weighing 660 tons by Henry Yevele (*c*.1320–1400), who also built the naves of Westminster Abbey and Canterbury Cathedral. Over the centuries the Palace of Westminster was extended, and once Parliament got into it in 1265, it never left, gradually pushing the kings out, until 1512, when a large part of it was gutted in a fire and Henry VIII moved out all together, building a new palace for himself in Whitehall (see p. 98), and leaving Westminster to Parliament. The Great Hall not only held parliaments, but feasts, celebrations, weddings, state trials and lyings in state as well. Lyings in state seem its most suitable use. It is dark and cold, like a cathedral without God in it. The Great Hall is all that survived the fire of 16 October, 1834. The rest of the Palace of Westminster had to be rebuilt. A competition was organized and Charles Barry won it. The design had to be either patriotic gothic or patriotic Tudor. With the help of the neo-gothic crusader, A. W. N. Pugin (1812–52), Barry compromised with a bit of both.

Best viewed from the south bank, the towers, pinnacles and neo-gothic sugar-coating on the Houses of Parliament stretch from Victoria Tower at the west end to the clock tower – commonly, if incorrectly, known as Big Ben – at the east end, with everything between them symmetrical; while a line of medieval kings, standing like saints in alcoves amid repeating patterns of windows, look down on the Thames as it flows softly by.

The interior is not so much neo-gothic as muscular Pre-Raphaelite, and there are times, standing in the Central Lobby, when you would be excused for thinking that you're in the Law Courts. Corridors leading from either side of the lobby lead to the House of Lords and the House of Commons. The frescoes on the walls are a historical compromise, with Charles I and Oliver Cromwell treated equally as heroes, and make you yearn for the passions of a Diego Rivera. The House of Lords is at one end, in undiluted neo-gothic, and the House of Commons is at the other, stark and leathery in its rebuilt post-war form, like an old first class railway compartment.

On the other side of St Margaret Street stands WESTMINSTER ABBEY, with St Margaret's Church to the north and the abbey precincts and cloisters to

ABOVE *Westminster Abbey, the mid thirteenth-century north transept.*

OPPOSITE *Charles Barry's and August Welby Northmore Pugin's Houses of Parliament and Clock Tower 'Big Ben', seen from the south bank. From Barry came the grand plan, and from Pugin the details and ornamentation, for what the critic John Pope-Hennessy calls 'this great and beautiful monument to Victorian artifice'.*

the south. Here for nearly a thousand years every English monarch save Edward V (1470–c.83), who was murdered in the Tower, and Edward VIII (1894–1972, reigned 1936), who abdicated, has been crowned.

The earliest Westminster Abbey of which remains can be seen was built by Edward the Confessor (1042–66) for Benedictine monks, in what was the 'foreign' Norman style, in vogue in the naive and pious court of the Confessor. His tomb is still here, lying in the Chapel of the Kings behind the High Altar. Harold II (1066), his successor, was crowned in the Abbey, and William the Conqueror rode up the aisle on horseback on Christmas Day 1066, and crowned himself while his Saxon subjects were being slaughtered by his Norman soldiers outside. Henry III (1216–72) rebuilt the Abbey in the Early English style. Ironically this was seen at the time as a French style, and hated for being modern and un-English. The cost bankrupted him.

Coming up to the west end of the Abbey, all you see is Nicholas Hawksmoor's early eighteenth-century neo-gothic, twin 225-foot towers, completely blocking Henry Yevele's high nave walls and held in place by giant buttresses. The Early English nave exterior is austere up to the far east end, the outside of the Henry VII Chapel, where the intricate patterns lighten the mood and the pinnacles are feminine rather than phallic, as suits a building on what was once the site of a Lady Chapel.

Inside, where the Unknown Warrior lies under a simple black slab by the entrance, your eyes soar upwards. The nave is high and narrow, and is the tallest in England. Eight bays with pointed arches, held up by pillars of marble, take you to the screen, pointedly neo-gothic and designed by Edward Blore (1787–1879) in 1834. Almost up against it Sir Isaac Newton (1642–1727) and the first Earl Stanhope (1673–1721), both carved by Rysbrack, look out over the nave. They are a perfect choice to prepare us for the statuary to come, for Westminster Abbey, like St Paul's Cathedral (see pp 70–73) and Highgate Cemetery (see p. 177), is not only the haunt of the famous, but of the almost-famous, and the vaguely-heard-of too.

Behind the screen is the choir, lined with Victorian stalls so theatrical that they look as if they have come from the House of Lords. Transepts open up on either side. The north transept is so crowded with statuary that it resembles a tube platform in the rush-hour. And as in a rush-hour crowd, only a few shapes and faces stand out. Here are three prime ministers: Lord Palmerston (1784–1865), Pitt the Elder (1708–78), and Sir Robert Peel (1788–1850); worthy epitaphs in three dimensions. More moving is Louis François Roubiliac's (c.1702–62) monument of Lady Elizabeth Nightingale sinking down as her husband tries to ward off Death's arrow.

On the other side of the nave, in the south transept, is Poets' Corner. Geoffrey Chaucer (1345–1400) has a reasonable and unostentatious tomb, John Milton (1608–74) a statue by Rysbrack, and Shakespeare (1564–1616) the clothes of a fop. Edmund Spenser (c.1552–99), William Camden (1551–1623), the antiquarian, and Ben Jonson (1572–1637), his name spelled incorrectly, are all remembered; there are somewhat pompous tributes to Samuel Johnson, John Gay, William Wordsworth (1770–1850), Samuel Taylor Coleridge (1772–1834) and Robert Southey (1774–1843); and a series of rather dull and sparse tablets to T. S. Eliot (1888–1965), Henry James, Dylan Thomas and assorted 'moderns'. The most beautiful of the monuments in Poets' Corner is not to a writer at all. It is Roubiliac's monument to the Duke of Argyll (1678–1743), the man who brought about the Union between England and Scotland in 1707.

To the east, beyond the crossing, is the resting place of sixteen kings and queens, their children, cousins, hatchet-men and hangers-on: the largest concentration of royal corpses in the country, buried in marshy ground – if Westminster Abbey wasn't a 'Royal Peculiar', it would have been closed down by a sanitary inspector years ago. First, behind the High Altar, close to the Coronation Chair, is the body of Edward the Confessor, in a marble tomb. A late Perpendicular screen embellished with scenes from his life separates his tomb from those of Henry III, Edward I (1272–1307) and Eleanor of Castile (d.1290), Edward III and Philippa of Hainault (c.1314–69), Richard II and Anne of Bohemia, and Henry V and Catherine of Valois (1401–37). She had been buried in the old Lady Chapel a century before Henry VII (1485–1509) built his chapel and left in a wooden coffin when the Lady Chapel was demolished. In 1669 the coffin was opened. Samuel Pepys watched the lid being levered off, bent down and kissed the corpse on the mouth, writing in his diary that evening, 'that this was my birthday 36 years old and that I did kiss a Queen'.

There are more royal tombs to come. In a tiny chapel off the north ambulatory, are those of queens Mary and Elizabeth, Elizabeth's with an effigy by Maximilian Colt, Mary's, as suits so sad and plain a queen, bare. Further on, at the end of the passage, are the bones of two children, found under a stairway in the Tower of London, supposedly the bones of Edward V and his brother, the Princes in the Tower. It is called Innocents' Corner.

In the side chapels off the south ambulatory, lie Mary Queen of Scots (1542–87), in the most extravagant tomb of them all, and Lady Margaret Beaufort (1443–1509), mother of Henry VII, her body beautifully carved, right to the veins on her hands, by Pietro Torrigiano (1472–1522), the man who has never lived down punching Michelangelo on the nose.

Around a corner from these tiny chapels, the whole edifice changes and lightens as you enter the Henry VII Chapel through a set of bronze early renaissance gates. The ceiling, with its delicate groin vaulting and pendants, appears to float above you. Henry VII, his wife Elizabeth of York (d.1503), Edward VI and George II (1727–60) are all buried beneath it. Henry VII's tomb, completed in 1518 and designed, like his mother's, by Torrigiano, is decorated with virginal cherubs, the earliest renaissance angels to arrive in England, and opening the way for the age of Baroque when the *putti* were anything but virginal. At the far end of the chapel Oliver Cromwell lay for

two years, before his corpse was disinterred, and hanged, drawn and quartered in 1661, after the Restoration of the Monarchy.

Beside the Abbey, to the south, are the cloisters and Chapter House in the precincts. The eastern passage off the four simple and unadorned vaulted cloisters, built in the thirteenth and fourteenth centuries, leads to the thirteenth-century octagonal Chapter House, its shape symbolizing the equality of all in the monastic community. The marble shafts are carved with foliage, six of the eight side walls are lit by enormous four-light windows, and around the walls are faded paintings depicting the Life of St John and the Apocalypse, showing such animals as the ostrich, wild ass, camel, reindeer, crocodile and deer.

Just to the north of the Abbey stands ST MARGARET'S CHURCH, a dwarf in comparison. It was built in the late fifteenth century and the stained glass in the east window is nearly 500 years old. Sir Walter Ralegh, William Caxton (c.1422–91), Admiral Blake (1599–1657), Cromwell's mother and another of his daughters, lie buried in the churchyard. Inside, the memorials along the nave walls are a delight, the kneeling effigy to Blanche Parry, Queen Elizabeth's maid, in her ruff, the most delightful of all.

Opposite, on the South Bank, past that riverside view of the Houses of Parliament that you've seen on a thousand chocolate boxes, you are confronted by the municipal baroque of County Hall – its sweeps suggesting Town Planning ennobled by the Gods and Goddesses of Foresight. Further on, Town Planning scores an overwhelming victory in that wasteland of concrete, the SOUTH BANK, housing the Royal Festival Hall, Queen Elizabeth Hall, Purcell Room, Hayward Gallery, National Film Theatre, the Museum of the Moving Image and National Theatre.

Return to the north embankment at Sir William Hambro Thornycroft's (1850–1925) statue of Boadicea in her chariot charging Westminster Bridge. VICTORIA EMBANKMENT is the grandest of all the embankments, built by Bazelgette between 1868 and 1872. Grand and monumental, epitomizing the Victorian era, it comes as a surprise to discover that it contains within it not merely an underground railway, but the biggest sewer in London.

This is perfectly logical given London's geography. London lies in a valley carved out by the Thames. For hundreds of years her sewerage came down the valley, in rivers like the Fleet and the Westbourne, and into the tidal Thames. Every day the tide shifted the sewerage some 20 miles downstream, then brought it 18 miles upstream. It took three weeks for the sewerage to reach open sea, and sometimes, as in the year 1858, it never got there.

The Great Stink of 1858 was the product of a low river, a long hot summer and the 369 sewers that emptied themselves into the Thames. Paddle steamers started churning up the muck and excursions on the river came to a standstill, the Law Courts considered evacuating to Oxford and the windows of the Houses of Parliament had to be hung with sheets soaked in chloride of lime while its members debated whether or not to move to Hampton Court. The lack of embankments made the problem worse, and low tide revealed miles upon miles of riverside mudbanks, sweating waste. You can see how much wider the Thames was before it was embanked by looking at York Watergate, built in 1626 and now all that remains of York House, in Embankment Gardens. Bazelgette realized that the only way to relieve London was to embank the River and build a series of gigantic sewers running parallel to it that would intercept the waste coming down the valley before it reached the Thames. Through the 1860s and 1870s six of these sewers, three north of the river and three south, were built, as only the Victorians could build them – unforgettable neo-gothic subterranean cathedrals, with weirs where the interceptory sewers crossed the main (north–south) sewers, so when an upper interceptory was ready to overflow the surplus poured over the sides and down to the next interceptory lower down the valley. The final sewer is the Embankment itself. A bust of the man who built it looks out from the Embankment opposite Northumberland Avenue.

The space between the old river bank and the Embankment is filled with four narrow gardens, packed with official-looking statuary of such famous names as the inventor of Sunday Schools, the writer of the best guide book on London and a blind Postmaster General. Only one, of Sir Arthur Sullivan (1842–1900), half of Gilbert and Sullivan, with the topless figure of Music embracing the pedestal, is at all memorable. Behind the line of statues the backdrop varies from the Scottish baronial of New Scotland Yard (formerly the headquarters of the Metropolitan Police), through Ministry of Defence brutalism and French renaissance fantasy, to the ghost of Adam's neo-classical Adelphi Terrace, and the Savoy Hotel. On the other side of the road, beside the river, is Cleopatra's Needle, given to Britain by Mohammed Ali (c. 1769–1849), maker of modern Egypt. Hieroglyphics down the column reel off its Pharaoh's victories. Inside, the Victorians, with a mind to future archaeology, placed a textbook on engineering, the Bible, a packet of newspapers, a photograph of Queen Victoria and Bradshaw's Railway Guide. The Savoy takes you almost up to Waterloo Bridge. It isn't the bridge of the movie, *Waterloo Bridge*, the bridge that Antonio Canova (1757–1822) called the most beautiful in the world, but one built during World War II.

Beyond Waterloo Bridge rises SOMERSET HOUSE. The original Somerset House was built by Protector Somerset and remained unfinished when he mounted the scaffold in 1552. It was rebuilt over decades by Sir William Chambers, the work starting in 1776, and turned into a magnificent Palladian mansion around four sides of a vast courtyard, with its best face to the river. From its entrance of three archways on the Strand, the courtyard opens up with statues of George III and Father Thames in the foreground.

A small door to the right under the entrance arch leads to the Courtauld Institute Galleries. A grand spiral staircase, from which you marvel at the delicate classical plasterwork, takes you to the uppermost floor: vast and high, and once the Royal Academy's Great Room where the Summer Exhibitions

The massive rusticated river-front façade of Somerset House dwarfs passers-by. It was built before the Thames was embanked in the nineteenth century and was originally much closer to the water's edge.

Sir William Chambers's magnificent Palladian Somerset House. Before the Thames was embanked the house's south terrace was on the water's edge.

were held, displaying, amongst other works, Georges Seurat's (1859–91) *Young Woman Powdering Herself*. Smaller rooms lead off from the Great Room; in one are twentieth-century English paintings by such artists as Walter Sickert, Duncan Grant (1885–1978) and Ben Nicholson (1894–1982); in another are early renaissance paintings, panels and triptychs, including masterpieces by Bernardo Daddi (*c.*1290–1350) and Fra Angelico (1387–1455). One floor down, beneath a neo-classical painted ceiling, hang Lucas Cranach the Elder's (1472–1553) *Adam and Eve*, Giambattista Tiepolo's (1697–1770) *Allegory of the Power of Eloquence*, lots of Rubens (1577–1640), a fascinating view of the Thames from Somerset House by Canaletto, Edouard Manet's (1832–83) *A Bar at the Folies-Bergère, Autumn Effect at Argenteuil*, and a version of *Le Dejeuner sur l'Herbe*, Edgar Degas's (1834–1917) *Woman at the Window*, Vincent van Gogh (1853–90) without the ear, Pierre Auguste Renoir's (1841–1919) *La Loge*, several Seurats, Paul

George Seurat's Young Woman Powdering Herself *(1889–90) hangs in what was the main exhibition room of the Royal Academy at Somerset House, and which is now part of the Courtauld Institute Galleries. The painting shows his pregnant mistress, Madeleine Knoblock, and originally had the artist's self-portrait in the mirror.*

Gauguin's (1848–1903) unforgettable *Nevermore*, and the Modigliani (1884–1920) nude that defined the female form for the twentieth century.

The river continues on the south bank to Bankside, past the bare red bricks of Sir Giles Gilbert Scott's (1880–1960) Bankside Power Station – built in 1960 and already a relic of an earlier era – where you get a splendid view of St Paul's Cathedral. In Hopton Street is a group of delightful early Georgian almshouses, built around a little garden of flowers and plane trees. A few minutes further on, by the old Bear Gardens – where bears were baited in Elizabethan times – stands the Anchor pub. Hester Thrale entertained Samuel Johnson there, and it was here 'at a little alehouse on the Bankside', that Samuel Pepys 'saw the fire glow, and as it grew darker, appeared more and more, and in corners and upon steeples, and between churches and houses, as far as we could see up the hill of the City, in a most horrid malicious bloody flame'. It was the Great Fire of London. A few years later, when

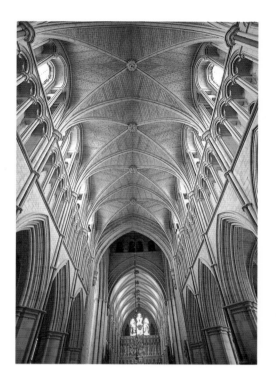

Southwark Cathedral's nave, by Sir Reginald Blomfield, erected between 1890 and 1897, is a meticulous copy of the thirteenth-century nave, demolished in 1830. At the bottom of the picture, at the far end of the nave, behind the altar, is the magnificent early Tudor screen, the much-restored figures in its niches representing saints, kings, bishops, clerics and other notables associated with the church.

London was being rebuilt, Sir Christopher Wren lived in a little cottage on the riverside a few yards from the Anchor, at number 1, Cardinal Wharf.

On the other side of Southwark Bridge is Park Street, where the foundations of the Elizabethan Rose Theatre were uncovered during building work in 1989. The Rose Theatre was built in 1587 and it was there that Christopher Marlowe's (1564–93) *Tamburlaine the Great* had its premiere in 1587 and William Shakespeare's *Titus Andronicus* was performed. At Clink Street, a few yards downstream, the river view disappears and the street becomes dark and Doréesque, closed in by high warehouses and hanging hoists, and made darker still by the Cannon Street railway bridge that runs over it. In Shakespeare's time Southwark, lying outside the jurisdiction of the City of London, was where the theatres and the whorehouses were. Since the suburb was owned by the Bishop of Winchester, the whores were called 'Winchester Geese'. Now Clink Street has a museum devoted to them, and to Clink Prison where the unlucky ones ended up. Does any other city in the world have a museum devoted to brothels? The remnants of the Bishop of Winchester's palace lie almost next to it, the ruins of the fourteenth-century Great Hall squashed between canyons of unpointed bricks, looking just like a church in the Blitz.

Southwark, at the head of the road to Canterbury, was a place of inns too. There was the Tabard (from where Chaucer's pilgrims set off), the King's Head, the Queen's Head, the Spur, the Bull, the St Christopher and the George. Part of the George still exists, just off Borough High Street, a topsy-turvy inn, rebuilt in the seventeenth century with three irregular galleries. Only one remains, but you can still eat and drink in it.

Almost hidden among the warehouses that grew up over the whorehouses is **SOUTHWARK CATHEDRAL**. Originally it was a monastery, the monks founding a hospital in 1173, dedicated to Saint Thomas Becket some three years after his murder. Their monastic church burned down in 1206 and in its place rose London's first gothic church. Its north and south aisles and the ambulatory still survive. The south transept came later, completed in 1420; while the lovely late gothic screen, honeycombed with niches now holding Victorian saints, and the four pinnacles on the tower, appeared a hundred years later still. The present nave is an exact copy of the original, a painstaking work of academic conservation by Sir Reginald Blomfield (1856–1942).

The tombs and memorials in Southwark Cathedral are boldly painted in bright colours, so they shine amid the grey stonework as the tombs and statues once shone in almost every church in pre-Reformation England. In the north aisle is the tomb of the medieval poet John Gower (*c.*1325–1408), 'the moral Gower', as Chaucer called him. Around the corner in the north transept is the charming memorial to Joyce Austen (d.1626), whoever she may be, with Agriculture standing amid sheaves of corn. In the north choir aisle, is the chapel dedicated to John Harvard (1607–38), founder of Harvard College, who was baptized here. On the other side of the choir, close to the memorial to

Shakespeare, lies Launcelot Andrews (1555–1626), the Anglican divine whose sermons contain some of the finest prose in the English language.

Outside, the cathedral precincts and the surrounding pavements are permanently covered in squashed fruit and vegetables. Southwark Market, a vast, almost Art Nouveau, late Victorian market arcade held up on solid cast iron pillars, is London's oldest fruit and vegetable market, originating from the 'Market of the Household', held on Old London Bridge. The new London Bridge, almost up against it, stretches effortlessly across the river.

On the north bank, the City begins at Temple Gardens (see p. 79), only a few hundred yards before the Embankment comes to an end at Blackfriars Bridge. There you leave the river and make your way up Queen Victoria Street, past Wren's **ST ANDREW BY-THE-WARDROBE** and along St Andrew's Hill, where the warehouses still retain their hoists. Beside the church is the Georgian rectory, at the unlikely address of $35\frac{1}{2}$ St Andrew's Hill.

Further on, past Morris Emmett's post-Fire College of Arms, called by the writer William Maitland 'one of the handsomest and best designed brick buildings in London', you rejoin the river at St Paul's Steps, where the modern buildings of the City of London School almost hide St Benet, Paul's Wharf, Wren's 'Dutch' church, topped by a cupola, lantern and spire.

You lose the river again within a few office blocks and as you walk down Upper Thames Street, the Wren churches and mostly Hawksmoor towers – St Mary Somerset, St James, Garlickhythe and St Michael Paternoster Royal – almost disappear amid the high-rise, high-tech office blocks. Only Edward Jarman's late renaissance Vintners' Hall, facing the river at Southwark Bridge, and the unadulterated Greek Revival **FISHMONGERS' HALL** (1831–4), offer some relief. Upper Thames Street was not always like this. In March 1668 Samuel Pepys 'walked all along Thames Street, which I have not done since it was burned, as far as Billingsgate; and there do see a brave street likely to be, many brave houses being built'.

To see Fishmongers' Hall at its best, you must stand on London Bridge and, after first looking upstream, at the Hall riding over the riverside and the dome of St Paul's behind it, look downstream, at one of the finest picture postcard views of London: the Pool of London, and the outlines of St Magnus Martyr, the old Billingsgate Fish Market, the Custom House, the Tower of London, HMS *Belfast* and Tower Bridge.

Fishmongers' Hall, dwarfed by office blocks. The hall was built by Edward Jarman after the Great Fire and rebuilt in 1827 in a similar neo-classical design (Sir George Gilbert Scott did the drawings) when London Bridge was demolished and re-erected. To the right rises Wren's Monument to the Great Fire of London.

2
The City and its Churches

....

ST STEPHEN WALBROOK *to* ST PAUL'S CATHEDRAL

The Port of London made the City and there is no better place to catch the spirit of that city than at Bank Station in the morning rush-hour. On the periphery of a whirlpool of clerks, secretaries, computer operators, shop assistants, tea-ladies, accountants and stockbrokers, eddies and slipstreams form at the station exits which pump out people to Prince's Street, Poultry, Queen Victoria Street, the Mansion House, King William Street, Lombard Street, Cornhill, Cheapside, the Royal Exchange and the Bank of England.

This is the financial heart of London. From any of Bank Station's exits a 360 degree view reveals a neo-classical circle, exuding confidence and longevity. It is broken only by the wedge on the corner of Queen Victoria Street and Cheapside, and by the spire of Wren's St Mary-le-Bow in Cheapside, a gothic steeple rising from a drum of twelve classical columns and bearing on its zenith a Greek cross. There is the Bank of England screen by Sir John Soane; the less elegant neo-classical 1930s Bank of England block by Sir Herbert Baker (1862–1946) behind Soane's screen; Sir William Tite's (1798–1873) exaggerated Athenian Royal Exchange; a touch of Edwardian baroque on the corner of Cornhill and King William Street; George Dance the Elder's (1700–68) Mansion House, and the reassuringly monolithic inter-war neo-classical banks on Poultry. Behind this circle the roofline to the west is low, kept down by Corporation of London decree so that nothing stands tall beside the dome of St Paul's. To the east the buildings shoot up into a coppice of skyscrapers: the Stock Exchange, Natwest Tower, Lloyd's Building, and attendant steel stumps.

Into these neo-classical edifices and post-modern tower blocks – and into the thousands of more modest Victorian, Edwardian, pre-war and post-war offices that surround them – pour half a million people, two-thirds of them women, every working morning, by bus, tube, train, car, bicycle and on foot.

OPPOSITE *Wren's west façade and dome of St Paul's Cathedral, the spire of St Martin, Ludgate and the NatWest Tower behind.*

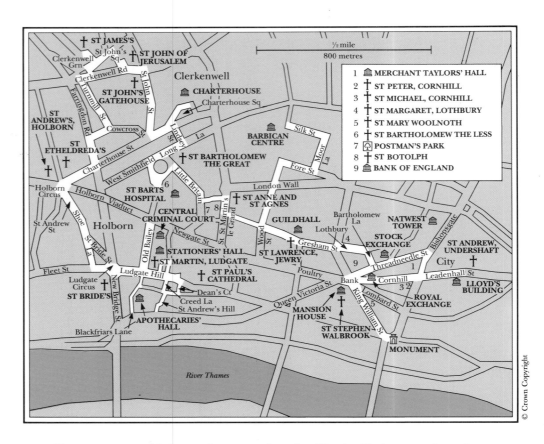

The map labels:

ST JAMES'S · St John's Sq. · ST JOHN OF JERUSALEM · Clerkenwell Grn · Clerkenwell Rd · ST JOHN'S GATEHOUSE · CHARTERHOUSE · Charterhouse Sq · Clerkenwell

½ mile
800 metres

1 🏛 MERCHANT TAYLORS' HALL
2 ✝ ST PETER, CORNHILL
3 ✝ ST MICHAEL, CORNHILL
4 ✝ ST MARGARET, LOTHBURY
5 ✝ ST MARY WOOLNOTH
6 ✝ ST BARTHOLOMEW THE LESS
7 🏠 POSTMAN'S PARK
8 ✝ ST BOTOLPH
9 🏛 BANK OF ENGLAND

ST ANDREW'S, HOLBORN · Farringdon Rd · Turnmill St · Cowcross · St John St · ST ETHELDREDA'S · Charterhouse St · West Smithfield · Long La · Little Britain · ST BARTHOLOMEW THE GREAT · Silk St · BARBICAN CENTRE · Moor La · Fore St · London Wall · Holborn Circus · Holborn Viaduct · St Andrew St · Shoe La · Holborn · ST BARTS HOSPITAL · 6 · CENTRAL CRIMINAL COURT · 7 8 · St Martin's le Grand · ST ANNE AND ST AGNES · Wood St · GUILDHALL · Bartholomew La · NATWEST TOWER · Bishopsgate · Newgate St · STATIONERS' HALL · ST MARTIN, LUDGATE · St Bride's La · Old Bailey · ST LAWRENCE, JEWRY · Gresham St · Lothbury · 14 · STOCK EXCHANGE · ST ANDREW, UNDERSHAFT · Fleet St · Ludgate Circus · New Bridge St · Ludgate Hill · Dean's Ct · Creed La · St Andrew's Hill · ST PAUL'S CATHEDRAL · Poultry · 9 · Threadneedle St · Bank · Cornhill · 1 · City · Leadenhall St · 3 2 · LLOYD'S BUILDING · ST BRIDE'S · APOTHECARIES' HALL · Blackfriars Lane · Queen Victoria St · MANSION HOUSE · King William St · Lombard St · ROYAL EXCHANGE · ST STEPHEN WALBROOK · MONUMENT · River Thames

© Crown Copyright

THE CITY

You cannot avoid them, they are what the City is all about, a city where you can be so mesmerized by the money-making that you can walk from one end to the other without noticing a single Wren church.

The City of London is not a theme park, and as long as sufficient people make sufficient money, and the pound does not totally collapse, it never will be one. The Wren churches that have survived, built in the days when the City was a residential district and the City churches were parish churches, have survived by accident. They continue to survive, in spite of their irrelevance to the mercantile spirit of the City, because Wren, like the Queen Mother, is beyond reproach.

Functionally, the City of London has been a series of markets since the Middle Ages, when stalls were selling honey in Honey Lane and poultry in Poultry. This is still so; only today they deal in different commodities, at the Stock Exchange, the Financial Futures Exchange, the Corn Exchange, the international currency markets and Lloyd's.

You can get some idea of the pace and the madness of the market place from the viewing gallery of the **LONDON INTERNATIONAL FINANCIAL FUTURES EXCHANGE**, housed in the **ROYAL EXCHANGE**. The first Royal Exchange was built by Sir Thomas Gresham (1519–79) in 1566. It was burned down in the Great Fire, and the building that replaced it, by Edward Jarman, was called one of the most beautiful in Europe. That burned down in 1838, and in its place is the present Greek Revival temple by Sir William Tite.

The Athenian interior has been turned from that of a temple into that of a market – a very modern market. The floor is crowded with dealers. There are banks of telephones along the walls and screens displaying the latest prices. The dealers do not fit the traditional image of the 'City gent'. They wear loud blazers, and each firm's blazers are a different colour (presumably so they will not deal against each other) and the colours congeal in the crowds around the computer screens. Looking down from the viewing gallery, the pink, red, yellow and purple blazers resemble a demented flowerbed.

The marketplace is everywhere in the City, although it rarely exposes itself so openly as at the London International Financial Futures Exchange. Each working day between 7.30 a.m., when the closing prices in Tokyo come in, and 10.30 p.m., when the closing prices in Wall Street come on the screen, the City is vibrant and living – horribly so. Outside those hours it slips into a long and lethargic sleep culminating on Sunday afternoons when it is so silent you can sometimes hear the choristers in St Paul's from Warwick Lane.

It is then that you notice the churches, although perversely you'll find most of them closed, for in the City of London the majority of the churches are open on weekdays but closed on Sundays. To experience the peace of their interiors you must return to them during the mayhem. One of these City churches, the most serene of all, **ST STEPHEN WALBROOK**, stands only a few yards from Bank Station, almost hidden behind the Mansion House. It is Wren's most exquisite church.

The square tower and spire are a light baroque joke. The door is simple and unobtrusive. Inside, through the wooden screen, is a rectangle with a four-sided aisle defined by tall stone Corinthian columns like a colonnade. Above the rectangle, springing up from the columns, is the dome, embellished in plaster rosettes. Beneath the dome, in the very centre of the rectangle, is Henry Moore's (1898–1986) altar, a simple stone slab on a chequered floor. The church is small, but the dome gives the appearance of great space, like the dome of St Paul's. This is intentional, for Wren used the St Stephen's dome as an experiment for St Paul's. The result is beautiful, so beautiful that Canova once said that if he ever returned to London it would be to see three things: Somerset House, St Paul's Cathedral and St Stephen Walbrook.

With its elbows up against St Stephen's, almost pushing it aside, is George Dance's **MANSION HOUSE**, the official residence of the Lord Mayor of London. The style is Palladian, designed by Dance in 1735. Its front faces the Bank of England, with a portico of six giant Corinthian columns supporting a pediment carved with 'London' trampling on 'Envy' and introducing 'Plenty'. Behind the Mansion House, running east of St Stephen Walbrook, is St Swithin's Lane, which takes you to where the crowds flow up the hill and down King William Street, and St Mary Woolnoth keeps the hour.

A short walk down King William Street, if you can negotiate the Cannon Street and Eastcheap crossing, will bring you to Wren's **MONUMENT**. It stands 202 feet high, close to the baker's shop where the Great Fire, which it

OPPOSITE *Wren's exquisite church of St Stephen Walbrook, with Henry Moore's simple altar in the middle beneath the dome. 'Perhaps Italy itself can produce no modern buildings that can vie with this in taste and proportion,' wrote* The Critical Review of Public Buildings in London *in 1734.*

commemorates, started. It is a simple Doric column, and the tallest isolated stone column in the world. On its base is a relief by Caius Gabriel Cibber (1630–1700) of Charles II in Roman dress overseeing the rebuilding of London. The 311 steps of the spiral staircase inside the column take you to the top. James Boswell (1740–95) found it 'horrid to be so monstrous a way up in the air, so far above London and all its spires'.

Return up the east side of King William Street and you come to ST MARY WOOLNOTH. It was built by Nicholas Hawksmoor between 1716 and 1727, and on the most difficult of sites, a wedge. John Betjeman (1906–84) calls it 'one of the most brilliant solutions to an awkwardly shaped site one could hope to see'. Its south and west sides were hidden until King William Street was cut through from the Bank to the new London Bridge in the 1830s.

Hawksmoor's front is heavy and monumental. The entablature above the entrance rises up then separates into two towers, where it sits with heavy baroque conviction. It is disconcerting, you expect more above: a spire, a dome, a trumpeting angel at least. St Mary's interior is square, its woodwork dark and its ceiling painted blue and dotted with stars. Hawksmoor's Corinthian columns play the same role here as Wren's do in St Stephen Walbrook, forming a four-sided aisle and suggesting a colonnade.

Amongst the memorials lining the nave wall of St Mary's is a simple brass oval to Edward Lloyd (d. 1730). He opened his coffee house in Tower Street in 1686, and it became the meeting place for all those wanting ships and cargoes to insure, and wanting insurers for their ships and cargoes. Ten years later he founded a newspaper, *Lloyd's News*, to provide shipping and trading news for his customers. It was suppressed for carrying parliamentary reports but in 1734 his successors brought out another newspaper, *Lloyd's List*, which is still published today. By then the coffee shop on Tower Street was too small, and Lloyd's had moved to Abchurch Lane off Lombard Street. They moved again in 1789 to Pope's Head Alley, between Lombard Street and Cornhill, and since then they moved half a dozen times, each time into bigger premises.

To get to the latest Lloyd's on the corner of Leadenhall Street and Lime Street, you can take a short-cut from St Mary Woolnoth through Pope's Head Alley into Cornhill. On the way you pass two Wren churches, St Michael, Cornhill and St Peter, Cornhill, both with quiet churchyards.

ST MICHAEL, CORNHILL was built by Wren in 1671, although the gothic pinnacled tower was completed by Nicholas Hawksmoor in 1722 when Wren was 90. Hawksmoor based it on his design for the tower of Magdalen College, Oxford. It was Victorianized by Sir George Gilbert Scott in 1858, and only the pelican feeding its young with its own blood, the iron sword rest and the organ on which Henry Purcell (1659–95) played, survived his zeal.

ST PETER, CORNHILL, almost lost among the shop fronts, was rebuilt by Wren in 1678, and although later Victorianized it has retained its marble font, pulpit, organ and beautiful wooden screen with the lion and the unicorn standing on top of it. Above it rises a brick tower, supporting a little cupola, a needle-thin steeple and a weather vane shaped like the keys of St Peter.

Then you pass Leadenhall Market, all iron and glass and built in 1881 by Sir Horace Jones; once the City's poultry market, and now selling chicken mayonnaise sandwiches to office workers at lunch time. A little further on, on the other side of the street is a third church, **ST ANDREW, UNDERSHAFT**, a rare pre-Fire City church. Built in the last of the late gothic styles between 1520 and 1532, and named after the tall Maypole shaft that the church kept in pre-Reformation days, St Andrew's was the last church to be consecrated in Catholic England. In 1549 the shaft was denounced as papist, chopped into pieces and consigned to the flames. St Andrew's was the parish church of John Stow. A tailor in Cornhill, he abandoned his trade to devote himself to recording the history and topography of London:

> It hath cost me many a weary mile's travel, many a hard-earned penny and pound, and many a cold winter night's study.
> (John Stow: *A Survey of London*, 1598)

A bust of him looks out from the nave, and every year the Lord Mayor of London places a quill pen into the sculpted hand at a memorial service.

Across the street from St Andrew's is Sir Richard Rogers's **LLOYD'S BUILDING**, his building-turned-inside-out facing the open piazza in front of St Andrew's and the P&O building. It is one of the most exceptional contemporary buildings in London. Yet it has produced none of the emotions of love and hatred that his Pompidou centre in Paris aroused – possibly because its understated grey blends with the weather of the English soul.

Behind the façade of Sir Edwin Cooper's inter-war neo-classical façade (with such 1930s kitsch as 'globe' and 'beehive' carved on it), Rogers's tower soars upwards, all glass, steel, pipes, shafts and ducts, its most intimate innards exposed to all. From the open piazza on the other side of Leadenhall Street you can view the edifice full on. There is a basic block, revelling in its external bracing, and three service towers shooting upwards, their tubular steel looking like vertebrae, carrying lifts, cables and air-conditioning ducts. Inside Rogers has achieved the intimacy, openness and space of the marketplace with an atrium the full height of the building, so the floors are like balconies facing inwards, and the whole building centres on the ground floor, where the Lutine bell is kept, rung once when an endangered ship has sunk and twice when an endangered ship has been reported safe.

As you return towards Bank Crossing up Leadenhall Street, Bishopsgate on the right gives you a short-cut to Threadneedle Street. There in Bishopsgate the stripes of steel and glass of the **NATWEST TOWER** soar upwards, the focus for the copse of towers and skyscrapers around it. Opened in 1980 and designed by Richard Seifert and Partners, it cost £72,000,000 and rises by 52 storeys to 600 feet, and is the tallest building in the City of London.

In complete contrast, lying in the shadow of the Natwest Tower, between Cornhill and Threadneedle Street, is **MERCHANT TAYLORS' HALL**, with more medieval remains than any other livery hall in London. It has been there since 1347, and still has its original medieval crypt and kitchen. The Merchant Taylors did well out of the Middle Ages, and became rich providing the padding to put under suits of armour. When all the hall save crypt and kitchen were destroyed in the Great Fire, they employed Edward Jarman to build them the present classical hall: its Court Room, Drawing Room and Hall forming a simple garden court with a fountain in the middle.

On the other side of Threadneedle Street rises the STOCK EXCHANGE, opened by the Queen in 1972 and already looking middle-aged. Its tower is 330 feet high, the whole thing is coated in pre-cast concrete panels. Beneath the Stock Exchange Tower, Soane's screen stretches around the Bank of England, neo-classical and chaste, save for a charming folly at Tivoli Corner.

On the far side of the Bank stands Wren's ST MARGARET, LOTHBURY. Wren finished it in 1690, building the church in white Portland stone, and giving it a square four-stage corner tower and a slender lead spire which rises 140 feet. Inside you are shoulder deep in wood. Its fittings are splendid, mainly because it has collected all the best fittings from Wren churches that have been demolished. The beautiful Grinling Gibbons carving of the lion and the unicorn, and the flowers and fruit carved on the screen and pulpit (with the pea-pod, Gibbons's personal signature), come from Wren's church of All Hallows, Bread Street, demolished in 1876; the font cover and reredos from St Olave, Jewry, demolished in 1888; the paintings of Moses and Aaron behind the altar from St Christopher-le-Stocks, demolished in 1782 when the Bank of England was extended. Only the beautiful seventeenth-century font, on a blue-veined baluster stem and carved with the images of Adam and Eve, Noah's Ark and the Baptism of Christ, is St Margaret's own.

West of Tivoli Corner and across Prince's Street, Lothbury continues a short distance past Victorian, Edwardian, pre-war and post-war offices before becoming Gresham Street. If the streets radiating from Bank Crossing represent the City's financial centre, Gresham Street, looked out on by the 600-year-old GUILDHALL, represents its administrative centre. Even the Guildhall's church, Wren's St Lawrence, Jewry, is sumptuously municipal.

There has been a Guildhall on the site since at least 1128. Here the Lord Mayor has been elected and the Common Council – a grey-suited oligarchy about as democratic as the Grand Council of Venice in the days of the Doges – have debated the City's affairs for 800 years. The present Guildhall, begun in 1411 and built in a Perpendicular style, was partly paid for out of the will of Mayor Richard Whittington, the Dick Whittington of the nursery rhyme, who became four times Lord Mayor of London. It contains the largest hall in England after Westminster Hall; where the poet Henry Howard, Earl of Surrey (c.1517–47), Lady Jane Grey and Archbishop Thomas Cranmer (1489–1556) were condemned to death. The 1666 Fire left the Guildhall standing, although gutted. For two days its insides had glowed, like 'a bright shining coal as if it had been a palace of gold or a great building of burnished

Magog looks down into the 600-year-old Guildhall from the west galley, with his brother, Gog (not in picture). The two giants were carved in limewood by David Evans, and replace the two earlier limewood statues of them, carved in 1708 by Captain Richard Saunders and destroyed on 29 December 1940.

brass', according to one eyewitness. Wren put on a temporary roof which lasted 200 years. Dance refronted the building in 1788 with buttresses and pinnacles set in an endearing mixture of classical and gothic, but left the medieval porch as it was. The Hall was again gutted in December 1940, and once again the medieval portions remained intact. A new administrative wing, containing the Guildhall's vast library on the history and topography of London, has now been built on the west side.

Between Gresham Street and the Guildhall stands ST LAWRENCE, JEWRY, 'called in the Jury because of old times many Jews inhabited thereabout', according to John Stow. It was Wren's most expensive City church, the City Corporation's own chapel; you can tell by the grand classical impedimenta of pillars and garlands on the east wall, the tower with obelisks and spire, and the weathervane shaped like a grid-iron, the symbol of St Lawrence.

Three livery halls follow on amongst the extremely ordinary post-war office blocks in Gresham Street. Two are post-war halls, Haberdashers' Hall and Wax Chandlers' Hall, and they lose themselves amongst the office blocks.

The sumptuous interior of Wren's St Lawrence, Jewry, the Corporation of London's own church; the interior was restored between 1954 and 1957 (most of the fittings were donated by the City Livery Companies) after it had been gutted in World War II.

The third is the august, **GOLDSMITHS' HALL**. The Goldsmiths' Company were founded in 1180, they were London's earliest bankers, and soon became the most wealthy and powerful of the City livery companies. The first Goldsmiths' Hall went up on the site in 1366 and was rebuilt in 1407. It burned down about 1633. The second, built by Nicholas Stone (1586–1647), was used by the Parliamentarians as their exchequer during the Civil War and Protectorate. It was gutted in the Great Fire and restored by Edward Jarman, but his building, too, was destroyed by fire. The present hall, in a rich neo-classical style, was built by Philip Hardwick in 1829.

Opposite it, and in complete contrast, is Wren's little church of **ST ANNE AND ST AGNES**, its tower crowned by turret with a vane shaped like the letter 'A'. Below it, at roof level, is a low dome. The walls are a homely red brick and the proportions so intimate that it could be mistaken for a doll's house. Its plan is a Greek cross, marked out by the four Corinthian columns supporting the dome, beneath which London's Protestant Latvian congregation worship on Sundays, and office workers listen to lunch-time concerts on Mondays.

North from Gresham Street dozens of tiny streets and alleys twist and turn in crooked northward directions towards the Barbican. One, Wood Street, still has a Wren tower, gothic and topped by six pinnacles, on an island in the middle of the street. It is all that is left of St Alban Wood Street, destroyed on 29 December 1940 when one-third of the City was burned down. The alleys stop abruptly at London Wall, which might have been a wall in Roman and medieval times, but is now a major thoroughfare, although you can still see stretches of the wall in Noble Street, behind the church of St Anne and St Agnes, and on the southern boundaries of the Barbican. The thoroughfare, each building facing diagonally on to the road, is a glittering display of reflective glass, a late twentieth-century triumphal way.

Behind it rise the three 400-foot residential towers of the **BARBICAN**, great blocks of brick and concrete of which the best that can be said of them is that they resemble the walls of a fortified city in the Middle Ages, which seems suitable for a development on the site of a Roman barbican. The Barbican did not always look like this. Lying just outside the City walls, it was heathland in the Middle Ages, where prostitutes, unlicensed traders, skilled men unable to break into the London guilds, and runaway serfs congregated. The old Barbican died in the fire of 1897. It was replaced by acres of cast-iron renaissance palaces and Art Nouveau warehouses looking more like SoHo in New York than a part of central London, which were entirely destroyed in a second great fire on 29 December 1940, save the late gothic church of St Giles, Cripplegate, where Oliver Cromwell was married and John Milton buried. Once again the area became a wilderness of rubble and fire weed, where prostitutes, army deserters, black marketeers and runaway children lived.

It was replaced by the present development. There had been hope that it could have become 'a genuine residential neighbourhood, incorporating schools, shops, open spaces and amenities, even if this means forgoing a more remunerative return on the land', as Sir Duncan Sandys, Housing Minister in the late 1950s put it. But the law of the market asserted itself, and only the wealthy can afford to live there. Londoners have got used to the buildings, and the harsh textures of glass, water and concrete, have been softened by grass, trees and bushes. The Barbican is no longer hated, merely disliked.

The **BARBICAN CENTRE**, on the north side of the complex, facing St Giles's Church across the pool, and the Museum of London on the south-west corner, are all that is left of the original ideal. In the Barbican Centre are concert halls, theatres, three cinemas, an art gallery, a library, the Guildhall School of Music and Drama, and a beautiful modern conservatory overgrown with exotic trees, plants and shrubs. In the south-west corner of the complex, by London Wall, the Museum of London tells the story of London, through the Roman finds in the Temple of Mithras found under Bucklersbury, a Viking tombstone, models of old St Paul's Cathedral (see pp. 70–73) and old Whitehall Palace (see p. 98), a diorama of the Great Fire of London, street scenes in the days of Dr Johnson and Queen Victoria and an Art Deco lift from Selfridges. The most haunting are Cibber's reclining figures of Madness and Melancholy, formerly in the Bethlehem Hospital (the lunatic asylum known as 'Bedlam'), and a cell from Newgate Prison. The most glittering is the Lord Mayor's four-ton coach, all but its panels gilded, and its panels exquisitely painted in classical make-believe by Giambattista Cipriani (1727–85).

A minute's walk west of St Anne and St Agnes, Gresham Street hits Aldersgate Street at right angles. On the other side of Aldersgate Street, where you can catch a brief glimpse of the dome of St Paul's, is the church of **ST BOTOLPH**, built between 1788 and 1791 by Nathaniel Wright, who gave it the little tower and bell-cote. The Venetian window and the classical accessories on the outside appeared about 40 years later. The interior is almost entirely Georgian, and the east window depicts the Agony in the Garden and is the only eighteenth-century painted window in the City. Above the altar the half dome is painted blue and gold, and meets a coved ceiling with plaster rosettes and foliage.

St Botolph's churchyard, behind the church, is now a public park, Postman's Park, a patch of trees and bushes about the size of a postage stamp where City workers eat their sandwiches in summer lunch-hours. At one end is a goldfish pond, and at the other an arbour, and a veranda built like an Arts and Crafts bus shelter. It is George Frederick Watts's (1817–1904) 'Shrine to Humble Heroes'. It is lined with tiles, each dedicated to a 'humble hero':

> Herbert Moconoghu. Schoolboy from Wimbledon aged 13. His parents in India, lost his life vainly trying to rescue schoolfellows who were drowned at Gloves Pool, Croyde, North Devon. August 28 1882.

> Frederick Alfred Croft. Inspector. Aged 31. Saved a lunatic woman from suicide at Woolwich Arsenal Station but was himself run over by the train. Jan 11 1878.

You come out on the other side of Postman's Park in Little Britain, unchanged in the 50 years since J. B. Priestley (1904–84) wrote of 'a gloomy street where dust and grit lay thick on everything' (*Angel Pavement*). One side is taken up by the back of St Bartholomew's Hospital, the other by alleys and passages like Bartholomew Close, still surrounded by those dowdy Victorian and Edwardian offices, 'too hot and airless in summer, too raw in winter, too wet in spring, and too smokey and foggy in autumn'.

At the end of Little Britain stands the half-timbered early Tudor gatehouse to St Bartholomew's Priory, with its statue of St Bartholomew above the entrance arch, the whole structure looking as all of London must have looked before the Great Fire, which did not get this far. Behind the gatehouse lies the churchyard of **ST BARTHOLOMEW THE GREAT**, alongside the old pre-Fire houses in Cloth Fair where the poet John Betjeman lived. Beyond the churchyard stand the remains of the Norman church, the oldest parish church in London, a mixture of black and white squares, Portland stone, brick, clunch and flint – like a church in East Anglia, as Betjeman once said.

The transepts, choir and Lady Chapel are now all that is left of St Bartholomew's. The nave, which took up the entire churchyard, was demolished after the Reformation. The priory had been founded in 1123 by Rahere (d.1144), variously described as a courtier, a jester and a prebendary at St Paul's. Inspired by a vision while suffering from malaria on a pilgrimage to Rome, he built the priory and a hospital 'to cure and comfort the poor'. After the Reformation the church was sold to Sir Richard Rich, the man who sent Thomas More to his death, but the hospital remained, refounded by Henry VIII. The priory church deteriorated, the nave was demolished and although a battlemented brick tower was built in the early seventeenth century, St Bartholomew's continued to decay. Its cloisters were turned into stables, its north transept into a blacksmith's forge and its Lady Chapel into a printer's where Benjamin Franklin (1706–90) served his apprenticeship. The church was rescued in the late nineteenth century, and meticulously and obsessively restored by Sir Aston Webb (1849–1930) to its original Norman. It is dark and stately, and as much a monument to Victorian architecture as to norman architecture.

The hospital that Rahere founded, rebuilt by James Gibbs in a sound Palladian style, still stands on the other side of Little Britain facing Smithfield. You enter through the gatehouse, built in 1702 by Edward Strong, a nephew of Wren's master mason, with a statue of Henry VIII by Francis Bird above the archway. Inside you enter a world of its own, at least a parish of its own, for the hospital's seven acres are a parish in themselves, where white-coated doctors, administrators, nurses, and cleaners, walk purposefully – for **ST BARTHOLOMEW'S** continues 'to cure and comfort the sick'.

To the left, after you come through the gateway, is **ST BARTHOLOMEW THE LESS**, the hospital's own parish church. The tower and vestibule were built in the fifteenth century, the body of the church – a playful Georgian 'gothick'

OPPOSITE *The west porch of St Bartholomew the Great, Smithfield, from the churchyard, which in pre-Reformation times, would have been the site of the nave. St Bartholomew's, built in the late Norman era, is the oldest church in London and a beautiful example of the architecture of the period.*

that looks as if it could have come straight out of Strawberry Hill (see p. 26), was built by George Dance the Younger (1741–1825); then rebuilt to exactly the same plan by Philip Hardwick in 1823, but given an iron-framed roof.

An eighteenth-century Palladian archway takes you into the main court. Around the quad Gibbs's three blocks, and a fourth 1930s neo-classical look-alike, give the quadrangle a sombre Augustinian air. On the first floor of the archway range is the great hall, and on the staircases are two vast paintings, donated by William Hogarth, a governor during Gibbs's rebuilding. One of the paintings is *The Good Samaritan*, the other is *The Pool of Bethesda*, in which every character displays the symptoms of an illness that can be identified – chlorosis, syphilis, gonorrhoea, rickets, blindness and a dozen others.

The circular green that St Bartholomew's looks out on, now the entrance to an underground car park, was the site of St Bartholomew's Fair from 1123 to 1855, the scene of tournaments where knights jousted in a spectacle that most civilized people would consider revolting. It was also the place where heretics were burned and criminals hanged in front of crowds of onlookers, which today we would consider just as revolting. On the far side of the green stands Smithfield Meat Market.

The three neo-renaissance blocks, linked to form a cathedral of iron and glass, with odd French chateau turrets and other romantic paraphernalia on the outside, were built by Sir Horace Jones, architect of Tower Bridge, Billingsgate Fish Market and Leadenhall Market. The best approach is along Grand Avenue where you can look through the cast iron gates at the nave-like interior. On the other side of Smithfield, Charterhouse Street leads to Charterhouse, past the Art Nouveau Fox and Anchor – open at 6.30 a.m., like most market pubs in London. Here, you are just across the borders of the City, in Clerkenwell, a suburb in Georgian times, where craftsmen have workshops, and the buildings seem sympathetic and on a human scale.

Charterhouse Square is still predominantly Georgian, in spite of the later Victorian and Art Deco arrivals. To the left two Queen Anne houses form a gatehouse, which leads you into the **CHARTERHOUSE**. The site was a plague pit in 1348. Twenty-three years later the Carthusians, the most rigorous and uncorrupted of the monastic orders, moved in, building the individual cells in which they ate, slept, prayed, meditated and eventually died. Thomas More spent four years living in one such cell, debating whether he should take the vows of the Order. He decided against it, though he continued to wear the Carthusian hair-shirt for the rest of his life. Whatever he had decided, his destiny would have been the same, for the Carthusian Charterhouse was virtually the only monastic house in England to stand up for its principles in the Reformation. Thirteen Carthusians were executed, Prior John Houghton and two of his fellow monks dragged to Tyburn on hurdles where they were hung, drawn and quartered – while still alive.

For three-quarters of a century after the Dissolution of the Monasteries, the Charterhouse passed from one nobleman to another, until it ended up in the hands of Thomas Sutton (1552–1611), Britain's first coal millionaire, who turned the buildings into an almshouse for 80 poor gentlefolk and school for 40 poor scholars. He lies in the Charterhouse chapel, below a sculpture of himself, '*Fundator Noster*', as W. M. Thackeray (1811–63) called him in *The Newcomes*, 'in his ruff and gown, awaiting the great examination day'.

The scholars have now moved, but the pensioners have stayed, although some of the accommodation is now rented out as offices. These newcomers have not destroyed the Charterhouse ambience, and walking through the tiny Jacobean gothic courts like Washhouse Court, the grander courts like Master's Court and Chapel Court, and the three gardens, so quintessentially English with their rose bushes, mulberry trees and creeping ivy, it is hard to comprehend that the City of London is only a few yards away.

From Charterhouse you must double back down Charterhouse Street, turn right into St John's Street and left into St John's Lane, to reach ST JOHN'S GATEHOUSE, the old Gatehouse of the Knights of St John of Jerusalem, in St John's Square. The gatehouse, built of Kentish ragstone and since tidied up and castellated like a set from *Henry V*, is all that remains of the Priory of St John of Jerusalem, once the largest and one of the richest of the monasteries surrounding London, 'the glory of north-west London', according to John

St John's Gatehouse is virtually all that remains of the Priory of the Knights of St John of Jerusalem. It was originally built in the late twelfth century, but has had some additions, like the vaguely Tudor hood-mouldings over the windows and doorways.

Stow, who remembered the whole as it had been during his pre-Reformation childhood.

The priory had been founded in 1185 by the Knights of St John of Jerusalem. That priory and all its buildings save the church crypt were burned down in the Peasants' Revolt of 1381, when the irate population, protesting at the imposition of a poll tax, dragged the unfortunate Prior Hales out of the priory and beheaded him. Priory and church were rebuilt, the buildings even more splendid than before. These passed to Protector Somerset after the Reformation and he used the priory's stones to build the first Somerset House (see p. 45). Only the gateway and crypt survived his vandalism, and by Shakespeare's time the gateway had become the office of Edmund Tilney, chief censor and Master of the Revels. The church was rebuilt in the eighteenth century and the gatehouse became the office of the *Gentleman's Magazine*, edited by Edward Cave (1691–1754), who was clearly not a gentleman since he insisted that the magazine's leading contributor, Samuel Johnson, eat his meals behind a screen so Cave's visitors would not be embarrassed by his shabbiness. The magazine moved and the gatehouse became a tavern until the late nineteenth century, when it was restored by the new Anglican Order of St John of Jerusalem, the founders of the St John's Ambulance Brigade, with whom they share the adjacent museum.

Through St John's Gate and on the other side of Clerkenwell Road is the **CHURCH OF ST JOHN OF JERUSALEM**, built on the site of the earlier priory church. Left a shell after the Blitz, its exterior facing St John's Square is red-bricked and modern, though you can see some of the Perpendicular south wall from the neighbouring garden; its interior is an assorted blend of Perpendicular, early Georgian and post-war styles. Beneath the church is the original Norman crypt, where beneath the stone-ribbed vaulting lies the sumptuous Spanish Renaissance tomb of Don Juan Ruiz de Vergera (d.1575), a worthy of the Order. On the other side of the altar rests Grand Prior William Westall (d.1540), the last Catholic head of the Order in England, who died of a broken heart when the Knights of St John of Jerusalem were suppressed. He lies in effigy above his tomb, depicted as a corpse, shrouded and withered.

Just a few blocks to the north and west, past the Georgian houses at the top of St John's Square, and via Jerusalem Passage, is Clerkenwell Green, overlooked by a church spire, surrounded by plane trees and as pretty as a village green. It is handsome and Georgian, from the neo-classical Middlesex Sessions House on the west side to the church of St James's on the north side. Even the Marx Memorial Library, where Lenin used to correct the proofs of *Iskra*, is Georgian. Off the Green run warrens of lanes lined with houses and workshops, the premises of watchmakers, precision instrument makers and hardware shops, joined by colonists from advertising agencies, presentation consultancies and public relations firms.

The church of **ST JAMES'S**, just off the Green and up a winding lane, is a Georgian delight, its square tower topped by balustrade, vases and an

A detail of one of the charming houses surrounding Clerkenwell Green. A village green in the Middle Ages, separated from the City by Smithfields, it lost its grass in the eighteenth century, but still retains its trees and its village tranquillity.

irreverent obelisk spire. Its architect, James Carr, was a local man, but his Palladian tastes were out of fashion by 1782, and the parishioners petitioned for it to be pulled down. It still stands, in Portland stone and yellow brick, with a plain god-fearing interior and surrounded by a generous churchyard.

From Clerkenwell Green you can meander south down Britton Street or Turnmill Street, then turn west down Cowcross Street, and down Farringdon Road and then west along Charterhouse Street – with its splendid view of the cast-iron Holborn Viaduct (1869) – to Holborn Circus, where Prince Albert (1819–61) on a horse and in military uniform raises his hat to the double-decker buses when he ought to be saluting them.

To the right, just before you reach the Circus, is another unexpected delight, ELY PLACE, protected from Holborn Circus by iron gates and a top-hatted commissionaire sitting in an eighteenth-century watchhouse. The houses are tall and mid-Georgian. Set slightly back, about half way down, is the oldest Roman Catholic church in London, ST ETHELDREDA'S.

The iron gates have a point. Ely Place is Crown Property, part of neither the City nor Holborn. Within living memory a nightwatchman tolled the hours every night, and like the Temple, no policeman may enter it without being invited in. Before the change in drinking laws the local pub, the Mitre, used to open at eccentric times, according to Cambridge licensing hours.

This is because Ely Place was once Ely Palace, home of the Bishop of Ely (whose diocese embraces Cambridge), to where John of Gaunt (1340–99), third son of Edward III, fled after his house, the Savoy, was burned down by poll-tax rebels during the Peasants' Revolt. Since then the palace has been the site of Henry VIII's and Catherine of Aragon's wedding feast, the home of the Elizabethan courtier, Sir Christopher Hatton (1540–91), a stable, a prison and a hospital. Most of the palace save the chapel had collapsed by 1770 when the tall Georgian houses were built. The chapel remained in its derelict state until 1874, when it was bought by the Roman Catholic church, lovingly restored to its dark late thirteenth-century glory and reconsecrated as St Etheldreda's, a fitting place for the church's prize relic, part of the hand of the seventh-century abbess from Ely whom the church is named after.

On the other side of Holborn Circus, where the church of ST ANDREW'S, HOLBORN stands, you are back in the City again, the part that lies outside the old City Walls, called the Liberties in the Middle Ages, because it was beyond the jurisdiction of the Lord Mayor of London. St Andrew's is late gothic on the outside, built in 1446 with money provided by John Thavies 'to maintain forever the fabric of St Andrew's'. It was one of the largest parish churches in London, 3108 parishioners dying in the Great Plague of 1665. The church survived the Great Fire a year later, but Wren rebuilt the interior (which was gutted in the War), leaving the tower as it was. It was by the tower, with the two Charity Children dressed in blue above the church door, that Dr William Marsden discovered a young girl dying from exposure in 1827 and founded the Royal Free Hospital; while inside the church, beneath the tower, a marble cherub weeps for Captain Thomas Coram, founder of the Coram's Children's Hospital. Outside, where the churchyard drops down into the Fleet Valley, is a relief of the Last Judgement, showing the dead rising from their tombs. It came from the entrance to the paupers' cemetery in neighbouring Shoe Lane, where the penniless poet Thomas Chatterton (1752–70), who poisoned himself was buried.

St Andrew's Street and Shoe Lane (not nearly as interesting as the name suggests) takes you south to Fleet Street, the wedding cake spire of Wren's St Bride's rising above the Art Deco steel and alternating lines of dark and clear glass of the Daily Express building. Fleet Street, the traditional approach to the City from the west provides a wonderful view of the dome of St Paul's Cathedral up Ludgate Hill.

The best thing about Fleet Street is **ST BRIDE'S**, boasting Wren's most outstanding spire. There has been a church here since the sixth century, when St Bridget came from Ireland and built the church on the foundations of a Roman house. It was rebuilt in the norman style and again in the perpendicular style. There the printer Wynkyn de Worde (d.1535) and the Royalist poet Richard Lovelace (1618–57) were buried, and Samuel Pepys was baptized. John Milton, John Dryden (1631–1700) and John Evelyn have knelt in the stalls. That church went up in smoke in 1666 and in its place Wren built this church, and topped it with the most exquisite steeple in London, four open octagonal stages on a square tower supporting a slender spire. Its interior was gutted by fire on 29 December 1940. But the walls and steeple still stood and its interior has been restored, minus its galleries, with simplicity and restraint. It is now the journalists' church, and on most days there is a candle burning in a side chapel remembering a journalist or correspondent lost, tortured, imprisoned, kidnapped or killed.

The Spire of St Bride's, Fleet Street, Wren's 'madrigal in stone'.

East towards St Paul's, Fleet Street becomes Ludgate Hill at Ludgate Circus, which may once have been a circus, but is now just a traffic jam. Beyond the Circus Ludgate Hill is as steep as it is crooked, a crookedness that Wren turned into a virtue, for by keeping the old street alignment of Ludgate Hill, and discarding any idea of a straight and intimidating baroque avenue, Wren ensured that the Cathedral gained in intimacy what it lost in formality.

On the south side of Ludgate Hill tiny streets and alleys lead down towards the river. One street, Blackfriars Lane, tumbles past **APOTHECARIES' HALL**, built in 1688 and set back from the lane in a classical 'Wrenaissance' courtyard which you enter through an archway. There is a Tuscan colonnade on the north side of the courtyard, a lamp in the centre and a staircase to the hall and formal rooms on the east side. Another alley takes you to St Andrew's Hill, which drops down to St Andrew's-by-the-Wardrobe (see p. 49). A third leads down Addle Hill and through an archway into a lovely paved and cobbled courtyard called Wardrobe Terrace.

North of Ludgate Hill Old Bailey leads to the **CENTRAL CRIMINAL COURT**, the Old Bailey, on the site of Newgate Prison, then Ave Maria Lane takes you

Stationers' Hall: rebuilt in 1673 after the Great Fire and refronted in 1800, it is one of the most splendid company halls in London.

to Stationers' Hall, the most sumptuous of the post-Fire halls in the City. Between the Old Bailey and the alley stands **ST MARTIN, LUDGATE**.

St Martin's stone-clad front porch projects slightly into the street and its lead spire, graceful and tapered, rising from a cupola and balcony, acts as a playful foil to the dome of St Paul's. Inside, Wren's church is dark, lofty, rectangular and galleried, and contains beautiful woodwork by William Emmett on the pulpit, altarpiece and organ case. Behind the altar is a triptych of St Martin cutting his cloak for the beggar. Beneath the Father Schmidt organ a pelican feeds its young with its own blood.

STATIONERS' HALL, which you reach through the tiny alley next to the church, is a pocket-sized palace. The hall is late renaissance and neo-classical, built after the Fire of London had destroyed the previous hall, and possesses a rich renaissance screen, a minstrel's gallery and some perfect plasterwork on the ceilings. The Stationers' Company is the company of the book trade, virtually the only City livery company whose members still practise the company's original profession. It was formed in 1403, established a monopoly over printing in 1476 and made most of its money out of *Old Moore's Almanac*. Until 1911 every book published in Great Britain had to be registered there.

Back on Ludgate Hill, the final gentle curve brings you up to the west front of St Paul's Cathedral. On the two sides of the cathedral stand the remains of the cathedral precinct, mostly hidden from view behind offices. On the north side is Amen Corner and Wren's Chapter House. Amen Corner, behind Stationers' Hall – 'an awkward name on a card, and an awkward annunciation to the coachman on leaving any fashionable address', according to one of its residents, the Revd Sydney Smith (1771–1845) – is a charming close of Queen Anne houses. In one house, number 2, Wren's brother-in-law, Canon Horder, lived, and it became Wren's second home after his daughter died. The Revd Sydney Smith found the place altogether too awkward and fled, giving his house to the Revd Richard Barham (1788–1845), author of *The Ingoldsby Legends*, who wrote of Amen Corner's garden as 'magnificent for London, containing the polyanthus roots, a real tree, a brown box border and muff-coloured jessamine, a shrub which is either a dwarf acacia or an overgrown gooseberry bush, eight broken bottles and a tortoiseshell tom-cat asleep in the sunniest corner'. Closer to the cathedral, facing its north wall, is the cathedral's Chapter House, modest, well-proportioned and built in the Wrenaissance manner in red brick.

On the south side, hidden from the cathedral by Edwardian offices and warehouse conversions, is the Deanery, equally Wrenaissance, built like a rather grand merchant's city house. Next to the Deanery is the part-neo-Italianate, part-Victorian Cathedral Choir School built in what the architectural historian Sir Nikolaus Pevsner (1902–83) calls 'South Kensington style'. The building is now a youth hostel, and the new choir school stands on the eastern side of the precincts, in the smooth and unobtrusively modern group of buildings beneath the tower of Wren's St Augustine's, which was all that was left of the church after a bombing raid.

A flight of 24 steps takes you up to the west doors of ST PAUL'S CATHEDRAL, set in a two-storeyed portico supported on pairs of Corinthian columns. Above the portico is the pediment, with a relief of the conversion of St Paul, by Francis Bird (1667–1731). Standing on top of the pediment are statues by Bird of St Peter, St Paul and St John, between Wren's two most baroque of baroque towers, the west towers of St Paul's Cathedral.

The first St Paul's was a wooden church, built by Mellitus, who had been consecrated Bishop of the West Saxons by St Augustine in 604. Erkenwald, Bishop of London, rebuilt it in stone 80 years later. The cathedral burned down and was rebuilt in 962. It burned down again in 1187. The new builder was Maurice, Bishop of London, and the cathedral he planned became the biggest in Europe. It took a hundred years to build the choir and nave, and twenty more to build the spire. Then the choir was rebuilt in the Perpendicular style in the 1260s. By the time it was complete it was 585 feet long and 290 feet across, and the tower and spire reached a height of 489 feet.

Queen Anne, before the west front of St Paul's Cathedral, the four figures around the base representing England, France, Ireland and North America.

It burned down in the Great Fire of 1666. The roof caught alight and its boiling lead dripped down the walls, expanding the stones until they exploded 'like grenades' (Pepys). Wren started rebuilding in 1675. His original plan (a model of it is in the cathedral crypt), based on a Greek cross, was rejected by the cathedral clergy as too unconventional. Wren compromised with a Latin cross. Its great baroque dome was to rival St Peter's in Rome. St Peter's took 120 years to build. Wren built St Paul's in 36.

Inside, the very size of the place is awesome. The vast nave, a procession of arches leading from the grey stone at the west end to a choir of gold and mosaics, seems to last forever. In the north aisle, beyond the unforgettable wood carvings by Jonathan Maine in the Chapel of St Dunstan's, loom statues of General Charles Gordon (1833–85) and Lord Melbourne (1779–1848), and memorials to the cannon-fodder of nineteenth-century colonial wars. Pride of place in the north aisle, however, goes to the memorial to the Duke of Wellington (1769–1852), its canopy with the bronze figures of Truth, Falsehood, Valour and Cowardice. At the top of the canopy the Duke balances on his horse. The designer, Sir Alfred Stevens (1818–75), claimed to have based it on Elizabeth I's tomb in Westminster Abbey.

The south aisle begins with the Chapel of the Order of St Michael and St George, also adorned with Jonathan Maine's superb woodwork. Further up the aisle lurk numerous nineteenth-century marble heroes in various stages of classical undress exposing themselves from behind the shadows of pillars. Two pious children being blessed by Bishop Middleton have turned their backs to all this, while Captain Westcott (whoever he might be) is so shocked he has swooned, and has to be held up by an angel. Against the aisle wall hangs the *Light of the World*, copied by Holman Hunt (1827–1910) himself in 1900, half a century after painting the original, which hangs in Keble College, Oxford.

At the crossing are four more statues: John Flaxman's (1755–1826) of Reynolds and John Bacon the Elder's of John Howard (1726–90), the prison reformer, Sir William Jones (1746–94), the jurist and orientalist, and Dr Johnson – all, except Reynolds, dressed up as Roman senators. In the transepts is yet more statuary, mostly remembering generals from the Napoleonic Wars. In the north transept General Houghton is being sent back into the front line by an angel. General Picton (1758–1815), who died at Waterloo, has brought a marble menagerie with him into the cathedral. Around those two warriors half of Wellington's General Staff and Divisional officers stand in relief. The other half, together with a dingy load of admirals, can be found in the south transept – which has a doorcase which Pevsner calls 'one of the most glorious pieces of woodcarving in London'. Nelson, carved by Flaxman, looks out at a maritime horizon while Britannia presents two small boys to him. General Cornwallis (1738–1805), who lost North America and saved India, doesn't look as if he knows where he's going. Admiral Collingwood (1750–1810) is laid out on the prow of his ship and Sir John Moore (1761–1809) lies like a warrior taking his rest with his martial cloak around him, as in the poem by Charles Wolfe (1791–1823).

Turning your back on the martial illustrious, return to the crossing, between the two transepts, and look upwards, to understand what St Paul's is all about. Above you is the gigantic dome, supported on eight arches, though seemingly suspended above you. The spandrels are filled with glittering nineteenth-century mosaics. Above them the dome is painted in grisaille by Sir James Thornhill (1675–1734), showing scenes from the life of St Paul.

Beyond the crossing the chancel continues eastwards, the high altar and the sanctuary separated from the two nave aisles by Jean Tijou's beautiful wrought iron screens. Grinling Gibbons's exquisitely carved choir stalls lead you to the high altar. The altar is modern and simple, though the view is complicated by the gilded oak baldacchino above it, which makes you think of four-poster beds. At the far east end of the cathedral stands the American Memorial Chapel, dedicated to the Americans who gave their lives in World War II. Wren's original altar, with a marble statue of the Virgin and Child on it, is nearby in the south choir aisle.

The dome and crossing of St Paul's, showing Sir James Thornhill's grisaille of scenes from the life of St Paul.

Below, the crypt stretches from one end of the cathedral to the other, the largest crypt in Europe. Here lies Wren, beneath his simple epitaph:

Reader, if you seek a monument,
Look about you.

Close by lie the cartoonist George Cruikshank (1792–1878), and the painters Holman Hunt, Sir John Millais (1829–96), Reynolds and Turner.

Finally there is the dome, and it is worth ascending to the top if you can, not only to experience one of the grandest views in London, but to understand its structure, for it is not one dome but three. The first is the shallow one we see from the crossing. It is made of brick. The viewing gallery here, the Stone Gallery around the drum of the outer dome, provides a spectacular vista of London, but for those who are adventurous a second and third staircase take you to the second dome, really a brick cone, which holds up the lantern, cross and outer dome (which is nothing more than wooden beams and a skin of lead). Wren needed his inner and outer domes (and the brick cone to support the lantern, cross and outer dome) because he recognized from the mistakes of St Peter's in Rome that a dome that looks right from the interior, looks too shallow from the exterior, and that a dome that looks right from the exterior, looks too high from the interior. A narrow staircase takes you up to the very top of the dome, from where Wren's lantern rises.

Immediately below is the fabric of the cathedral itself, and you can see how Wren used the cathedral walls to screen off the untidiness of single-storey aisles and a two-storey nave, and conceal behind the walls the buttresses he needed to support his drum and dome.

Beyond St Paul's, in all directions, London stretches out below you. To the south the River Thames meanders across London. You can see it bend at Westminster and straighten out at Waterloo, flow under Tower Bridge, and make its oxbow bend at the Isle of Dogs. To the east, the spires of St Augustine, St Mary Aldermary, St Mary-le-Bow and innumerable office blocks, lead the eye out to the East End and Dockland. To the north, the spires and steeples of St Vedast, Foster Lane, Christ Church, Newgate Street and St Sepulchre without Newgate, squeeze upwards, jostling against counting houses as far as that concrete fortress, the Barbican. To the west Ludgate Hill and Fleet Street, punctuated by St Bride's steeple, cut through London to Westminster, and to the flashes of green, the Royal Parks beyond.

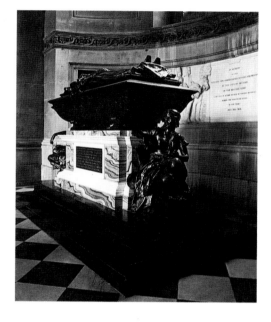

The tomb of Lord Leighton of Stretton, the seventh President of the Royal Academy, in the crypt of St Paul's almost completely overshadows the monument to 'officers, non-commissioned officers and privates of the cavalry regiments of the British Army . . .' behind.

The view west from the dome of St Paul's, showing one of Wren's two west towers, and the River Thames beyond.

3
Legal London

....

THE INNS OF COURT *to* DICKENS'S HOUSE

Stretching northwards from the river mid-way between the City and Westminster, as befits a profession that claims to act as the intermediary between people and Crown, the barristers' four Inns of Court – the Inner Temple, the Middle Temple, Lincoln's Inn and Gray's Inn – present a stretch of courts, gardens and quads from the Thames to Holborn, broken only by Fleet Street and High Holborn.

In the thirteenth century, the Inns of Court were hostels, inns where the law students stayed. Each inn was independent, like the Oxford and Cambridge colleges they so resemble, governed by 'Benchers', who alone decide which of the students will be called to join the 6645 members of the Bar, the barristers' own guild, although some would call it a 'closed shop'.

To be a member of one of the Inns of Court is to be a member of an extremely exclusive club, though no one called to the Bar would be so vulgar as to put it like that. A new law student's working environment, the Inns of Court, is little different from the Oxford or Cambridge college he (and increasingly she) might have just left. There is the same quiet mixture of architectural styles in the quads and courts, the same quiet contempt for the rest of the world, and the same quiet pecking order, with the Benchers in the same role as the Senate, the judges as the dons, the silks (senior barristers) as fellows, and the young men carrying squash racquets and walking around in dark suits 'such as be of a sad colour' (according to the Benchers' rules) as the undergraduates.

The most southerly two of the four Inns of Court, the **INNER TEMPLE** and **MIDDLE TEMPLE**, set between the Embankment and Fleet Street, contain the oldest buildings. The Temple had originally been the home of the Knights Templar, whose round church still survives. Nine knights established the Order in the earliest years of the eleventh century, during that short period when Jerusalem was in the hands of the Crusaders. They saw themselves as a

OPPOSITE *Lincoln's Inn Fields, with the stone-clad Sir John Soane's Museum, mixing classicism and gothic, at the far end.*

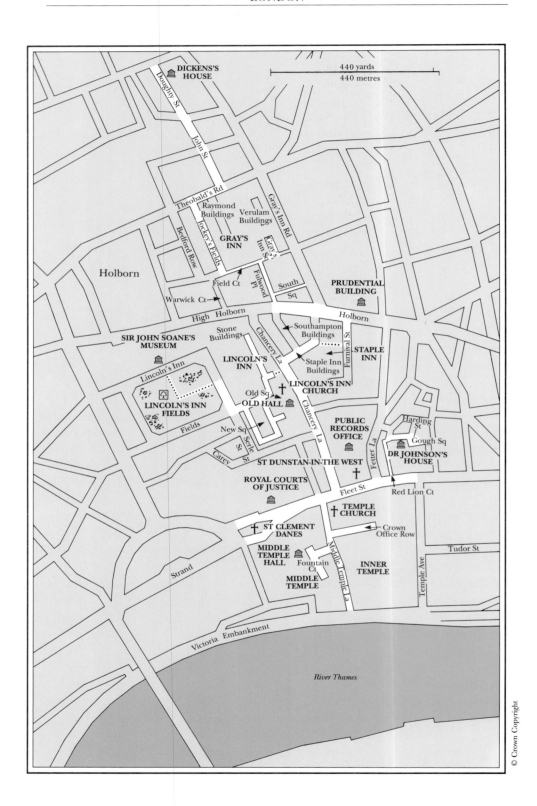

LEGAL LONDON

© Crown Copyright

part-religious, part-military brotherhood-in-arms, epitomized by the red cross on the white tunic, pledged to a life of poverty and chastity, and protecting pilgrims from bandits and Jerusalem from the Moslems.

They first established themselves in London at Holborn, then moved to the meadows between Fleet Street and the Thames in 1162 where they built their monastic barracks, giving it two grand halls, one for the knights and one for the priests, and a church, round like all the Knights Templar churches, based on the ground plan of the Holy Sepulchre in Jerusalem.

Once Jerusalem had been retaken by the Moslems in 1244, and it was clear that they were going to stay there, the Knights Templars' reason for existence had disappeared; but still they continued, growing rich from the covenants the worthy left them in their wills. Within half a century the ideals of poverty and a 'free' Jerusalem had withered, while their vows of chastity were regarded as only prohibiting them from enjoying the female sex. They became one of the leading bankers in Christendom, with 'so great and so large privileges, liberties, and immunities for themselves', according to the lawyer Sir Edward Coke (1556–1634), that 'no other Order had the like'.

Anxious for money, jealous of the Templars' claim to be exempt from the jurisdiction of anyone save the Pope, and impressed by the success of Philip the Fair of France (1268–1314) in suppressing the Parisian Templars on charges of sodomy, heresy and witchcraft (charges which were only half true), Edward II (1284–1327) confiscated the Order's wealth and imprisoned its members in the Tower. The Temple passed to the Knights Hospitaller, a less militant religious order, who leased part of their grounds to the lawyers, an unpopular profession, whose buildings were enthusiastically burned down in the Peasants' Revolt. The Hospitallers were suppressed with the other orders in the Reformation and in 1609 the Inner Temple and Middle Temple came into the hands of the Crown, who granted it to the lawyers in perpetuity, on condition that they maintain the round church and Master's House. They have been there ever since.

From the Embankment you get a splendid panorama of the Temple, the eye travelling west to east, from Middle Temple Gardens, past Crown Office Row and the neo-Elizabethan Paper Buildings, where Sir John Chester lived in Charles Dickens's (1812–70) novel *Barnaby Rudge*, to King's Bench Walk, where the houses at the top end were built by Christopher Wren, or someone from his stable. But the view fails to bring out the intimacy and smallness in scale of the courtyards and halls. To capture that you must wander through the Temple, up Middle Temple Lane, which is the approximate boundary between the Middle and the Inner Temples; but you must be patient. The first building you encounter at the archway from the Embankment is out of character, Temple Gardens Buildings, all Beaux Arts and looking like a very expensive hotel. On the other side of the arch the buildings in Middle Temple Lane are post-war neo-Georgian, smug and bland, and a reminder of how much of the Temple was destroyed in the War.

ABOVE *Middle Temple retains a predominantly Tudor architectural style, and is still gas-lit in parts.*

Take the first turning right from Middle Temple Lane and you will be in Crown Office Row, where the writer and critic Charles Lamb (1775–1834), whose father was a Bencher's clerk, lived as a child with his tragic sister Mary before she killed their mother.

> I was born, and passed the first seven years of my life, in the Temple. Its church, its halls, its gardens, its fountains, its river ... these are my oldest recollections. . . . A man would give something to have been born in such a place. (Charles Lamb: *Essays of Elia*)

The row where he lived was destroyed in the Blitz, like the Inner Temple Hall and Library (now replaced by neo-Georgian imitations) that follow on from it. The view has not changed, however, of the sloping lawns and rose bushes of Inner Temple Gardens. These were the gardens where the Earl of Somerset and Richard Plantagenet first quarrelled in Shakespears's *Henry VI, Part I*, their supporters plucking red and white roses from the surrounding bushes and precipitating the Wars of the Roses. At the bottom of the slope is the Benchers' own memorial to Charles Lamb, a boy reading a book with four words engraved on the open pages: 'Lawyers were children once'.

At the end of Crown Office Row, you come to King's Bench Walk, and on the other side of the parked cars are the dignified and unostentatious Wren houses. The Irish poet and playwright Oliver Goldsmith (1728–74) lived at number 3 before moving to Brick Court in the Middle Temple, and Harold Nicolson (1886–1968) and Vita Sackville-West (1892–1962) lived their interesting lives at number 4 when they were in town.

So far, though, you will have seen nothing of the essence of the Temple. To find that, you have to turn left and left again, behind the neo-Georgian hall and library, and into Church Court, an intimate and irregular quadrangle, its northern side taken up by the Temple Church.

The earliest portion of the **TEMPLE CHURCH**, the round part, is romanesque. Building started in 1162 in a part Norman style and part transitional gothic style. It was consecrated by Heraclius, Patriarch of Jerusalem in 1185. Some 55 years later a Decorated gothic chancel was added, consecrated on Ascension Day 1240, giving the church the shape of a keyhole. In spite of restoration by Sir Robert Smirke and his son Sydney (1799–1877) in the nineteenth century, and by Walter Godfrey after World War II, its cold and military spirit has survived – the embodiment of muscular Christianity.

Inside the circular nave it is dark and sombre, the roof held up by six Purbeck marble pillars and surrounded by the rib-vaulted ambulatory, the triforium and clerestory. Around the ambulatory 60 grotesques carved on the wall depict heaven (a complacent monk, a bored man) and hell (a woman with a toothache, a man being sodomized). On the stone floor of the nave lie the effigies in Purbeck marble of some of the Order's most illustrious benefactors, lying in their armour and chain mail, some holding their swords to their chests like crucifixes, others drawing them for God: Geoffrey de

OPPOSITE *The Temple Church, circular like the Dome of the Rock of Jerusalem, seen from Goldsmith's Buildings.*

Mandeville (d.1144), Robert de Ros (d.1227), William Marshall, Earl of Pembroke (d.1219), and his sons, William (d.1231) and Gilbert (d.1241), who never even reached the Holy Land but died in a tournament.

Between chancel and nave, looked down on by the five-foot punishment cell where Walter le Bacheler, Grand Preceptor of Ireland, was starved to death, and placed so the malefactor can starve and participate in the Mass at the same time, lies another effigy, to Edmund Plowden (1518–85). He was the first lawyer to maintain records of previous judgements, was regarded as having the greatest legal mind in his day, and became treasurer of the Temple. He lies there, a Catholic in a Protestant church, at his own request, so he would always be near his beloved Temple.

East of Plowden's tomb, the Decorated gothic ribs, columns, carved foliage, lancet windows and pointed arches of the chancel extension are exquisite, built like a cathedral's retrochoir. On the north window is the crest of the Middle Temple, the *Agnus Dei*, the lamb of God, and on the south window is the crest of the Inner Temple, *Pegasus*, the winged horse. At the far end is Wren's screen, renaissance and classical, like a beautiful woman in the wrong clothes and in the wrong place.

Outside in Church Court, north of the church, Inner Temple Lane runs up to Fleet Street. Boswell had chambers there, and regarded the situation as 'the most agreeable in the world for a single man'. The lane takes you through the timber, plaster and brick gateway into Fleet Street, Inner Temple Gate. Above the gate in the gatehouse is Prince Henry's Room. Once a tavern, it was rebuilt in 1610 and named after Henry, Prince of Wales (1594–1612). Later it became the waxworks that inspired Charles Dickens to write *The Old Curiosity Shop*. It has a superb Jacobean plastered strapwork ceiling decorated with flowers, and a grating in the window bay so you can see the people walking up and down Fleet Street without them seeing you. Back in Church Court, north-east of the Temple Church, is the Master's House, looking domestic and Dutch, with seven bays and three floors, and its own front garden. It is a brick by brick rebuild of the 1667 house which was destroyed in the War. On the western side of Church Court are three exits; the most northern, a small entrance opposite the deeply recessed west door of the Temple Church, takes you into Hare Court. It is where the notorious Judge George Jeffreys (1648–89), James II's 'hanging judge', had his chambers. The court is quiet and intimate, laid out in gravel with miniature trees and bushes in pots, and looking like a very large window box.

Just to the south of the entrance into Hare Court, a neo-classical cloister of two rows of Tuscan columns, rebuilt after the War to exactly the same design as the original by Christopher Wren, reminds you of Francesco di Giorgio Martini's (1439–1501/2) renaissance painting, *Perspective of an Ideal City*. It leads to Pump Court, where the north side was built by Wren, but there is no pump. The final western exit from Church Court, the most southern, leads down a flight of steps to Elm Court, blitzed in the War and replaced with rather suburban-looking neo-Georgian blocks. All three courts, Hare Court, Pump Court and Elm Court, lead you eventually back into Middle Temple Lane, and across the lane into Middle Temple.

The best place to start any wander around the Middle Temple is from Fountain Court, where a fountain beside a crooked tree draws sparrows and pigeons to drink and bathe. Charles Lamb remembered the fountain with affection. It was the same fountain where Tom Pinch met Ruth Pinch, 'with the best little laugh on her face that ever played in opposition to the fountain', in Dickens's *Martin Chuzzlewit*.

Part of the south side of Fountain Court, the part nearest the fountain, is open, giving you a view down on to Middle Temple Gardens and the Thames beyond it. The remainder of Fountain Court's south side is taken up by the red-bricked, buttressed and pinnacled Elizabethan **MIDDLE TEMPLE HALL**. It was built between 1562 and 1573, financed by Edmund Plowden (whose bust stands in front of the screen), and has a splendid Tudor double hammerbeam roof and one of the most magnificent Tudor oak screens in the country. The

Middle Temple Hall, built in 1573, where Shakespeare's Twelfth Night *was performed on 2 February 1601.*

screen, shattered into a jigsaw of thousands of pieces in the Blitz and meticulously put together again, displays pillars, wreaths and caryatids on both its storeys. Above the 29-foot-long Bench Table, a gift from Queen Elizabeth, made from a single oak tree, are paintings of Charles I, the Duke of York, Charles II, Queen Anne, William III and George I (1714–27). The suits of armour and the busts of the Caesars are Elizabethan. The hall was not only used by the lawyers to eat in. Shakespeare's *Twelfth Night* had its premiere in front of Elizabeth I here on 2 February 1601. Today, law students are required to dine in the hall at least three times each term, as in an Oxford or Cambridge college, the sound of a horn calling them to dinner at 6.30.

On the north-west side of Fountain Court a flight of stairs leads to New Court and Devereux Court, the most westerly of the Temple's courts and quads. New Court was a speculative enterprise laid out in 1675 by Dr Nicholas Barebone, the speculative builder who made a vast amount of money after the Great Fire of London putting up the jerry-built blocks that are now all protected by preservation orders. An archway on the eastern side takes you to Essex Court and Brick Court, two courts before the War when there was a range running north-to-south between them, now effectively one large court graced by a couple of trees and a car park. The two separate names are a postman's anachronism. Oliver Goldsmith lived in Brick Court, at number 2 on the second floor, and wrote *She Stoops to Conquer* there in 1773. When he gave parties, which was frequently, Judge Blackstone (1723–80) of *Blackstone's Commentaries*, who lived downstairs, complained about the noise. Goldsmith died of fever aged 45, penniless but not friendless; and when he was buried in the old churchyard by the Temple Church half of London's whores and a quarter of the city's destitutes came to mourn him.

Finally, Middle Temple Lane takes you to Middle Temple Archway on Fleet Street, built in 1693 and dignified with Ionic pilasters and a pediment depicting the *Agnus Dei*. Just before you reach the archway at the top of the lane, the overhangs on the houses are held up by iron pillars that Dr Johnson, in his 'little shrivelled, unpowdered red wig, which was too small for his head' (James Boswell: *Life of Johnson*) clasped as he waddled up to Fleet Street.

Dr Johnson had rooms in the Temple from 1759 to 1765. Before then – apart from a brief period renting lodgings in Staple Inn (see p. 93) – he lived on the other side of Fleet Street, in Gough Square. Later he lived in Lincoln's Inn (see p. 87). Now simply called **DR JOHNSON'S HOUSE**, the house in Gough Square is accessible through the maze of courts north of Fleet Street: Hen and Chicken Court, Crane Court, Three King's Court, Fleur-de-Lys Court, Hind Court, Johnson Court (no relation, though he did live there in 1765 and 1766) and Wine Office Court, home of the Cheshire Cheese (one of the oldest pubs in London, rebuilt in 1667) where Johnson and Boswell supposed to have drunk, and generations of journalists and tourists have drunk since.

Johnson lived in the corner house in Gough Square for eleven years compiling his dictionary, in an unpretentious late seventeenth-century brick

Middle Temple: New Court, built by Nicholas Barebone, seen from Fountain Court.

house that at times must have seemed too small for his vast bulk. He lived there, he said, to be close to his printer in Great New Street, a sentiment not shared by the printer, who, asked about his feelings when he received the last pages of the proofs, could only reply: 'Thank God I have done with him.' The great reference work was put together in the attic, 'fitted out like a counting house', according to Boswell, Johnson's six clerks working in a row at a long table. The three floors below the attic were his living quarters, where he produced his twice-weekly *Rambler* from 1750 to 1752, where his wife died of drink and opium, where he agonized about falling in love with Mrs Thrale, and where he despaired at his failures. The rooms in which he entertained the politicians Edmund Burke (1727–97) and Charles James Fox (1749–1806), the actor David Garrick (1717–79), the painter Sir Joshua Reynolds and Oliver Goldsmith, are full of Johnson memorabilia, his chair, a portrait of his black servant Francis Barber, and a piece of the Great Wall of China. The walls are lined with paintings: *Dr Johnson with Flora Macdonald*, *Dr Johnson with the Vicar of Wakefield*, *Dr Johnson with Mrs Siddons*, *Dr Johnson with John Wesley* and *Dr Johnson at Uttoxeter Market*. It is also a sad house, sad but not cold, as befits the house of a fragile genius who was crippled by lack of love as a child, lack of self-confidence as a young man, lack of money as a middle-aged man, and lack of happiness as an old man, yet still retained his humanity.

To the west of Middle Temple Gateway, on an island in the Strand (the westerly continuation of Fleet Street), where a statue of Dr Johnson stands looking out over the Fleet Street that he would now loathe, is Wren's church of **ST CLEMENT DANES**, the church of the nursery rhyme, *Oranges and Lemons*, where once a year, in Lent, what local children can still be found are each given an orange and a lemon. The first St Clement Danes was a wooden church, and according to Stow was so called because Harold Harefoot, the Danish king, was buried there. A stone church was built in its place about 1000. In 1189 it was given to the Knights Templar, then taken over by the Austin Friars (the Augustinians) after the Knights Templars' suppression. In 1617 the metaphysical poet John Donne (c.1572–1631) was vicar there for a short time before taking up the post of Reader at Lincoln's Inn. St Clement's survived the Great Fire, but the church was so old, and in such bad state, that Wren rebuilt it in 1680, keeping only the tower, which he faced in Portland stone. In 1719 James Gibbs was commissioned to raise the tower by 25 feet, and he gave it the three diminishing octagonals culminating in the cupola. Wren, an old man by then, thought it was beautiful. Fifty years later Samuel Johnson was churchwarden here. His seat was number 18 in the north gallery, near the pulpit. Boswell attended a service with him on Good Friday 1773.

> His behaviour was, as I had imagined to myself, solemnly devout. I never shall forget the tremendous earnestness with which he pronounced the awful petition in the Litany: 'In the hour of our death, and at the day of judgement, Good Lord deliver us.'

Wren's church, with its handsome entrance hall and domed lobby, was gutted in May 1941. Within a few weeks of the destruction, the rector, the Revd William Pennington Backford and his wife (the daughter of the previous incumbent who had lived there all her life), died 'from shock and grief'. There is a modest memorial to them. Since then St Clement's has been restored and is now the church of the Royal Air Force. You can see the names and crests of all the squadrons of the Air Force set in Welsh slate in the aisles and turn the pages of the Memorial Book that contains the names of all the men and women of the RAF who died in World War II.

On the north side of the Strand, diagonally across from Middle Temple Gate, are the **ROYAL COURTS OF JUSTICE**, or simply the **LAW COURTS**, built by George Edmund Street (1824–81), and so vast they could be mistaken for a neo-gothic railway station, or the Houses of Parliament. Asymmetrical, but never undisciplined, only their irregularity and fantasy saves them from pomposity. The hall, 250 feet long and 82 feet high, vaulted in stone, lit by a clerestory and with a statue of Judge Blackstone at one end, is awesome. It is supposed to be. Running off from the hall, three and a half miles of corridors lead to a thousand rooms.

Street left school at the age of fifteen in 1839. He had ambitions to be a clergyman but by the time he was twenty he was a failed painter. George Gilbert Scott gave him his chance, employing him as his assistant. Five years later he started his own practice, establishing his unique ecclesiastical gothic style. In 1866 a competition was announced for the design of the new Law Courts. He entered it and won, with much bad grace from his former mentor George Gilbert Scott, who lost. The foundations were laid in 1871 and work began in 1874. For his followers it was the ultimate in 'noble architecture'. To his detractors it was 'the grave of gothic'. By the time it was finished in 1882 Street had already been dead for a year. He had died of a stroke brought on by the controversy, the details and the delays.

Behind the Law Courts stretch Lincoln's Inn and Lincoln's Inn Fields, accessible from Chancery Lane. The way there takes you past the fairy-tale gothic of the old **PUBLIC RECORDS OFFICE** on the right, completed in 1851 by Sir James Pennethorne, with further extensions by him in the 1860s. It was the main repository of the nation's records until 1977, when the majority of them were moved to the new Public Records Office at Kew. It still displays the most important historic documents of the nation's collective memory, including the Domesday Book, the *Magna Carta* and the last will and testament of William Shakespeare, in a small museum.

A small alleyway by the side of the Public Records Office leads to Clifford's Inn. Established in 1345, on land leased to the lawyers by Lady Clifford, widow of the sixth Baron Clifford, it was an Inn of Chancery, effectively a preparatory school for the Inns of Court, until it ceased functioning in 1903. Ten years later it was the home of the writer Virginia Woolf (1882–1941). The mid seventeenth-century inn was virtually entirely

The City's symbol, the Dragon, perched on top of the Temple Bar, with G.E. Street's spectacular neo-gothic Royal Courts of Justice behind.

demolished in 1934; only the garden with its view of the Public Records Office, and the gateway into Fleet Street survived the vandalism.

On the far side of the gateway stands ST DUNSTAN-IN-THE-WEST, its best face towards Fleet Street. There has been a church on the site since 1185, although the present one was built in the 1830s, which makes it the most modern church in the City. In the early Middle Ages it had been known as St Dunstan-Against-the-New-Temple and was later known as St Dunstan-in-the-West to distinguish it from St Dunstan-in-the-East.

William Tyndale (d.1536), the translator of the Bible, preached regularly here; so did John Donne, who was rector from 1624 until his death in 1631, and preached some of the most moving sermons in the English language from St Dunstan's, 'weeping sometimes for his Auditory, sometimes with them; always preaching to himself'. Busts of the two men, Tyndale and Donne, look out from either side of the porch.

The church escaped the fire, which burned itself out a few yards away to the east. Five years later, in gratitude at their deliverance, the parishioners erected the clock that stands over Fleet Street, with its two mechanical figures, Gog and Magog, striking the quarter hour. It was the first clock in London to have the minutes marked on the dial.

That church was demolished in 1829 so Fleet Street could be widened and a new one, the present octagonal one, was built by John Shaw in Regency 'gothick' between 1830 and 1833. Outside, over the vestry door, is a rare statue of Queen Elizabeth I, one of the few sculpted in her lifetime.

On the other side of Chancery Lane, opposite the Public Records Office, is the neo-classical Law Society building, erected in 1831, and few yards further north stands the early Tudor red-bricked gatehouse to Lincoln's Inn. LINCOLN'S INN is greener than the Temple, and more expansive, a collection of gardens rather than courts. Originally the site had been a Dominican Priory, then in 1272 the Dominicans moved to Blackfriars, selling their ground to Henry Lacy, Earl of Lincoln (d.1311). In 1412 Lacy's successor leased the old Dominican site to the lawyers, who bought the freehold in 1580. Lacy's arms are displayed above the massive oak doors of the square-towered gatehouse, built in 1518 and facing Chancery Lane. Beside them are the arms of Henry VIII, the reigning monarch when the gatehouse was built, and Sir Thomas Lovell, Speaker of the House of Commons, Chancellor of the Exchequer and a Bencher at the Inn.

On the other side of the gatehouse you enter an irregular rectangle, everything built between the late fifteenth and early seventeenth centuries, and everything except the chapel in red brick. The gatehouse range of 1518 extends to the south-east corner, where another Tudor range, also of red brick and stone dressing, and with Jacobean additions, continues along the south side. The poet and playwright Ben Jonson worked as a bricklayer with his stepfather on the Jacobean additions, 'having a trowel in one hand, he had a book in his pocket', according to the antiquarian Thomas Fuller (1608–61).

Sir James Pennethorne's neo-Tudor fantasia, the old Public Records Office. From the 1660s until a new Public Records Office opened at Kew in 1977, it was the main depository for the nation's state papers. It still contains some of the most important historical records of the nation, including one of the four surviving original copies of the Magna Carta.

ABOVE *The neo-Tudor west gateway from Lincoln's Inn Fields into Lincoln's Inn, built by Philip Hardwick in the 1840s.*

OPPOSITE *The Jacobean gothic undercroft of Lincoln's Inn Chapel, where the law students could 'walk and talk and confer for their learning'.*

The west side of the rectangle is taken up by the Lincoln's Inn Old Hall, late Perpendicular, and built between 1490 and 1492, an odd-looking hall with buttresses on the sides, two bay windows at each end and a Victorian neo-gothic lantern perched precariously on top. Inside, the roof is arch-braced with collar-beams and the walls are lined with linenfold panelling, their simple rhythms in sharp contrast to the early seventeenth-century double-decker screen. On the north wall hangs Hogarth's biblical epic, *St Paul Preaching Before Felix*, which shows what even a great artist is capable of when he needs the money. The hall was the meeting place of the Court of Chancery until it moved to the Law Courts, and the scene of the wrangles between Jarndyce and Jarndyce in Charles Dickens's *Bleak House*.

On the northern side of the rectangle stands LINCOLN'S INN'S CHAPEL, with an open vaulted undercroft, the scene of the sword fight in Tony Richardson's film *Tom Jones* (1963), though merely intended as a place where law students could 'walk and talk and confer for their learning'. John Thurloe (1616–68), Cromwell's Secretary of State, lies here, and it was here, nine years before his interment, that 80 members of parliament met to take the first tentative steps towards the restoration of the monarchy.

The Jacobean gothic church above was built in the then-fashionable style of Inigo Jones. In 1620 John Donne laid the foundation stone and in 1623 he consecrated the church, which was much restored by Christopher Wren in 1685 and later by James Wyatt in 1791. Inside is a gallery, the most Perpendicular of tracery, a tunnel-vaulted roof painted a rich red and a hexagonal pulpit carved in the reign of Queen Anne. Much of the original early seventeenth-century stained glass by the Flemish van Linge brothers was destroyed in World War I, but some of it has survived. Other, more modern, windows depict former Benchers of Lincoln's Inn: Thomas More, Thomas Cromwell (*c.*1485–1540), William Pitt the Younger (1757–1806), Horace Walpole, Cardinal Newman (1801–90), George Canning (1770–1827) and Herbert Asquith (1852–1928).

North of the church is a second rectangle, surrounded by Sir George Gilbert Scott's neo-Elizabethan ranges of 1873–6, forming a slightly too precious courtyard with a tree in the middle. Further north of Scott's gentility, and in staid contrast to it, is Stone Buildings, stark, stone-faced and Palladian, built by Robert Taylor (1714–88) around a paved cul du sac between 1774 and 1780.

The lawns open up to the west of Stone Buildings, revealing a Victorian 'English garden' with dappled trees and spotless grass slopes, in front of Philip Hardwick's (1792–1870) neo-Elizabethan New Hall and Library. Hardwick's New Hall and Library (started 1843) have an authority that Gilbert Scott's neo-Elizabethiana lacks, and not just because the New Hall and Library are so big. It is pure romance, romance in red brick. The hall has two bay windows at one end and two towers at the other. On the walls of the hall, beneath the Victorian hammerbeam roof is George Frederick Watt's

pre-Raphaelite fresco, *The Lawgivers*, both romantic and Raphaelesque, depicting Moses, Minos, Mohammed (570–632), Charlemagne (742–814), King Alfred and Edward I. To the north of the hall, forming an 'L' shape with it, is Hardwick's library, equally tall and romantic, and linked to the hall at right angles by an octagonal room.

To the south of this group is New Square, a perfect rectangle of trees, shrubs and lawn, with a round pond in the middle. It is open to the north and closed in on the other three sides by identical four-storey brick ranges, and looks exactly like a London square is supposed to look. New Square was laid out in the 1690s by Henry Serle, a barrister and a property speculator. It was one of London's first squares. Originally it had nothing to do with Lincoln's Inn, even though Serle was a barrister. He just wanted to make money. The lawyers took it over and have maintained it unchanged since. It is simple and beautiful, and in one of the houses overlooking the square, Charles Dickens worked as a legal clerk. He hated it. At the south-east corner is a small archway bearing the arms of Henry Lacy and Henry Serle. It was built in 1697 and leads to Carey Street and the back of the Law Courts. The legal bookshop, Wildy's, has been in this archway for 160 years.

Immediately to the west of Lincoln's Inn is another expanse of lawn, LINCOLN'S INN FIELDS. In the Middle Ages it had been two patches of waste land, Purse Field and Cup Field, a recreation ground for the law students at Lincoln's Inn. Purse Field belonged to the Hospital of St Giles, and Cup Field to the Hospital of St John. The waste land reverted to the Crown in 1537 and effectively became common ground, where law students still went for recreation and local inns grazed their customers' horses. It was here that the Catholic Anthony Babington (1561–86) was hanged, drawn and quartered. Babington was still alive when he was 'drawn' (disembowelled) and the crowds were so shocked that Queen Elizabeth allowed his fourteen accomplices merely to be hanged – seven one day, seven the next. Two years later the Catholic martyrs Robert Morton and Hugh More were hanged here, and a hundred years after that Lord William Russell (1639–83) was wrongfully executed here for treason. It remained common ground and when a building developer petitioned King James I in 1613 for permission to build houses on the fields, the Benchers of Lincoln's Inn quickly put a stop to it. A few years later another developer, a Mr William Newton, secured permission from Charles I to build on the fields. This time the Benchers, sensing a shift in the balance of power, petitioned Parliament, and the Commons ordered a halt to 'any further building in Lincoln's Inn (especially by Mr Newton)'. By this time, however, the houses were creeping up on the north and south sides. But the lawyers prevented any further encroachments on the open space, reinforced by a decree signed by Oliver Cromwell in 1656, and kept the houses on the west side at a distance.

By the early eighteenth century it had become a fashionable London square, its inhabitants including Edward Montagu, Earl of Sandwich

(1625–72), the Earl of Leicester, the Earl of Lindsey, the Duke of Newcastle (c.1650–1712), Lord Coventry and the Countess of Sunderland. With residents like that it attracted criminals from all over London.

> *Where Lincoln's Inn, wide space, is rail'd around,*
> *Cross not with venturous step; there oft is found*
> *The lurking thief, who, while the daylight shone,*
> *Makes the walls echo with his begging tone,*
> *That crutch, which late compassion moved, shall wound*
> *Thy bleeding head, and fell thee to the ground.*
> *Though thou art tempted by the linkman's call,*
> *Yet trust him not along the lonely wall,*
> *In the mid way he'll quench the flaming brand*
> *And share the booty with the pilfering band.* (John Gay: *Trivia*)

On the west side of the square there is still an original pre-Restoration house, Lindsey House, its five bays separated by Ionic pilasters and surmounted by a balustrade, probably designed by Inigo Jones. It is grand and built of red brick, although the brickwork is now hidden behind stucco. Spencer Perceval (1762–1812), the only British prime minister to be assassinated, lived in apartments there for seventeen years in the early nineteenth century. Next to it is number 58, an early Georgian house built in 1730. It was the home of the Earl of Sandwich, and later of John Forster (1812–76), the friend and biographer of Charles Dickens. Dickens used the house as the setting for Mr Tulkinghorn's rooms in *Bleak House*.

> It is let off in sets of chambers now, and in those shrunken fragments of its greatness, lawyers lie like maggots in nuts.

Next to it stands Newcastle House, built of red brick and stone dressing in 1720 and with an intimidatingly formal staircase at the entrance. In 1930 it was completely gutted, its insides rebuilt by Sir Edwin Lutyens (1869–1944), but you wouldn't know to look at it from the street.

The south side of the square is neo-classical, neo-Georgian and medical, dominated by the Royal College of Surgeons, built in 1806 and graced by George Dance the Younger's Ionic portico. Inside the college those connected with the medical profession will find an unexpected gem, the Hunterian Museum of Medicine, which holds, in addition to the various human parts pickled in jars, Holbein's drawing of Henry VIII and the Barber-Surgeons, paintings by Reynolds and Hogarth, and three perfect studies of a rhinoceros, baboon and monkey by George Stubbs (1724–1806).

Opposite, the north side of Lincoln's Inn Fields is almost entirely Georgian, real Georgian, with windows lined up like regiments, intricate ironwork on the balconies, and that eccentric touch of classical and Gothic on the façade of number 13, the **SIR JOHN SOANE'S MUSEUM**, which gives the houses their authenticity. The museum, shamelessly displaying its classical and

A detail of the exterior of Sir John Soane's Museum in Lincoln's Inn Fields, showing one of his coade-stone copies of the caryatids of the Erechtheum in Athens.

William Hogarth's series of satirical paintings, The Rake's Progress, *gained a wide audience through being engraved and sold relatively cheaply. Here, the Rake is arrested for debt. The companion series,* The Harlot's Progress, *is relatively unknown.*

gothic eccentricities, is the focal point on the northern side. It catches the eye, though staying in line with its neighbours, as Soane wanted it to.

Sir John Soane bought number 13 Lincoln's Inn Fields in 1792, and lived there until he died in 1837. Over the years he purchased the two neighbouring houses and filled all three with his remarkable collection. He was Professor of Architecture at the Royal Academy and Surveyor to the Bank of England, building the Bank its chaste and beautiful neo-classical screen (see p. 51). By a special Act of Parliament, them and their contents were bequeathed to the nation. The houses, with their shallow domes and mirrored recesses, intricate passages and cellars full of treasure, have not changed since he died. Packed into them are the fruits of all his enthusiasms, first cultivated on his Grand Tour through Italy from 1777 to 1780 and nurtured until his death. There are paintings by Canaletto, Reynolds and Turner, Hogarth's *Rake's Progress* and *Election* series, a portrait of Napoleon (1769–1821) commissioned by Josephine (1763–1814), 8000 architectural drawings by Robert and James Adam, classical paraphernalia of every description, first editions of Milton and Shakespeare, and the sarcophagus of Seti, father of Rameses the Great, with an inscription informing him of the places he will pass through on his journey through the underworld.

Returning through Lincoln's Inn and continuing up Chancery Lane, a side street on the right takes you to **STAPLE INN**, where there is the garden and the fountain which the American novelist Nathaniel Hawthorne (1804–64) called his 'little island of quiet' in the middle of London. Behind the fountain, separating the garden from the cobbled courtyard, is the buttressed Tudor hall of 1581. Inside is an original hammerbeam roof, a minstrel's gallery and a five-bay oak screen. The hall, built of red brick, is small and unimposing. Originally it had been a wool merchant's warehouse. Wool was England's staple industry, thus the name, Staple Inn. It became an Inn of Chancery in 1378. Dr Johnson had chambers there in 1759 when he was writing *Rasselas* and penniless, and so did Mr Grewgious in Dickens's *Edwin Drood*.

Coming out of Staple Inn into Holborn, you get a spectacular view of Alfred Waterhouse's (1830–1905) gigantic, gothic and gabled terracotta Prudential Building, built on the site of Furnival's Inn, another redundant Inn of Chancery, and so symmetrical it could be described as Mechanical Perpendicular. But you have to cross Holborn, to get the best view of Staple Inn's front, two Tudor half-timbered houses, displaying seven gables beneath a line of shops, the finest example of Tudor timber-framing in London.

On the northern side of Holborn, a little to the west of Gray's Inn Road, is the unobtrusive archway built in 1688, into **GRAY'S INN**, the fourth of the Inns of Court, established in the fourteenth century on land belonging to the de Greys, whose family had provided generations of lawyers, including one who was King John's chancellor.

The arch leads into South Square, where a bronze statue of Sir Francis Bacon (1561–1626), the philosopher and statesman, stands in the middle. He was Gray's Inn's treasurer and her most illustrious Bencher. Its south and west sides were once lined with late seventeenth-century brick chambers, built in 1685 after the fire that destroyed so much of Gray's Inn. But the War tore out most of them, now only number 1, where Charles Dickens was a clerk for Ellis and Blackmore, is original. Blackmore remembered Dickens, and described him as 'a bright, clever-looking youth, and several instances took place in the office of which he must have been a keen observer, as I recognized some of them in his *Pickwick* and *Nickleby*'. Next door at number 2 David Copperfield's smug little friend Traddles, had his chambers.

The north range of South Square is taken up by the Hall and Chapel, the east range by the library. All three were bombed on 11 May 1941. The chapel and library were wrecked, but much of the hall, where Shakespeare's *Comedy of Errors* was performed in 1594, survived. It has a hammerbeam roof, and an Elizabethan screen made from the wood of a Spanish galleon.

North of the hall and chapel is Gray's Inn Square, elegant, open and spacious. Until 1676 it had been two courts, Chapel Court and Coney Court, then the range between them was pulled down, opening up the vast rectangle. To the north, west and east Gray's Inn Square is lined by identical Queen Anne brick ranges, a few on the northern side are genuine, the majority are exact post-war rebuilds, like the one that replaced the house where Mr Perker, Mr Pickwick's solicitor, had his offices.

Bacon's statue in South Square, Gray's Inn. Francis Bacon, Earl of Verulam, who entered Gray's Inn in 1576 and was called to the Bar in 1582, was the Inn's most illustrious Bencher. The hall is to the left of the picture.

West of South Square, through a tiny arch, is Field Court, a paved and intimate contrast to the wide green spaces in which Gray's Inn abounds. Here are late seventeenth-century houses and their twentieth-century clones. To the north, Field Court opens up into Gray's Inn Fields through early eighteenth-century wrought iron gates displaying the crests of Gray's Inn and the Inner Temple. Like Lincoln's Inn, Gray's Inn had fields in the Middle Ages, where law students went for recreation and the Trained Bands, London's militia, practised archery. It had its own windmill and looked out over open country to the villages of Hampstead and Highgate to the north.

Charles Dickens's house at 48 Doughty Street, where he lived from 1837 to 1839 is now a museum devoted to his life and work.

Francis Bacon laid out the ground, The Walks, in 1606, planting the catalpa tree that stands on crutches at the far end. Later in the century it became one of the most fashionable spots in London. Samuel Pepys was a frequent visitor. 'When church was done, my wife and I walked to Gray's Inn, to observe fashions of the ladies, because of my wife's making some clothes.' At other times he went alone, and 'was very well pleased with the sight of a fine lady that I had often seen walk in Gray's Inn Walks'. It is a fine place to stroll, up and down the lawn's slopes and along The Walks lined with plane trees where office workers eat sandwiches at lunchtime – 'still the best gardens of any of the Inns of Court, my beloved Temple not forgotten' (Charles Lamb).

Lamb was not the only lover of the Inns of Court. Dickens loved them too, and on the far side of The Walks, across Theobalds Road and past the Georgian houses in John Street, is **DICKENS'S HOUSE**, at 48 Doughty Street.

Charles Dickens moved there in the spring of 1837, and within a month he witnessed the death of his seventeen-year-old sister-in-law and reputed lover Mary Hogarth from heart seizure. She became the model of Little Nell. In the first floor study, next to Mary's room, he wrote the final parts of *Pickwick Papers*, *Oliver Twist*, *Nicholas Nickleby* and the opening of *Barnaby Rudge*.

The house is full of Dickens memorabilia, sketches by Cruikshank and Phiz are everywhere, and in Mary Hogarth's room is R. W. Buss's wonderfully kitsch *Dickens's Dream*, showing Dickens in his study thinking, while Traddles, Ruth Pinch, Little Nell, Squeers, Mr Micawber, Mrs Fathersham and the rest of them ooze their way out of the bookshelves. Many of them are characters that had paced the Inns of Court, as plaintiffs, barristers and victims, and the house is packed with references to the Temple, Lincoln's Inn, Staple Inn and Gray's Inn. On the landing is a portrait of Mr Tulkinghorn of Lincoln's Inn Fields. In the Morning Room on the ground floor is the desk at which Dickens worked as a clerk in Gray's Inn, and the petty cash book with such names as Weller, Corney, Rudge, Bardell and Newman Knott. And in the library are rare editions of all his works, including *Barnaby Rudge*, which tells us that:

> There are still worse places than the Temple, on a sultry day, for basking in the sun, or resting idly in the shade. There is yet a drowsiness in its courts, and a dreamy dullness in its trees and gardens. (Dickens: *Barnaby Rudge*)

4
The Royal Parks

....

ST JAMES'S PARK *to* KENSINGTON PARK

From Horse Guards Parade a quartet of royal parks forms an almost uninterrupted lawn nearly three and a half miles long as far as Kensington Palace. St James's Park, Green Park, Hyde Park and Kensington Gardens, are very English parks, arranged landscapes, their essence grass and water. Unlike French and Dutch gardens, which are formal and symmetrical transformations of nature into street plans, the royal parks of London are an escape from the city.

Three of the royal parks started out as Henry VIII's hunting grounds, which stretched as far west as Kensington and as far north as Hampstead, and we should be grateful for this tyrant's whim, preventing the land being built on. Open fields like Lincoln's Inn Fields have always been important to Londoners, and throughout the Middle Ages the City of London always protected the rights of its citizens to recreation grounds.

Charles I found that he had unintentionally opened up St James's Park and Hyde Park to the aristocracy by issuing too many invitations to garden parties. It was Cromwell who opened them up to the public, but within a couple of years Parliament was short of money and privatized them. In 1652 Evelyn was complaining in his diary of having to pay 'a shilling, and a horse sixpence, to the sordid fellow who has purchased it'.

They went public again after the Restoration, and have been regarded as Common Land, in spite of being 'Royal', ever since. In the nineteenth century the eccentric Lord Dorchester insisted on putting his cow out to grass in Hyde Park under the supervision of a groom. No one was able to stop him. Right up until World War II sheep grazed there. Only once, in the days when a 'crown' was another name for five shillings, did the Crown think of taking them back, and Queen Caroline, who loved the parks and had financed the excavation of the Serpentine, asked the prime minister of the day, Sir Robert Walpole, what they would cost her. 'Three crowns,' he replied. 'England's, Ireland's and Scotland's.'

OPPOSITE *Whitehall and the domes and pinnacles of Sir George Gilbert Scott's Foreign Office, from the bridge across the pond in St James's Park.*

This vast lawn begins in **WHITEHALL** at Horse Guards Parade. Wolsey had built a palace there, stretching down to the river, so it was easily accessible from Hampton Court (see p. 21), and like Hampton Court, it was taken by the King when Wolsey fell. There is a model of Whitehall Palace in the Museum of London (see p. 61). It shows an early Tudor palace, like Hampton Court, built of warm red bricks. There is a turreted gateway from Whitehall, gardens, orchards, tennis courts and a tiltyard. In 1619 Inigo Jones built a **BANQUETING HALL** in a classical style. It was the first classical building in England since Roman times. His friend Rubens was commissioned to paint the ceiling, a hymn to James I, showing the monarch being led to heaven by Justice while Peace and Plenty embrace. A quarter of a century later later his son Charles I, stepped out on to the balcony of the Banqueting Hall and was beheaded. In 1698, a palace laundrywoman laid out some linen by a fire to dry and the linen caught alight. Only the Banqueting Hall survived.

A generation later Kent's Horse Guards and Treasury were laid out on the west side of Whitehall opposite the Banqueting Hall. They were in the same Palladian style. Horse Guards was built as the headquarters of the British army, and behind it was marked a great open space, a parade ground that had once been the palace's tilt-yard and now doubles up as a car park. The space still manages to impose, surrounded on three sides by monumental government buildings. On the north side is the Admiralty and the Admiralty Blockhouse, part covered in ivy. On the east side is Kent's Horse Guards itself, stern and restless, with a busy broken roofline. On the south side are the Queen Anne backs of Downing Street and Sir George Gilbert Scott's Italianate Foreign Office. Only to the west is Horse Guards Parade open, as if embracing four great parks in a single gesture.

The first of the great parks is **ST JAMES'S PARK**, in what were the grounds of the hospital of St James's, a leper hospital for women until Henry VIII turned it into the eastern stretch of his hunting grounds. Today St James's Park forms a triangle, its base at Horse Guards Parade, its apex at Buckingham Palace. From the middle of the base to the apex meanders the lake, shaped like a spanner, with an island, Duck Island, at the Whitehall end linked by an isthmus to the mainland. Before the lake had been naturalized by most artificial means, it had been a canal, and Pepys, the diarist and Secretary to the Admiralty, 'lay down upon the grass by the canal and slept awhile' as generations of civil servants from the Ministry of Defence have done since. On the island is a tiny neo-gothic park keeper's cottage designed by John Nash and looking like a Victorian almshouse that had been sent to the wrong postal district. It must have been the most idyllic home in London once; now it's used as changing rooms by the bandsmen. The pond is the home of 36 species of water fowl, including pelicans and black swans, and on Duck Island is a flock of chickens who act as wet-nurses for the ducks' eggs. The pelicans have been here since the 1660s, when the Russian ambassador brought over a brace for King Charles II. A slim and graceful bridge (1957) has been cast

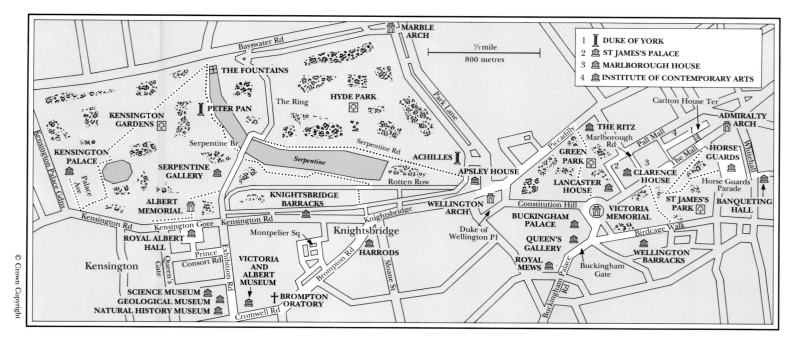

effortlessly across the handle of the spanner. The bridge provides two of the most striking views in London: the Italianate skyline of the Foreign Office and the domes and spires of Whitehall framed by weeping willows to the east, and Sir Aston Webb's Victoria Memorial and Buckingham Palace to the west.

James I turned the eastern end of the park into a zoo, and kept a couple of crocodilles in it. Walk across the park from St James's Palace to Horse Guards Parade and you will be following the route that his son Charles I took on his journey to the executioner's block. The park suffered neglect in the Commonwealth, and its trees were cut down for fuel. But Charles II loved the park, swam regularly in its canal for all to see and walked daily through its glades. The ducks prospered. Evelyn wrote of 'numerous flocks of several sorts of ordinary and extraordinary wild fowl', as well as 'deer of several countries – white, spotted like leopards, antelopes, an elk, red deer, roebucks, stags'.

King Charles considered remodelling the .park, and asked the famous French landscaper, André Le Nôtre (1613–1700), who was responsible for Versailles, for advice. Le Nôtre, showing sensitivity to a landscape and diplomacy to a monarch, 'was of the opinion that the natural simplicity of this park, its rural and, in some cases, wild character, had something more grand than he could impart to it, and persuaded the king not to touch it'.

It remained fashionable into the new century, and the fashionable strutted there. Cows grazed in St James's and fresh milk cost a penny a mug. By Boswell's time, the 1760s, whores grazed there too, and he went there regularly. In 1814, in a premature celebration of the European peace, the Battle of the Nile was re-enacted by rowing boats dressed up with frames and canvas to resemble ships-of-the-line. The Prince Regent and his architect John Nash organized it and they put a bridge across the canal and built a Chinese pagoda out of theatre props. Canova called the bridge a 'trumpery affair' and the pagoda caught fire in the firework display. Twelve years later Nash remodelled the canal in a romantic style, in its present spanner-shape.

On the north side, the park comes to an end at THE MALL, laid out by Charles II as a place to play 'pell mell', a fashionable game that came from France and was a bit like croquet. In 1733 Baron von Pollnitz wrote:

> The grand walk they call the Mall is full of people every hour of the day, especially in the morning and evening and their Majesties often walk in it, with the Royal Family, who are attended by only half a dozen Yeomen of the Guard and permit all persons without distinction of rank or character to walk there at the same time with them, for which reason the crowd is sometimes too great, and it forms one of the most diversified scenes imaginable.

The Mall may have been grand by the standards of London, but it was hardly grand by the standards of European baroque. In Paris, Berlin or Vienna it would have been turned into a triumphal way from the symbol of government (a palace) to the seat of government (Whitehall), something as uniform as it was magnificent, a line as straight as a rifle shot, on which kings on white horses and marching columns can look both noble and intimidating. The Mall was spared that; partially because there was no grand palace at the end of it (Buckingham Palace had yet to be built and St James's Palace, at right angles to the Mall, looked embarrassingly domestic); and partially because the English Revolution of 1642–60 and the political compromise of 1688 that followed it made the kind of absolute rule needed to carry out such architecture impossible. But although London has been spared the absolutism and totalitarianism of full-blown Baroque, it has not been spared neo-Baroque. In 1901, when Queen Victoria died and the British Empire had already passed its zenith (Germany and the USA had overtaken Britain in steel production a decade earlier), a great chunk of St James's Park was appropriated and Sir Aston Webb turned the Mall into a grand and self-conscious Processional Way, starting at a victory arch, Admiralty Arch, and ending at the Victoria Memorial and Buckingham Palace.

The Mall's south side is bordered by the park. On the north side Nash's CARLTON HOUSE TERRACE, painted white and dripping with Corinthian columns, stretches to almost half-way down the Mall. At number 12, Nash House, the home of the Institute of Contemporary Arts, Carlton House Terrace is broken in two by the steps leading up to Waterloo Place. At the top of the steps is the statue of Frederick, Duke of York (1763–1827), the one who marched his men to the top of the hill. He stands 124 feet up on a pink granite column, supposedly high enough to keep the noble duke out of the reach of his creditors. The terrace stands on the site of Carlton House, built in 1709 and

Nash's Carlton House Terrace, almost as grand from the back as from the front.

bought by Frederick Prince of Wales in 1732. It became the home of his widow, Augusta, who founded Kew Gardens (see pp. 29–30), and she lived there until her death in 1772. Her son, George III, gave it to his son, the future Prince Regent and George IV, who commissioned Henry Holland (1746–1806) to spend a fortune turning it into 'the most perfect palace in Europe' (Horace Walpole). Not everyone liked it. Robert Smirke thought it 'overdone with finery'. But when the owner came to the throne he found it inadequate and the place was demolished, the Ionic pillars ending up as the portico of the National Gallery (see p. 136). The magnificent terrace was built by Nash to replace it, and he used it as the base for his own Regent Street scheme leading up to Piccadilly Circus and on to Regent's Park.

Carlton House Terrace ends at the brick wall of **MARLBOROUGH HOUSE**. Behind the wall, and originally part of St James's Palace, is the Queen's Chapel, built by Inigo Jones as a Catholic chapel for Queen Henrietta Maria, and served by a friary of Capuchins. The chapel is classical and galleried, one gallery reserved for royalty, and has a coved ceiling with a rich cornice highlighted in gold. The proportions are perfect, a double cube.

Marlborough House had been built by Christopher Wren to house Sarah Churchill (1660–1744), Duchess of Marlborough and wife of the great general, John Churchill (1650–1722), Duke of Marlborough. It is 'strong, plain and convenient', as she insisted, which is what you would expect from someone who so hated the baroque extravagance of Blenheim Palace that she refused to set foot in it after her husband died. Later she tried to improve the access by building a driveway from the Mall. Sir Robert Walpole (1676–1745), the future Prime Minister, bought the lease on the intervening house just to spite her. She was furious. She had already built the arch, which still stands, blocked and unused inside the garden.

In 1863 it became home to Edward, Prince of Wales, later Edward VII (1901–10), before becoming the traditional London residence of the Dowager Queen, until 1959 when the Crown donated it to the Commonwealth Secretariat, who use it as their headquarters.

The house still bears traces of some of its former inhabitants. Marlborough's victories painted by Louis Laguerre (1663–1721) spread across the walls, Blenheim (1704) in the saloon, Ramilles (1706) on the west staircase and bloody Malplaquet (1709) pushed out of the limelight on to the more dowdy east stairs. The Prince of Wales's smoking room is lined with bogus books, and Muff, Joss and Tiny, Queen Alexandra's (1844–1925) dogs, still rest peacefully under their headstones in the garden. A delightful and totally unexpected Art Nouveau statue of her stands outside the wall looking across Marlborough Road at **ST JAMES'S PALACE**.

The palace of dark red brickwork with blue diapering was built by Henry VIII for Anne Boleyn on the site of St James's leper hospital, to be near his new hunting grounds. The gatehouse of two flanking octagonal brick towers facing St James's Street, like a section of Hampton Court, and the Chapel

The multitude of early Tudor turrets on St James's Palace, built by Henry VIII on land acquired by him in 1532 from the leper hospital of St James's.

Royal's ceiling by Holbein are the only major parts of the Tudor Palace to survive the alterations of Wren, Hawksmoor, Kent and William Morris. Henry VIII's first daughter Queen Mary died here and his second daughter Queen Elizabeth held court here, as did James I, and his son, Charles I, who spent the night before his execution here. When Whitehall Palace was burned down in 1698, St James's became the monarch's principal London seat, and remained so until the reign of King William IV (1765–1837), who moved to Buckingham Palace. It is still the statutory seat of the monarchy. The accession of a new sovereign is proclaimed from St James, and ambassadors to the Court of St James are formally received by the monarch in the Throne Room, where two exquisite garlands of fruit and flowers carved by Grinling Gibbons are hung.

West of St James's Palace two grand mansions impose themselves before the open space of St James's Park, Clarence House and Lancaster House. **CLARENCE HOUSE**, standing beside St James's Palace, is gracious, stuccoed and well-preserved, as befits the home of the Queen Mother. It was built by Nash for George III's third son, William Duke of Clarence, only a couple of years before he became William IV, and he continued to live there while Buckingham Palace was being built. Later it was used by the present queen as a family home before her accession as Elizabeth II.

LANCASTER HOUSE, its golden Bath stone marking the beginning of Green Park, has gone by almost as many names as it has had owners, Godolphin House, York House, Stafford House and finally Lancaster House. The first house on the site belonged to the Godolphins. It was rebuilt by Robert Smirke for Frederick, Duke of York, the second son of George III, when he became heir to the throne. But George IV, who regarded himself as regally qualified to interfere in the architectural taste of his relatives, so hated Smirke's design that he sacked him and replaced him with Benjamin Dean Wyatt (1747–1813). The house, a straightforward rectangle with the obligatory classical pillars, was still unfinished when the unfortunate duke died.

The government, irritated by the royal family's architectural extravagence, sold the lease and gave the house to one of the duke's numerous creditors, the Duke of Stafford. His son re-employed Smirke on the interiors, which were decorated in the style of Louis XV. Called Stafford House, it became a centre for liberal politics under the highly political Stafford offspring, and Lord Shaftesbury (1801–85), the pioneer in child reform, Garibaldi (1807–82) and William Garrison (1805–79), the American abolitionist, were entertained there. In 1912 the house was sold to the soap millionaire William Hesketh (1851–1925), First Viscount Leverhulme of Unilever, who renamed it Lancaster House in honour of the county he was born in, and gave it to the nation.

On the other side of St James's Park, **BIRDCAGE WALK** forms the the park's southern boundary. This was where James I kept his aviary. The walk was created during Charles II's remodelling of the park and up until 1828 only members of the royal family (and their Hereditary Grand Falconer) could drive down it. The houses present their backs to the park. To see their fronts, London's finest example of domestic architecture built in the reign of Queen Anne, you must turn into Queen Anne's Gate, They are built of dark mellow bricks, and still have their porches, iron railings and torch snuffers. Amongst those who have lived in them are Lord North (1732–92), Jeremy Bentham (1748–1832), John Stuart Mill (1806–73), Lord Palmerston (1784–1865) and Sir Edward Grey (1862–1933). Today its most illustrious residents are the National Trust and the Director of Public Prosecutions.

Beyond Queen Anne's Gate, and facing the park without flinching, is **WELLINGTON BARRACKS**, regimental home of the Brigade of Guards, the monarch's personal troops. Its central block, like a regiment of the line, was built in 1833, significantly, by an military engineer, with some help from Philip Hardwick. To the east is the surprisingly light and graceful Guards' Chapel, built in 1962 on the site of the nineteenth-century chapel that had been destroyed in the War. To the west stands the new barracks, built in the 1970s. The three blocks, chapel, Regency barracks and modern barracks, form a parade ground, screened off from the street by cast-iron railings.

The best view of **BUCKINGHAM PALACE** is the obvious one, from the Mall. In front of it rises the Victoria Memorial – a neo-baroque ending to Sir Aston Webb's triumphant Mall, topped by a golden Victory above the old queen, with Truth, Motherhood and Justice standing beside her, while Military Power, Science, Art, Peace, Agriculture, Industry, Consistency and Courage hover on the edge like unimportant courtiers. Buckingham Palace itself, is set far back, behind cast iron railings and sand-blasted pillars, and with a cold and formal neo-classical front, put up by Sir Aston Webb to 'harmonize' with the grandeur of his Victoria Memorial and the Mall.

In the Middle Ages the site had been a swamp, watered by the River Tyburn. King Henry VIII drained it for his hunting ground and King James I, wanting to create a silk industry, turned it into a mulberry garden. It was an expensive failure. Silkworms feed on white mulberry trees, not black ones, and the king in his ignorance had ordered the wrong ones. It soon became the most fashionable pleasure garden of the seventeenth century. A house was built by the mulberry garden, grander than some of the royal palaces, going under the names of its successive owners: Goring House, Arlington House and Buckingham House. In 1761 it was sold to George III.

His son, George IV (1820–30), had it completely rebuilt by John Nash, who had to appear before two parliamentary committees to answer for the cost. His original palace was a three-sided extravaganza, with imitation pillars 'partly red like raw sausages, partly blue like starch', according to a German visitor, its open side facing the Mall and St James's Park. The courtyard was enclosed by a fourth block in 1847. The palace was unfinished when William IV came to the throne. He so disliked it that when the Houses of Parliment were burned down in 1834 he offered it to them, but they turned it down. It remained unloved until Victoria became queen. 'I have been so happy here', she later wrote. Her son Edward was born and died there, but it was not until 1912, after his death, that Sir Aston Webb added the present facade to the 1847 front with funds left over from the Victoria Memorial. He refronted the place in a mere twelve weeks, while George V (1910–36) and Queen Mary were out killing grouse in Scotland.

Apart from the Royal Mews and the Queen's Gallery, Buckingham Palace is not open to the public. Some, however, have visited the palace without an invitation. In 1841 a lad called Jones, an apothecary's errand boy, was found under a sofa next to the Queen's bedroom by Elizabeth Lilley, Queen Victoria's 'monthly nurse', after he had wandered through the kitchens and helped himself to what was in the larder. It turned out to have been his third visit. A few years later the Queen, passing through the Picture Gallery, noticed a man she had never seen before. She asked him who he was. 'One of the workmen laying the carpets, madam.' 'No you are not,' the Queen responded. 'A workman would call me "Your Majesty".' The man explained he was an art lover and *had* to see the royal collection. The queen invited him to stay for the rest of the day.

In June 1914 an engineer's fitter from Pimlico was found outside King George V's apartment. He had climbed over the garden wall and through a basement window, and had stopped off in the servants' quarters and exchanged his clothes for those of one of the occupants. Later in the reign of George V a man was found inside the palace gardens. He explained that he had climbed over the wall in search of a runaway hat.

The summer of 1982 was a busy time for Buckingham Palace. First a party of German tourists were found camping in the Palace gardens in the middle of the Falklands campaign, then a few weeks later the queen awoke to find a dishevelled hippy sitting on her bed and drinking from a bottle of wine that he had taken from the cellar. He told her that his name was Michael Fagan and he wanted a chat. The most recent intrusion was in December 1990. A 22-year-old unemployed Irishman, Eugene Smith, climbed over the garden wall to tell the queen that he was in love with her.

North and east of the Palace, the two triangles of Buckingham Palace gardens and Green Park form a rectangle of green as far as Hyde Park Corner, cut diagonally by Constitution Hill.

Laid out on the burial grounds of the St James's Hospital for lepers, GREEN PARK'S 53 acres grow no flowers. There is only grass, and crowds of lime, hawthorn and dappled plane trees. There was once a river flowing through it, the Tyburn, which left its own valley, but the river was buried and turned into a sewer. Henry VIII enclosed the land as an extension of his hunting grounds and Charles II laid it out as a park, excavating a subterranean ice house, London's first refrigerator, so he could drink cool drinks in summer. Nash landscaped it and built a revolving Temple of Concord and a make-believe gothic castle, to celebrate the make-believe peace of 1814. Six years later the

OPPOSITE Green Park, once a leper graveyard, where lamp posts and plane trees stand in orderly lines, but no flowers grow.

suitably named Mr Green (see p. 34) made a balloon flight from here to celebrate George IV's coronation, ending up at Potters Bar.

The eastern base of the Green Park triangle is marked by Queen's Walk, named after Queen Caroline who had a library in a small pavilion there. Overlooking Queen's Walk is Spencer House built in 1756–65 by John Vardy and Robert Adam, and one of the finest Palladian buildings in London.

> I do not apprehend there is a house in Europe of its size, better worth the view of the curious in architecture, and the fitting out and furnishing great houses, than Lord Spenser's in St James's Place (wrote Arthur Young). I know not in England, a more beautiful piece of architecture.

Beyond it, on the corner of Piccadilly, stands the inimitable RITZ, by Charles Mewes and Arthur Davis (1878–1951), treating Green Park as its own back garden. The Ritz is Beaux Arts like its sister in Paris, which was also built by Mewes, and has an arcade lined with shops on the Piccadilly side reminiscent of Paris's rue de Rivoli. The interiors are luxurious and Edwardian, with palms and pillars and marble and mirrors. Everyone should have tea there just once in their lives.

Piccadilly, along the north side of Green Park, is mostly in the styles of the twenties and thirties, with aspirations towards imperial Rome. There are several very imperial-looking gentlemen's clubs, the odd post-war airline office and a couple of expense account hotels. Behind them Shepherd Market, a little village of narrow streets, covered alleys and twisting lanes, has retained its Georgian charm.

West of Piccadilly, standing by itself and looking out over Hyde Park Corner, is APSLEY HOUSE. As the first house after the Hyde Park Corner turnpike, it was known as Number One, London. Built in 1771 by Robert Adam, it was refaced in Bath stone and given a Corinthian portico by its most famous resident, Arthur Wellesley (1769–1852), Duke of Wellington. He also gutted all the Adam rooms in the house save the Piccadilly Drawing Room and the Portico Room, but then, according to his friend Mrs Arbuthnot, his tastes in interior decoration were appalling.

The interior has been turned into the Wellington Museum. In the Muniment Room, on the ground floor, is the exquisite Meissen, Sèvres and Berlin porcelain given to him by the grateful monarchs of post-1815 Europe, the gold Waterloo Vase and the field-marshal's batons of seven nations. The grand staircase is guarded by a naked Napoleon, sculpted at twice his normal size by Canova. Napoleon himself had rejected the piece, on the grounds that the gilt figure of Victory in the palm of his hand was looking away from him, which was prophetic in a way.

Wellington's great picture collection, loot taken from Joseph Bonaparte after the Battle of Vittoria (1813), begins at the top of the staircase where portraits of the emperors Frederick the Great (1712–86) and Napoleon, and the kings Charles X of France (1757–1836, r. 1824–30) and John VI of

Portugal (1816–26), hang. Dutch paintings by Nicolaes Maes (1632–93), Jan Steen (1626–70), Pieter de Hooch (c.1629–c.1684) and David Teniers the Younger (1610–90) line the Adam Drawing Room. Numerous portraits, including those of Napoleon and Josephine, and Bonnemaison's copies of four Raphael cartoons hang in Adam's Portico Room.

Then comes the Waterloo Gallery, and the finest paintings of all: Antonio Correggio's (c.1494–1534) *The Agony in the Garden* (the duke's favourite), Diego de Silva y Velazquez's (1599–1660) *Water Seller of Seville* and *A Spanish Gentleman*, and others by Bartolomé Murillo (1618–82), José de Ribera (1588–1656), Rubens, Reynolds and Claude Lorraine. Amongst them is Francisco José de Goya y Lucientes's (1746–1828) portrait of Wellington on horseback. The duke looks surprised. He should. Originally Goya's portrait had been of Joseph Bonaparte, to celebrate his expected victory. The face had to be rapidly overpainted when news of the ultimate victory arrived. Joseph Bonaparte appears himself in the Yellow Drawing Room, painted by Lefèvre. Beside his brother Napoleon, hangs the Empress Josephine (also by Lefèvre) and the 'Iron Duke' himself, looking at a bust of Napoleon. The Striped Drawing Room is devoted to the Battle of Waterloo (1815), with portraits of Wellington's generals and Sir William Allan's (1782–1850) panorama of the battle. 'Good – very good; not too much smoke', was the duke's reaction when he first saw it.

Outside Apsley House the traffic roars around Hyde Park Corner and its seemingly purposeless arch. Previous plans for a triumphal arch here had been put forward by Robert Adam, Jeffry Wyatt (1766–1840) and Sir John Soane. It was finally erected in the post-Waterloo euphoria by Decimus Burton. In 1843 an oversized statue of the Duke of Wellington on his horse Copenhagen, 30 feet long and 40 tons in weight, was put on top of it. Forty years later the statue was taken down and given to the British Army, and it now sits on the Round Hill at Aldershot. The arch stayed, and the oversized Wellington was replaced by a statue of Peace, erected, somewhat ironically, in the early summer of 1914.

North-west of the roundabout, behind Decimus Burton's elegant classical screen into Hyde Park, is the Achilles statue by Sir Richard Westmacott (1775–1856), supposedly of the Duke himself and commissioned by a 'Committee of Ladies' on behalf of 'the women of Great Britain'. You can't miss it, all 20 naked bronzed feet of it. At first there was not even a fig leaf on the noble Duke, and he appeared ... well ... under-endowed. In fact he was so under-endowed that one French visitor exclaimed: '*Enfin, on est vengé*'. National pride asserted itself and the Duke was given his fig leaf.

The first thing you notice about **HYDE PARK** is its size, 340 acres (or 630 acres if you include Kensington Gardens which the park becomes west of the Serpentine Bridge); and the sight of tiny people walking over a flat two-mile landscape beneath a wide open sky is a reminder of the immensity and the sheer loneliness of London.

The Long Water (at the west end of the Serpentine, from the Italianate fountains by Bayswater.

Everyone has their own association with Hyde Park, bleak or beautiful, depending on the weather in your soul: lovers on the Serpentine, Gulf Arabs on horses, rabbits in the Dell, the Rolling Stones Concert, Sinn Fein orators at Speakers' Corner, people shouting at trees. But whatever the association, it always happens beneath a wide open sky.

Hyde Park was the haunt of boars and wild bulls in the Middle Ages. Henry VIII acquired it as an extension of his hunting grounds. In the north-east corner, the hunting grounds stopped at the gallows of Tyburn, a few yards from Nash's Marble Arch, built in 1827 and based on the Arch of Constantine in Rome – yet another triumphal arch of George IV's decades of architectural extravagance. Hyde Park became the centre for fashion every May Day in the reign of Charles I, and remained fashionable in spite of revolution and privatization, to the fury of the radicals and extreme Puritans. One pamphleteer complained of 'many hundreds of coaches and gallants in attire but most shameful, powdered hair, men painted and spotted women'. Cromwell, on some issues a most tolerant man, rode there regularly both on horseback and in his one-man carriage. He nearly died once, when his horses bolted and he was flung from his carriage and dragged along, his foot caught in the tackle and his pistol going off in his pocket. In spite of the accident people have been parading with horses in Hyde Park ever since.

Charles II took the park back into royal hands and reopened it to the public free of charge. Once again it was the centre of fashionable society. It was still fashionable when William III was king and hung 300 lamps from St James's Palace to Kensington Palace along the *route de roi*, or Rotten Row.

Queen Caroline had the Serpentine formed in 1730, by damming the River Westbourne and linking together its small ponds. It was a revolutionary break from the formal and geometrical waters in other royal parks like Hampton Court. In 1816 Percy Bysshe Shelley's (1792–1822) pregnant and deserted wife, Harriet Westbrook, went to the Serpentine and took her own life. Four years later Princess Lieven complained that 'good society no longer goes there except to drown itself'.

South of the Serpentine stood the Crystal Palace in 1851, that extraordinary glass structure which housed the Great Exhibition. It stood in front of what is now Sir Basil Spence's (1907–1976) Horse Guard Barracks. The idea of the Great Exhibition, to bring together all the artistic and industrial achievements of the world under one roof, was taken up enthusiastically by Prince Albert, the Prince Consort. The building in which this was all housed, designed by Sir Joseph Paxton, was the most stupendous of all the exhibits, a cathedral of iron and glass in prefabricated parts, with a dome that was larger that St Peter's in Rome. *Punch* dubbed it 'the Crystal Palace' and the name stuck. Six million people visited it, the octogenarian Duke of Wellington going every day it was open.

North of the Serpentine, Hyde Park presents vast open spaces, broken only by a smattering of Georgian and neo-Georgian park buildings and the bird sanctuary, the Green Mansions, where Jacob Epstein's (1880–1959) relief of Rima, the half-human and half-forest spirit, once shocking and now merely anorexic, looks out over trees and water. To the west stretches the Serpentine Bridge, from where you get that view of 'extraordinary nobleness' (Henry James), with Big Ben rising above the treeline beyond the Serpentine.

South of Hyde Park, from Hyde Park Corner to the Brompton Oratory, is **KNIGHTSBRIDGE**, once a bridge over the River Westbourne. In 1783 Knightsbridge was still 'quite out of London'. Thirty years later it was a favourite spot for highwaymen. In the 1900s Knightsbridge was an upper-middle class suburb. Now it is part of central London and the only people who can afford to live there are diplomats, debutantes, and dowagers.

A single name symbolizes Knightsbridge: **HARRODS**, the grandest dowager of them all. Charles Digby Harrod was the man who made Harrods. In 1861 he brought a small grocery store from his father and was so successful that by 1880 he employed nearly 100 assistants. His reputation grew, and shot up in

December 1883 when Harrods was destroyed by fire. 'I greatly regret to inform you that, in consequence of the above premises being burned down, your order will be delayed in the execution a day or two', he wrote to his customers. Every Christmas order arrived on time. A new Harrods grew up over the embers, the fairytale terracotta building that has become its own logo. Inside, the unforgettable Art Nouveau food halls, where the smells of salmon, strong cheeses and expensive scent coagulate at the counters, have remained unchanged since 1905.

In the streets around, Sloane Street, Brompton Road, Pont Street, and Beauchamp Place, are dozens of chic shops, feeding off the crowds coming out of Harrods, their window displays a chronicle of each year's fashion: Harvey Nichols and the Scotch House in Knightsbridge; Karl Lagerfeld, Fiorucci, Esprit, Hermes, Joseph, Giorgio Armani, Issey Miyake and Kenzo in Sloane Street. Virtually the whole length of Sloane Street – where prep school children in maroon plus-fours and mustard-coloured jerseys walk in crocodiles from the park, and old ladies complain about their Filipino servants – is lined with such shops. The most exclusive don't even have names on the outside, only signatures scrawled on windows. Katharine Hamnett doesn't even have that, merely a fish tank. It was not always like that. Next door to the New Art Centre used to be the Empire Food Store, run by a one-legged colonel and his batman. Now it is a boutique.

But outside the main shopping ground, particularly in the alleys and mews around Montpelier Square, between Brompton Road and Hyde Park, the acquisitive crowds disappear and you can lose yourself amongst delightful Georgian doll's houses and forget for a moment just how ugly people wearing fur coats and Gucci shoes can be.

To the west of the Montpelier Square quarter, is the **BROMPTON ORATORY**, its best face looking south to Brompton Road, beside Chavalliaud's simple and life-like statue of John Henry, Cardinal Newman (1801–90). The Oratory was completed in 1884 at the height of the Roman Catholic Revival, in full-blown Italian neo-Baroque. It is faced in Portland stone and the size of a cathedral. Inside, overflowing Italianate chapels glow from both sides of the nave. Between the side chapels stand Giuseppe Mazzuoli's (1644–1725) late baroque marble apostles, recovered from a Genoese warehouse after being discarded by Siena Cathedral, restless and dramatic, the face of Judas so ordinary that it could be you or me. The music of the Oratory choir, at High Mass on Sundays and at Christmas and Easter, is exquisite, and the Oratory shares with the Russian Orthodox Church, a couple of hundred yards to the north in Ennismore Gardens, the accolade for producing the most beautiful church music in London.

Beside the Oratory the **VICTORIA AND ALBERT MUSEUM** stretches as far as Exhibition Road, marking the beginning of the great museum quarter of South Kensington: the Victoria and Albert, the Natural History Museum, the Geological Museum and the Science Museum.

OPPOSITE *The Brompton Oratory: pure Victorian baroque, its interior is like the inside of a cathedral in late renaissance Italy.*

The 'V and A' opened as the Department of Oriental Art in the Museum of Manufactures, then housed in Marlborough House. In 1857 it moved to South Kensington, where 80 acres of land had been bought with the profits of the Great Exhibition. Its aim was to extend 'the influence of Science and Art upon Productive Industry'. The collection was first housed in an enormous glass and corrugated iron shed known as the 'Brompton Boiler', which has since been dismantled and re-erected at the Bethnal Green Museum of Childhood (see p. 149), where it looks, in hindsight, surprisingly post-Modern. The present building by Sir Aston Webb, its bulk ponderous and its roofline a festival of domes and spires, was not started until 1899. Queen Victoria laid the foundation stone. It was her last public engagement.

Inside is a delightful mish-mash. From the foyer at the Brompton Road entrance, the hall leads you to a central space devoted to early medieval religious art. A corridor to the left leads to the seven Raphael Cartoons, the most treasured exhibit of the museum. Commissioned by the Medici Pope Leo X (1513–22) in 1515 to be copied on tapestry for the Sistine Chapel, they were bought by Charles I in 1623 for his tapestry works at Mortlake. To the right the view opens to a gallery crowded with statuary by Flaxman. Chantrey, Rysbrack, Cibber and Joseph Nollekens (1737–1823), and including Louis-François Roubiliac's (1705–62) statue of Handel, the first in Europe of a living artist, and the closest in likeness to the composer.

Further into the middle of the building are rooms on either side of the entrance hall devoted to Islamic and Sino-Japanese art. Beyond the Islamic Room is displayed Indian art, including the exquisite second-century figure of the god, Bodhisattva, a synthesis of Indian and Greek traditions, and a reminder of the far-flung influence of Alexander the Great. At the end of the corridor is the museum's Dress Collection, a fascinating chronicle of fashions from the eighteenth century to the present day. Deeper into the museum is a charming central courtyard, the Pirelli Garden, with its own fountain, surrounded by galleries displaying gothic and renaissance art including works by Michelangelo (1475–1564), Donatello (c.1386–1466) and Giovanni Bologna (1529–1608).

The Lower Gound floor is given over to European art from the Renaissance – paintings, sculpture, embroidery, porcelain and furniture – and leads to the Henry Cole Wing, which exhibits painting by Gainsborough, Reynolds, Romney, Rossetti, Rembrandt, Degas, Blake, and Jean-Auguste Ingres (1780–1867). It also has what is probably the most comprehensive collection of drawings and paintings by John Constable (1776–1837).

On the Upper Gound Floor you can find British art, including Grinling Gibbons's superb *Crucifixion* and the Great Bed of Ware, mentioned by Shakespeare in *Twelfth Night*, and said to have held 26 butchers and their wives on the night of 13 February 1689. More British art and furniture can be found on the first floor, and here are galleries devoted to the V and A's collections of textiles, tapestries, jewellery and glass. There is also the National

John Constable lived in Hampstead for many years, and the Victoria and Albert's picture galleries contain many of his paintings and sketches of the heath.

Art Library, a reference library of over 300,000 publications, while on the second floor are galleries displaying porcelain ranging from the Inca Empire to Royal Worcester.

The eight miles of corridors form a series of collections, and house so much that the museum's guardians have given up trying to give it any sense of order. 'Any visitor to the Victoria and Albert Museum today is likely to be bemused as to what exactly is the central thread that animates these discrepant if marvellous collections,' a former director, Sir Roy Strong, wrote. 'The answer is that there is none. For over a century the museum has proved an extremely capacious handbag.' It is a handbag best visited without a guidebook; that way you will never cease to be surprised at the contents.

The V and A comes to an end at Exhibition Road, where a procession of museums, colleges and other institutions of learning line up between Exhibition Road and Queens Gate culminating at the Royal Albert Hall. The first and largest of these, facing Cromwell Road, is the NATURAL HISTORY MUSEUM, imposing and ecclesiastical in buff and blue terracotta, a Darwinian encyclopaedia between romanesque covers.

The origin of the museum is the natural history collection of Sir Hans Sloane, which he bequeathed to the British Museum. With the South Kensington site available after the Great Exhibition, Captain Fowke, the engineer/architect of the Royal Albert Hall, was commissioned to design a new museum. Fowke died and the commission passed to Alfred Waterhouse, the Liverpool Quaker who built the Pru (see p. 93). His choice of style came after careful consideration; and he decided that late Romanesque with its carvings of trees and leaves, fish and mammals. seemed the most suitable.

In the central hall, a neo-romanesque Great Hall, you are greeted by the reconstructed skeleton of the dinosaur, *Diplodocus*, who lived 150 million years ago, was 84 feet 9 inches (nearly 26 metres) long and weighed 50 tons. On the left, is a gallery filled with stuffed birds, from humming-birds to Golden Eagles. From the end of it another corridor, exhibiting species of marine life at its most primitive, leads to the mammal room, nine tenths of it taken by a gigantic Blue Whale. In the Great Hall's upper gallery, is a motionless zoo of stuffed monkeys, baboons, gazelle, tigers, and even a polar bear.

North of the Natural History Museum on Exhibition Road, squashed and almost lost between it and the Science Museum, is the GEOLOGICAL MUSEUM, infinitely more fascinating that its name suggests, boasting a collection of over a million minerals and fossils and the 'earthquake room'.

Beside it, as every London schoolchild will tell you, is the SCIENCE MUSEUM. The entrance hall is filled with the great dinosaurs of the steam age – beam engines by Boulton and Watt, the oldest steam locomotive in existence, 'Puffing Billy', and Stephenson's 'Rocket'. From there you jump in time to the immediate present, and find yourself in a lunar landscape crowded with space capsules including Apollo Ten. A few feet from Apollo Ten you go back in time again, to the late nineteenth and early twentieth centuries. There is an

A detail from Alfred Waterhouse's patterned terracotta Natural History Museum, showing the lively imagination of the sculptor, as well as the state of knowledge about pterosaurs at the time. Waterhouse chose the romanesque style because its traditional carvings of plant and animal life seemed the most suitable for a building devoted to natural history.

1888 Benz, the first motor car, fire engines from the very earliest hand pumps, and a London Underground tube train. Close by is a staircase, and from the stairwell, the Foucault Pendulum demonstrates with every silent swing that the earth rotates on its axis.

The first floor is concerned with iron and steel, the development of machines and time, from the 1392 clock of Wells Cathedral to a modern Marconi beam transmitter. There is an astronomical star dome, and a space known as the Launch Pad designed for children to make discoveries of their own. On the second floor are displays given over to marine engineering, computing, chemistry and nuclear physics. The third floor is the most dramatic, ending in a gigantic aircraft hangar housing aircraft from the 1903 Wright Brothers flying machine, through Alcock's and Brown's Vickers 'Vimy' (the first plane to cross the Atlantic), and the earliest helicopter to the Whittle turbo-jet aero-engine that powered the first jet aircraft. The smaller floors above are devoted to the history of medicine.

Outside the Science Museum, Exhibition Road rises gently up the slope to Hyde Park and Kensington Gardens. On the left is the Imperial College of Technology followed by Prince Consort Road, and on the corner of Prince Consort Road is Sir Aston Webb's monumental Royal School of Mines, whose entrance presents a neo-baroque gap that can only be explained by assuming that the Victoria Memorial has been cut out of it, and transported to the Mall. Prince Consort Road makes the best approach to the ROYAL ALBERT HALL, up the grand flights of steps, flanked by the curves of Norman Shaw's Albert Hall Mansions, so that the red brick and oval hall, with its shallow iron and glass dome, and frieze celebrating the Triumphs of the Arts and Sciences, confronts you full on.

Proposed, like its foil the Albert Memorial, in memory of the Prince Consort, who died in 1861, the foundation stone was laid in 1868 by Queen Victoria. Two years later it was opened by the Prince of Wales, his mother being too overcome by emotion to attend herself. The Prince declared the hall open and the hall echoed back 'open'. Its echo became famous, and until 1968, when the acoustics were improved by saucer-shapes suspended from the dome, it was said to be the only concert hall in the world where a composer could be guaranteed to hear his work twice.

Here have been held concerts conducted by Richard Wagner, and concerts led by Bob Dylan, fascist rallies, and world heavy-weight boxing competitions, Coronation Balls attended by 80 members of royal families from all over Europe, and the spectacular Chelsea Arts Club balls of the 1920s which turned into carnivals. Surprisingly, the most famous concerts associated with the Albert Hall, the Promenade Concerts, or Proms, did not come to the Albert Hall until 1941, when Queen's Hall was bombed.

West of the hall, and coming as a great relief after its dull brick morality, is the Royal College of Organists, a charming mixture of classical and Venetian styles, in cream and maroon and pale blue sgraffito, delightful in its

OPPOSITE *The Albert Hall: a detail of the frieze celebrating 'the Triumph of Art and Letters'.*

*William Kent's neo-classical Summer
House in Kensington Gardens.*

unworldliness. Next to it, and much larger, looms T. H. Cadbury-Browne's
and Sir Hugh Casson's uncompromising, modern Royal College of Art,
which provides one of London's best fashion and design shows of the year.

The main entrance of the Albert Hall, on the north side facing
Kensington Gore, gives you a perfect view of the **ALBERT MEMORIAL**, completed
in 1872, 'that wistful unique monument of widowhood,' as Sir Osbert Sitwell
(1892–1969) called it.

The gothic icing spire is 175 feet high. Beneath it sits a gigantic bronze
statue of the Prince reading the catalogue of the Great Exhibition. Guarding
the four corners are marble groups representing Africa, Asia, America and
Europe. Around the pediment, where Agriculture, Engineering, Commerce
and Industry survey the tourists from the corners, is a frieze of 178 figures:
painters on the east, architects on the north, sculptors on the west and poets
and musicians on the east. They are surprisingly unpompous. Hogarth has his
dog, Pythagoras is solving a geometrical problem, Lorenzo Ghiberti
(1378–1455) and Luca della Robbia (*c.*1400–82) are gossiping.

Beyond the Memorial, hidden from it by the rich herbaceous borders behind, open up **KENSINGTON GARDENS**, the fourth of the royal parks. You get a better class of person in Kensington Gardens – gardens, note, not just a common park. It is said that the dogs in Kensington Gardens are better dressed than the people in Hyde Park.

North from the Memorial, past the Serpentine Gallery, the Serpentine curves into a Claudian landscape. A little to the north-west, in the alcove of trees by the Serpentine shore where nannies double-park their prams, stands the Peter Pan statue by Sir George Frampton (1860–1928), a memorial to J. M. Barrie's (1860–1937) 'Boy Who Never Grew Up', blowing his pipe on an art nouveau spiral populated by fairies, rabbits, birds, mice, squirrels and owls, and still innocent. The pilgrims who attend the statue seem predominantly middle class, indeed the whole Peter Pan cult seems middle class, which would have pained Barrie. 'Quite common boys also picnic (in Kensington Gardens),' he once said, 'and the blossom falls on their mugs just the same.' Across the water stands a lonely abstract by Henry Moore. It remains untitled, although those who work in the gardens have christened it 'Arse on Stilts'. At the head of the Serpentine the waters end with the flourish of French Italianate fountains and their disporting sea-nymphs, overlooked by an Italian Pavilion which hides a pumping station at the back of it. To the right is the shell-shaped Queen Anne's Alcove, designed by Wren.

The further west Kensington Gardens go, the more they discipline themselves, gradually discarding the romantic landscape of the Serpentine, first for a formal classical landscape, and then for something even tighter, closer to a Dutch garden. Queen Mary did lay out a Dutch garden, at the far end of Kensington Gardens, where it is overlooked by Kensington Palace. It was her husband William III who purchased the house, and commissioned Wren to rebuild it. He said that the palaces at Whitehall and St James's were bad for his asthma. Mary supervised the planting of the box and yew hedges, and the orange, lemon and myrtle trees along the walks. Queen Anne, who succeeded William and Mary, disliked the Dutch style and had much of it uprooted. She commissioned Charles Bridgman to redesign the larger part of the palace gardens into a less formal style in the late 1720s, laying out the Broad Walk and excavating the Round Pond.

KENSINGTON PALACE itself, 'noble but not great', according to John Evelyn, stands beside Hawksmoor's Orangery and a charming sunken garden, excavated in 1909, dropping down three levels to a lily pond inhabited by koi carp and surrounded by a bower of lime trees. The palace is domestic and unpretentious, rambling round several courtyards. Even the additions by Hawksmoor on the south side are without grandeur. A generation later Kent tried to give the palace a more baroque style, gutting the rooms in the north-east corner of the building and replacing them with three grand state rooms for George I, but they did not alter the essence of Kensington Palace, and Wren's domesticity still predominates.

Sir George Frampton's Peter Pan statue in Kensington Gardens, art nouveau, still innocent and not yet grown-up, a memorial to the lost childhoods of the English middle-classes.

You enter the palace through a door built by Wren's master mason, Thomas Hill. To the left, a passage leads through an exhibition of court costume to the nineteenth-century rooms, designed by James Wyatt for the Duke of Kent (1767–1820), Queen Victoria's father, and including both the room where the future Queen Victoria was born on 24 May 1819, and the room where she first heard, raised from her bed, that she had become queen.

Up the stairs, designed by Wren, are the Queen's Apartments. Here is the Queen's Gallery, 84 feet long, with its beautiful Grinling Gibbons woodwork and the portraits on the wall of Peter the Great (1672–1725) by Kneller, and William III, Queen Mary and Anne Hyde, all by Lely. Further on is the Closet, where the clash of wills between Queen Anne and the Duchess of Marlborough, which destroyed their long friendship, took place.

Beyond are the great state rooms by Colen Campbell and William Kent: the Privy Chamber, the Presence Chamber, the King's Staircase and the King's Gallery. The ceilings of the Privy Chamber and Presence Chamber are painted by Kent in classical make-believe, with George I (1714–27) as Mars in the Privy Chamber. They lead to the King's Grand Staircase, built by Wren and with a balustrade by Tijou. Painted on the walls, in a *trompe l'oeil*, so they look as if they are almost hanging over the balustrade, are some of the faces of the English court, including Kent (the man who painted it), his mistress Elizabeth Butler, and Peter the Wild Boy (the feral child found in the woods of Hanover and adopted by the court), while mischievously climbing up the wall is Lady Suffolk's page.

Further on, on the ceiling of the King's Gallery, Kent depicts the story of Ulysses. The subject is eminently suitable for a trading nation, and above the fireplace is a map of Europe with a wind dial centred on England, connected to a vane on the roof, so that the monarch could discover which way the wind was blowing – and whether it would bring commerce or invasion.

The final room to visit (though it means doubling back) is the King's Drawing Room, with its ceiling painting of Jupiter. From the central window you can see at a glance the formality of Kensington Gardens, the Round Pond aligned to the window, and the avenues radiating out from it. Beyond the trees, grass and water stretch out eastwards through Kensington Gardens, Hyde Park, Green Park and St James's Park as far as Whitehall, and the ghost of Whitehall Palace which King William rejected in favour of Kensington Palace some 300 years ago.

ABOVE *The sunken garden in Kensington gardens lined on its four sides by an alley of limes, their branches intertwined, and laid out it 1909 in imitation of the formal gardens that so delighted William and Mary.*

OPPOSITE *The statue of William III given to Edward VII by Kaiser Wilhelm II, outside Kensington Palace.*

5
The Squares

·····························

MANCHESTER SQUARE *to* BLOOMSBURY

The eighteenth century created London's squares, giving them that period's suggestion of a contrived and controlled countryside on your doorstep. They epitomize Georgian elegance, genteel uniformity and bourgeois respectability. The finest lie in Mayfair and the quarters off it, Marylebone, St James's, Soho and Bloomsbury, and nineteenth-century copies of them can be found all over London.

From the 1630s when Francis Russell, the Fourth Earl of Bedford, commissioned Inigo Jones to lay out Covent Garden, there had been a gradual movement westwards by the aristocracy, away from the poky, polluted streets of the City, first to the Strand, and then further west into Mayfair and, as the eighteenth century turned into the nineteenth century, onward into Belgravia, Kensington, Chelsea and beyond.

Covent Garden was London's first square. Formerly it had been the gardens of the Abbey of St Peter at Westminster. It passed to the Earls of Bedford after the Dissolution of the Monasteries. About 100 years later, in 1630, the Earl of Bedford, seeing an opportunity for profit, commissioned Inigo Jones to design a plan for seven acres of his ground. Jones proposed new houses, tall and narrow, set in two arcades north and east facing a rectangular square after Paris's Palais Royale (now Place des Vosges). The style was to be classical. On the south side Bedford House was to stand, and on the west side there was to be a church, St Paul's. Little except the reconstructed church remains. The Earl had wanted to save money on it. 'I would not have it much better than a barn,' he told Jones. 'You shall have the handsomest barn in England,' Jones replied. And he did. Five years later Leicester Square was laid out in front of Leicester House. Bloomsbury Square followed in 1665, Soho Square in 1681, St James's Square in 1684, Grosvenor Square in 1695 and Berkeley Square in 1698. But these were only the vanguard. Hanover Square appeared in 1714, Cavendish Square in 1717, Portman Square in

OPPOSITE *St James's Square, one of the most perfect of London's squares, looking towards the statue of King William III in classical dress.*

121

1764, Bedford Square in 1775, Manchester Square in 1776, Fitzroy Square in 1792 and Russell Square in 1800.

The motives of these squares were as uniform as the layout. They began as grand houses for noble families, built in open country with a wide space in front to make an impressive approach to the house. The noble families were followed by the merchants, lawyers, tradesmen, shopkeepers and servants who fed off the aristocracy. Uniform ranges were built on three sides of the open approach, forming a square, enhancing the original mansion and – once rented out – enhancing the bank balances of the mansions' owners. These Georgian houses, built of dark grey London bricks and broken only by lines of absolutely symmetrical sashed windows, were reserved for the high bourgeoisie. Behind them were smaller, meaner houses, cramped in narrower streets for the lower-middle class. Squeezed in behind them were the mews and alleys, reserved for horses and servants. James Boswell, writing in his *London Journal* in the 1760s, had no illusions about the London square:

> Behind these gracious houses, however, with no gardens to insulate them, were closely-ranged houses and tenements of a baser sort, so that the back windows of 'the Squares' looked out on a solid prospect and were looked in upon by many pairs of eyes, some envious, some hostile.

MANCHESTER SQUARE, a little to the north of the western half of Oxford Street, is one of the least changed of all central London's squares. Laid out to the south of Hertford House, only in the north-west corner is the Georgian uniformity of grey brick and sashed windows on the other three sides of the square broken. Manchester Square was created by the Duke of Manchester who, with a nice touch of vanity, named it after himself. He had planned a church for the middle of the square, but it was never built. The Duke's residence, Manchester House, renamed Hertford House in 1797 when the Second Marquess of Hertford bought it, is now the home of the **WALLACE COLLECTION**, containing the greatest collection of seventeenth- and eighteenth-century French paintings assembled outside France.

Hertford House is a joy to wander through, like walking through someone's private house. The collection is the fruit of five generations of Hertford family acquisitiveness and taste. It was started by Francis Seymour-Conway (1719–94), the First Marquess of Hertford, who purchased the views of Venice by Canaletto, and to whom George III gave the portrait of himself by Allan Ramsay. His son, the second Marquess, continued the collection, adding French boulle furniture, the exquisite Sèvres porcelain, Reynolds's *Nelly O'Brien* and Gainsborough's *Mrs 'Perdita' Robinson*, given to him by the Prince Regent in return for the favours of the Marchioness.

The third Marquess, the dissolute and eccentric Francis Seymour-Conway (1777–1842), who succeeded to the title in 1822, and was the model of the fascinatingly evil Lord Steyne in Thackeray's *Vanity Fair*, enlarged the collection further, buying up French furniture, the French and Italian

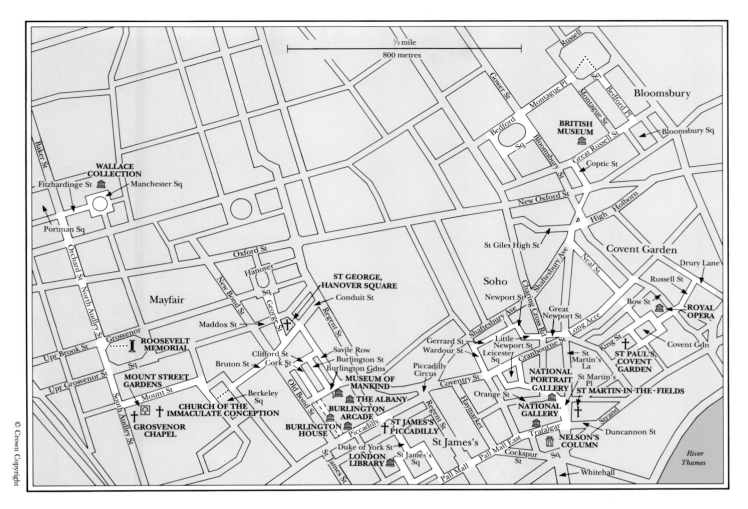

bronzes, the exquisite renaissance miniatures, and such paintings as Netscher's *The Lace Maker*, and Titian's (*c.* 1487/90–1576) *Perseus and Andromeda*. His son, the fourth Marquess, lived as a recluse at his château on the Bois de Boulogne just outside Paris and devoted his life to his collection. His pride was his French eighteenth-century paintings, and he gathered up the buxom and baroque subject matter of François Boucher (1703–70), Jean Antoine Watteau (1684–1721) and Jean-Henri Fragonard (1732–1806). But his appreciation was wider than that, and he added to the collection Rubens's *Rainbow Landscape*, Velazquez's *Lady with a Fan*, Rembrandt's *Titus*, Gaspard Poussin's (1615–75) surreal *Dance to the Music of Time*, Franz Hals's (1584–1666) engaging *Laughing Cavalier*, the dozens of seventeenth-century Dutch works, landscapes by Claude Lorraine, eight paintings by Murillo, as well as works by the Marquess's contemporaries, Jean Meissonier (1813–91), Alexandre Decamps (1803–60) and Paul Delaroche (1797–1856). He died in August 1870, and his illegitimate son, Richard Wallace (1818–90), expanded the collection further, adding the illuminated manuscripts and the splendid European, African and Oriental arms and armour. It was his French widow, Julie, who left the collection, by then one of the finest private collections in existence, to the nation in 1897.

West of Manchester Square, Fitzhardinge Street leads to **PORTMAN SQUARE**, built between 1764 and 1784. Apart from number 20, which was built by Robert Adam for the eighth Earl of Home, and is graced with wall paintings by Antonio Zucchi (1762–95) and Angelica Kauffmann, and a few other mid-Georgian houses, standing out like white teeth in a mouth full of gold fillings, the square has been entirely rebuilt.

South from Portman Square, Orchard Street takes you to Selfridges on the corner of Oxford Street, opened in 1909 by the American Harry Gordon Selfridge (1857–1940) and one of the great department stores of London. Gordon Selfridge from Chicago epitomized Selfridges. For though it was grand (as grand as the Greek temple it was supposed to look like), it was also democratic, and inside it all English types can be found, the gnarled old and the puppy-skinned young, the West Indian and the East Ender, the company director and the office tea lady.

Oxford Street is older than it looks. Since Roman times it has been the traditional road out of London to the west. It was the road to Tyburn, and you can follow the route of the notorious highwaymen Jack Sheppard (d.1714) and Jonathan Wild (d.1725), as they were taken on the execution cart, past Oxford Circus to the spot marked in the pavement on the traffic island immediately north of Marble Arch, where the gibbet stood.

Buildings grew up on either side of Oxford Street in the eighteenth century, but only Stratford House in Stratford Place, a couple of blocks to the east of Selfridges, built in the 1770s and looking like a piece of stage scenery, still stands. Oxford Street was turned into a major shopping street in the nineteenth century, dominated by drapers until the arrival of the big department stores towards the end of the century. They are still there, John Lewis, British Home Stores, Marks and Spencer and D. H. Evans: middle-priced, middle-range, middle-class and – just a little bit – middle-aged.

Cross Oxford Street and you come into Mayfair, which takes its name from the May Fair which was held for fifteen days each May until the local residents ensured its suppression for disorderliness in the 1760s. By then the quarter had become the recognized London home of the aristrocracy, an image Mayfair has retained ever since, even though it is now almost all given over to prestigious offices and exclusive shops. Today it is still the centre of fashionable London, graced by three beautiful squares, Grosvenor Square, Berkeley Square and Hanover Square.

Continue down North Audley Street on the south side of Oxford Street and you come to **GROSVENOR SQUARE**, marked by the statue to Franklin Delano Roosevelt (1882–1945). Begun in the 1720s and taking 30 years to complete, it is the largest of Mayfair's three great squares. Except for number 9 in the

Sir William Reid Dick's statue in bronze of Franklin D. Roosevelt in Grosvenor Square.

north-east corner, the residence of John Adams (1735–1826), the United States's first ambassador to Britain and the second president of the USA, and number 38, now the Indonesian Embassy, the square has been entirely rebuilt, the whole west side taken up by Eero Saarinen's (1910–61) United States Embassy, completed in the year of his death.

Grosvenor Square, according to its historian, Arthur Desant, 'was strewn with the strawberry leaves and the blue ribbons of the Garter' throughout the eighteenth century (*A History of Grosvenor Square*, 1935). Number 38 was occupied by Ehrengard Melusina, Baroness von de Schulenburg, Duchess of Kendal and mistress of George I. Lord Chesterfield (1694–1773), whose cynical and practical epistles to his illegitimate son earn him a leading place in any study of English male chauvinism, lived at number 45. So did Madame d'Elitz, mistress of George I, George II and Frederick, Prince of Wales. At number 35, that 'Friend of Liberty', John Wilkes (1727–97), lived from 1790 until his death. Lord Harrowby, the Foreign Secretary, lived at number 44, and it was there that the cabinet heard of the victory of Waterloo in 1815. Five years later when the entire cabinet was dining there one night, the 'Cato Street conspirators' failed in their attempt to assassinate the lot of them and launch a radical revolution.

On the other side of Grosvenor Square, South Audley Street leads you down to the **GROSVENOR CHAPEL**, built in 1730, in a simple early Georgian style by Benjamin Timbrell, a local builder who had previously worked for James Gibbs in the building of St Martin in the Fields (see p. 136). From South Audley Street you see an unpretentious brick tower containing an octagonal bell-stage and squat green zinc spire. Below is a four-columned Tuscan porch. The chapel's interior is simple and classical, flooded by light from two tiers of arched windows on either wall. Galleries run round three sides beneath a coved ceiling painted white and picked out in gold. The Lady Chapel, set behind a screen of Tuscan columns where the Holy Ghost depicted as a dove descends in glory, is all blue. The Grosvenor Chapel is chaste and homely, almost Colonial in style, which seems suitable for a chapel that has become the worship place for the American community in London. Inside are buried Lady Mary Wortley Montagu and John Wilkes, who has a tablet by Flaxman, while amongst those who have worshipped here are the Duke of Wellington, Prince Albert, Florence Nightingale (1820–1910) and General Dwight David Eisenhower (1890–1969).

Hidden behind the chapel is a virtually unknown public garden, Mount Street Gardens, an L-shaped green under an umbrella of beech trees, and at the south-east corner is the back entrance to a second church, its style a complete contrast to Grosvenor Chapel, the Church of the Immacuate Conception, known by most London cabbies as simply 'Farm Street'. The mother church of the Jesuit community in Britain, it was built in 1844, in a variety of medieval styles. Inside, the nave is lined with side chapels leading up to the high altar, a medieval cascade of saints and scholars designed by

Augustus Pugin. Behind the altar is a spectacular stained-glass rose window, modelled on the east window of Carlisle Cathedral.

Return into Mount Street Gardens, and come out in the north-east corner, almost opposite the Connaught Hotel in Mount Street, and follow the street east to the north-west corner of **BERKELEY SQUARE**. Once Berkeley Square was beautiful, now, it is surrounded by automobile showrooms and advertising agencies. Saatchi and Saatchi takes up the whole south side. It stands on the site of the gardens of Berkeley House, built in 1665 by the Royalist general, the first Lord Berkeley, and demolished in 1924. Growing within the square are 30 tall plane trees, each over 200 years old. Apart from them the square has only two adornments, a Chinoiserie pump-house, built about 1800, and a statue of a nymph pouring water into a basin, sculptured by the pre-Raphaelite, Alexander Munro.

You can get an idea of the eighteenth-century elegance that Berkeley Square once had, when sedan chairs were parked in ranks like taxi cabs and nightingales sang, from the early Georgian houses that have survived on the west side. At number 45, which shares a splendid stone-faced front with its neighbour, number 46, Robert Clive (1725–74), Clive of India, lived until he took his life with an overdose of laudanum. Next door, number 44, the Clermont Club, has been called by the architectural historian, Nikolaus Pevsner, 'the finest terraced house in London'. It is by William Kent, started in 1741 and completed in 1744. Its exterior is modest, brick and stone, no different from the exteriors of the other houses that had once lined the square. Inside, it is breathtaking and palatial, although only club members are allowed in without a prior appointment. From the hall a staircase of Portland stone, with a delicate wrought iron balustrade, turns gracefully as it rises, divides at a half-landing into two sweeping arcs, then passes through a screen of Ionic columns and continues to the first floor, and then on to the minstrels' gallery, beneath a coffered dome of glass and gilded plaster. Horace Walpole called the staircase 'as beautiful a piece of scenery, and, considering the space, of art as can be imagined'.

East of Berkeley Square, Bruton Street, looked down on from the north side by a line of elegant early Georgian survivals, takes you to New Bond Street, which is Mayfair's high street. At number 165–9 is Asprey's the silversmiths, founded in 1781; at number 147 is Sotheby's the art auctioneers, founded in 1744; at number 139 is their rival Phillips, founded in 1796; at number 6 is Mappin and Webb the jewellers – and all of them neighboured by shops that make Harrods look tatty.

Across New Bond Street, where Bruton Street becomes Conduit Street, St George Street, on the left-hand side, opens up on to **HANOVER SQUARE**, marked by the statue of William Pitt the Younger, with the cool and sedate church of St George's Hanover Square on the right-hand side.

The square, named in honour of the dynasty of the new king, George I, was the third of the great Mayfair squares to be laid out, and a few of the

OPPOSITE *Berkeley Square: William Kent's number 44, 'the finest terraced house in London', stands on the left of the picture.*

original houses still stand on the south and west sides. It was begun in 1714, and in 1717 the *Weekly Medley* was reporting:

> Round about the new square which is building near Oxford Road, there are so many fine edifices that a whole magnificent city seems to be rising out of the ground, and one would wonder how it should find a new set of inhabitants.

It found the inhabitants and Hanover Square became an extremely fashionable address in the eighteenth and nineteenth centuries, where Johann Sebastian Bach (1685–1750), Franz Joseph Haydn (1732–1808), Nicolo Paganini (1782–1840) and Franz Liszt (1811–86) played at the Hanover Square Rooms (demolished in 1900), and Elizabeth Chudleigh, lover of George I and half his court, arrived at a masked ball as Iphigenia wearing so little she was 'in a state almost ready for the sacrifice' (Horace Walpole).

While Hanover Square was Mayfair's most fashionable square, St George's Church was Mayfair's most fashionable church. Two future British prime ministers, a future president of the United States, and one of England's sharpest novelists were married here. Benjamin Disraeli married Mary Lewis, Herbert Asquith married Margot Tennant, Theodore Roosevelt (1858–1919) married Edith Carow and George Eliot married John Cross.

St George's, built between 1720 and 1724 by John James, was, like Hawksmoor's St Anne's Limehouse, one of the 'Queen Anne' churches built under the Act of Parliament of 1711 to ensure that every London suburb was blessed with a church. Its front is one vast portico of six Corinthian columns projecting out into the street. It takes up the entire pavement but no one has tried to remove it. The same cannot be said for the two cast-iron dogs by Sir Edwin Landseer (1802–73) that used to lie by the steps. All too frequently they have been taken for walks, so they now lie safe in the porch.

Inside, beneath the tunnel-vaulting of the nave, is a reredos of *The Last Supper* by Kent, and an east window made of sixteenth-century stained glass. The central pulpit has its own iron stairway and there is a splendid organ case bearing the royal arms. It is a perfect early eighteenth-century church, galleried, simple, and spacious.

Return south down George Street and cross Conduit Street to Savile Row, once part of the estate of Lord Burlington. Its top end is uninteresting: a fortress (Fortress House, the home of English Heritage, the government-run preservation agency) and a police station. Further south at Clifford Street you have a choice of continuing down Savile Row, where many of the original 1730s houses still line the street, or turning right and coming down Old Burlington Street or Cork Street. Savile Row south of Clifford Street is taken up by tailors. There is Gieves and Hawkes at number 1, Huntsman's at number 11, Hardy Amies at number 14, where the dramatist Richard Brinsley Sheridan (1751–1816) lived, and Stricklands at number 15. Some are so exclusive that they would regard it as a vulgar to put their name on the lapel. One is supposed to be able to recognize the tailor of any given suit by the cut of the cloth.

Old Burlington Street, running parallel to Savile Row, does without shop fronts in the same way that Savile Row does without labels. Building started in 1719 and was completed by 1730. A few early Georgian houses still survive, including numbers 31 and 32 which were designed by Colen Campbell.

Parallel to Old Burlington Street is Cork Street, which contains some of the most interesting commercial art galleries in the country. Walk down the street, gaze into the front windows, and wander around inside; no one will mind if you don't buy anything. The street is lined with galleries: the Waddington Galleries, the Redfern Gallery, the Richmond Gallery, the Nicola Jacobs Gallery and the Mercury Gallery, and you cannot fail to come across the odd Picasso, Chagall or Man Ray, though you may not be able to afford to take it home with you.

All three streets end at Burlington Gardens, which is not a garden at all, but a short street. Two buildings dominate it. On the north side is Uxbridge House, stately, stone-faced, classical and a little boring. It was built in 1723 for the third Duke of Queensbury, who called it Queensbury House. In 1785 the Earl of Uxbridge bought it, renamed it and rebuilt the exterior, giving it a front of six great pilasters. Directly opposite it stands the massive Italianate thirteen-bay MUSEUM OF MANKIND, built in the 1860s by Sir James Pennethorne (1801–71) in the gardens of Burlington House. The two floors of the museum contain some of the most fascinating ethnographical and anthropological artefacts in the world, ranging from phallic statues from the Pacific islands to Eskimos' gut anoraks, from West Africa jewelry to Red Indian head-dresses.

The portico of Sir James Pennethorne's Museum of Mankind, built in 1869.

Running along the two sides of the Museum of Mankind, from Burlington Gardens to Piccadilly, is the Albany on the east side and Burlington Arcade on the west. The Albany is the most exclusive blocks of flats in London, reserved for bachelors (and now single women). Among its former residents are the Albany's architect Henry Holland (1746–1806), the statesman Lord Palmerston, the architect of Belgravia George Basevi (1794–1845), the writer Aldous Huxley (1894–1963), the broadcaster Malcolm Muggeridge (d.1990), the actress Dame Edith Evans (1888–1976), the novelist J. B. Priestley, the art critic Lord Clark (1903–83), and the twentieth-century politician and diarist Sir Harold Nicolson, and among its present residents is the former prime minister Edward Heath. It had originally been built in 1774 by Sir William Chambers for the First Viscount Melbourne, the father of Queen Victoria's first prime minister, but in 1803 Henry Holland converted the house into chambers for bachelors. It is Holland who is responsible for the almost collegiate ambience, adding the two ranges on either side, forming an 'H', and garden flanked by covered walks.

BURLINGTON ARCADE on the other side of the Museum of Mankind, is still the most elegant shopping arcade in London, specializing in everything you can do without: Havana cigars, embroidered waistcoats, camel-haired jerseys, diamond encrusted jewellery and extremely expensive toy soldiers. The arcade was opened in 1819, and remains effortlessly Regency in spite of the twentieth-century 'improvements'. It is overseen by two beadles. Once they were recruited from the 10th Hussars, now they come from all branches of the Armed Forces, charged, according to the terms of their employment, to keep the peace, prevent singing, whistling and running, and to deny entrance to drunks, beggars and people carrying large parcels or open umbrellas.

The arcade comes to an end at Piccadilly. Beside it, and facing Piccadilly, is **BURLINGTON HOUSE**, almost the last remaining example of the great houses that lined Piccadilly in the late seventeenth century. The house was built in 1664, then drastically altered between 1717 and 1720 by the Third Earl of Burlington, of Chiswick House fame (see p. 31), who commissioned Colen Campbell to remodel it on the plan of the Palazzo Porto in Vicenza. The front was faced in stone and the height of the first floor rooms was raised to give them proportions in accordance with the laws of Palladianism and Taste. It was, pronounced to Colen Campbell, 'without Dispute, the finest structure in the World'. Burlington House became the centre of Taste in London. Burlington gave Kent, Campbell and George Frederick Handel rooms there. Pope, Gay, and the actor David Garrick were frequent visitors.

The house was remodelled again – some would say vandalized – by Sydney Smirke in 1872, who wrecked the house's Palladian proportions by adding a second floor. Worse, Burlington's beautiful colonnade in the front, designed by Colen Campbell, and 'one of those edifices in fairy tales that are raised by a genii in a night-time' (Horace Walpole), was torn down. In spite of Smirke, enough of the inside of the house survives to reflect its former glory, in particular the magnificent painted ceiling of *The Wedding Feast of Eros and Psyche* and Michelangelo's *Madonna and Child with the infant St John* which stands beneath it in the saloon.

Burlington House is now the home of the **ROYAL ACADEMY** and half a dozen learned and obscure societies, with such names as the Linnean Society and the Society of Antiquaries (historians, to you and me). The Royal Academy had been founded by George III in 1768. Its first president was Sir Joshua Reynolds, whose statue stands in the forecourt, and it seems an appropriate body, with its winter shows and summer shows and special exhibitions, to take over the saloons where once Kent, Campbell, Flitcroft and a dozen other Palladian aspirants disputed the meaning of Taste.

In front of Burlington House Piccadilly stretches from Piccadilly Circus to Hyde Park Corner. Like Fifth Avenue and the Champs-Elysées, it is one of the most famous streets in the world. Piccadilly first came to the attention of Londoners in 1612 when Rober Baker, a tailor who had made a fortune out of selling 'pickadils' (a fashionable frilly collar of the period), built a house just to the north of where Piccadilly Circus now stands. Not a man to be ashamed of the origins of his wealth, Baker called it Piccadilly Hall. The name stuck and by the 1730s it referred to the whole street. The Circus at the east end of the street, which we now so closely associate with Piccadilly, did not appear until 100 years later, laid out by Nash as a punctuation mark in his Regent Street scheme. The statue of Eros is even more recent, sculpted in 1893, as a memorial to the philanthropist Lord Shaftesbury. The sculptor, Alfred Gilbert, spent £7000 on the statue and was paid only £3000. Naturally he was bitter, and suggested that the statue should be sold as scrap, the money raised providing 'shelters for the poor creatures who, year in and year out, congregate on the Embankment nightly'.

The great houses that once lined Piccadilly had gone long before Eros was erected, replaced by buildings now housing airline offices, hotels and expensive shops, which are Piccadilly's greatest magnet. Cross the road from Burlington House, and there is Fortnum and Mason, probably the most exclusive grocery shop in the world. It was founded by William Fortnum, who had once been footman to Queen Anne. Every hour a model of him on the clock above the Piccadilly pavement rings out the hours, then turns and bows to his partner Mason. A little to the east is Hatchards, the 'carriage trade bookshop'. It has been selling books since 1797 and regular customers have included Lord Byron (1788–1824), Palmerston, Wellington, Gladstone, Thackeray, Oscar Wilde (1854–1900), Graham Greene (1904–91) and most of the kings and queens of England who could read, since Queen Charlotte. Further to the east is Simpson, selling conservative chic, as Art Deco as an ocean liner, launched in 1936 and the first welded steel-framed building in London.

Between Hatchards and Simpson, set back behind cast-iron railings in a paved courtyard, is Wren's church of **ST JAMES, PICCADILLY**. It is unpretentious, unlike some of its neighbours, built between 1676 and 1684, of plain brick with Portland stone dressing. St James's is the only London church Wren built on a completely new site, unhindered by cramped spaces. 'I think it may be found beautiful and convenient,' he told Parliament in 1708.

Inside, the nave ceiling is barrel-vaulted and delicately plastered. There is a curved gallery and a marble font, where William Pitt the Elder and William Blake were baptized. It was carved by Grinling Gibbons, as were the organ case and the limewood reredos behind the altar. According to John Evelyn, 'there was no altar anywhere in England, nor has there been any abroad, more handsomely adorned'. Among those buried in St James's are Charles Cotton (1630–87), the writer and angler; James Dodsley, Dr Johnson's long-suffering publisher, who has a tablet by Flaxman; the two William van de Veldes, father (1611–93) and son; James Christie (1730–1803), the auctioneer and founder of Christies; and James Gilray (1757–1815), the cartoonist.

The south wall of St James's overlooks Jermyn Street, laid out in the 1680s as part of a property development stretching from Piccadilly to Pall Mall. Its author was Henry Jermyn, Earl of St Albans and lover of the Dowager Queen, Henrietta Maria. He was granted the lands by Henrietta Maria's son,

Charles II, after the king's return from exile in 1660, and there is a relief of the king handing over the deeds to Jermyn on the front of number 73, at the corner of Bury Street. Though once residential – Isaac Newton, Sir Thomas Lawrence (1769–1830), William Gladstone and Thomas Wall (the founder of the ice cream empire), all lived here – Jermyn Street is now lined with men's shops and food shops. Turnbull and Asser, the shirtmakers, is at number 70 and Paxton and Whitfield, the *fromagerie*, at number 89.

Across Jermyn Street, Duke of York Street, which contains one of the most exuberant cut-glass-and-mahogany Victorian pubs in London, the Red Lion, leads to ST JAMES'S SQUARE. It was developed by Jermyn at the same time as Jermyn Street, over what had previously been called St James's Fields. The houses were of plain red brick. Their glory was their uniformity, and for 50 years St James's Square, so conveniently close to the Court at St James's Palace, was the most glamorous address in London. Yet the square itself was one of the most squalid spots in London. Lord Macaulay (1800–59), the historian, described it as 'a receptacle for all the offal and cinders, and for all the dead cats and dogs of Westminster'. Squatters moved in, living in makeshift sheds of packing cases. The residents did not notice, or if they did, they did not care, and in 1721 St James's Square was housing six dukes and seven earls. But by 1800 almost all the houses had been rebuilt. Today, in spite of the nineteenth- and twentieth-century additions, the square – with its bronze statue of King William III dressed like a Roman on horseback by the two John Bacons, father and son (1777–1859) – has retained both its well-bred air and its local tramps.

Number 1 on the corner of Charles II Street was built by Mewes and Davis, who gave London the Ritz Hotel. On the site of number 3 have been houses built by Hawksmoor and Soane. Number 4, originally built by the property speculator Nicholas Barebone, was rebuilt by Hawksmoor and later became the home of Nancy Astor (1879–1964), the first woman to be elected to the House of Commons. Numbers 9, 10 and 11, on the northern side, Chatham House, is now the home of the Royal Institute of International Affairs. It has been the home of three prime ministers, Pitt the Elder, William Gladstone and Edward Stanley, Earl of Derby (1826–93), and its library has been the study-place for half a dozen more.

Number 14 on the west side is the narrowest house on the square. It was built in the 1770s and much changed in the 1890s, an endearing mixture of Georgian, Victorian, neo-Elizabethan and neo-classical. Since 1845 it has been the home of the London Library. The library was founded by Thomas Carlyle (see p. 35), who got impatient at the amount of time he had to wait for books from the British Museum's Reading Room, and at not being able to take the books home with him. Carlyle himself was the most antisocial of borrowers. He scribbled in the margins, crossed out paragraphs that he did not agree with, and hoarded books. In spite of Carlyle the library now holds well over a million books.

OPPOSITE *Wren's St James's, Piccadilly, 'beautiful and convenient', according to the architect. The Renatus Harris organ had been made for James II's Chapel Royal in Whitehall. Grinling Gibbons worked on the organ case and Henry Purcell tested it after its installation here.*

Next door, at number 15, lived the beautiful Frances, Duchess of Richmond, the model of Britannia on the old penny coins and almost the only woman to refuse to sleep with Charles II. It was in the neighbouring house, the very Greek Revival number 16, where the Prince Regent was attending a ball on the night of 21 June 1815, that Major Percy arrived, exhausted and bloodstained, in a carriage overflowing with captured French flags and eagles, bearing news of Wellington's victory at Waterloo.

Halifax House, at number 17, was the home of Queen Caroline in 1820 when the House of Lords was investigating her alleged adultery. It was from one of the upper windows of Halifax House that she emerged on the first morning of her 'trial' to the roar of thousands of Londoners chanting 'The Queen! The Queen!', and from Halifax House she left each morning, driving in state to the House of Lords, past Carlton House (see p. 100), the home of her estranged husband, George IV (the former Prince Regent), where to the delight of her supporters the sentries presented arms. Two years later, the occupant of the neighbouring house (18), Britain's greatest Foreign Secretary, Robert, Viscount Castlereagh (1769–1822), took his own life, using fingernail clippers to cut his carotid artery 'with anatomical accuracy'.

Number 20 was built in 1775 by Robert Adam, who considered the house one of his best, and number 21 was the home of two of James II's mistresses, Arabella Churchill, and the difficult Catherine Sedley – of whom Charles II said she must have been inflicted on his brother by his Catholic priest as a penance. Later Mewes and Davis turned the house into an exact copy of number 20, so the two houses look like exquisite Siamese twins.

South of St James's Square runs Pall Mall, home of the most sedate of London's gentlemen's clubs: the Travellers', the Reform, the United Service and the Oxford and Cambridge. The most sedate of all is the Athenaeum, which stands on the corner of Waterloo Place, designed by Decimus Burton in 1828, pink and neo-classical, with a Doric porch and a blue and white frieze running around it. Inside, to the right of the hall, is the grandest drawing room in London.

Pall Mall was laid out in 1661, and was the most fashionable street in Restoration London. Nell Gwynne (c.1650–87), Charles II's most vivacious 'horizontal', lived at number 79. As befits a king's bed companion who was her own mistress, her house was the only one in the street that did not belong to the Crown. The houses dropped in value through the eighteenth century, and writers such as Laurence Sterne (1713–68), Edward Gibbon, and even the political radical, William Cobbett (1763–1835), moved in. Today there are no Bohemians or radicals left in Pall Mall. It is now the preserve of clubs, offices and a few extremely select shops. Turn east down Pall Mall, along the route that Queen Caroline took to her 'trial', and you come to Trafalgar Square, which is not a square at all, more a *grande place*.

In the Middle Ages TRAFALGAR SQUARE was the Royal Mews and stables, and Geoffrey Chaucer was at one time Clerk of the Mews. Later, in 1723, the ubiquitous William Kent rebuilt the stable block where the National Gallery now stands. It was demolished in 1830 to make way for Trafalgar Square, planned by John Nash, although he died before he saw the result. The square was laid out ten years later by Sir Charles Barry. He levelled the slope and built a terrace on the north side. The 185-foot high memorial to Admiral Horatio Nelson was raised in 1842. He stands on the top, three times his height, the column's base guarded by lions cast by Landseer, and displaying four reliefs cast from captured cannon depicting Nelson's victories at St Vincent (1797), the Nile (1798), Copenhagen (1801) and Trafalgar (1805).

Here the Mall, Pall Mall East, St Martin's Place, the Strand, Northumberland Avenue and Whitehall (see p. 98) meet. Sir Robert Smirke's Canada House, neo-classical, built of warm Bath stone and completed in 1847, takes up the west side of the square. Sir Herbert Baker's less interesting South Africa House, built in 1933, and just saved from tedium by the carvings of African

The National Gallery and its neo-classical extension, which opened to the public in July 1991, seen from Trafalgar Square.

wildlife on the front, fills the east side. William Wilkins's (1778–1839) neo-classical National Gallery and its post-modern neo-classical extension, opened in 1991, sit comfortably on the north side. But the most graceful building occupies the north-east corner, Gibbs's church of **ST MARTIN IN THE FIELDS.**

St Martin's looks out on Trafalgar Square through a gigantic portico of six Corinthian columns, the height of the nave. Above the portico a pediment bears the Royal Arms (for Buckingham Palace lies within the parish of St Martin's). Immediately behind the pediment is the tower, rising through five stages to a pillared octagonal lantern, and continuing upwards into a needle spire. This vast portico and west tower were new in church architecture when Gibbs designed St Martin's in 1722, and served as a model for the eighteenth-century 'colonial' churches built all over New England.

The interior is galleried around three sides, and has a barrel-vaulted ceiling decorated with plaster scrolls and cherubs by Giovanni Bagutti and Giuseppe Artari. The altar lies behind a screen of Corinthian columns. To the left of the screen is a relief by Rysbrack of the church's builder, James Gibbs. Close by, on the west wall, is a painting by Francesco Solimena (1657–1747) of St Martin, as a Roman soldier cutting his cloak in two and giving half to a beggar. A statue in bronze of the same scene by Josephina de Vasconcellos stands in the side chapel by the south wall. Buried in the church are Francis Bacon, Nell Gwynne, Nicholas Hilliard, Louis Laguerre, Sir Joshua Reynolds, Louis Roubiliac and Thomas Chippendale (1718–79), the cabinet maker. Beneath the nave the crypt has been turned into a soup kitchen.

The **NATIONAL GALLERY**, which looks out on Trafalgar Square from the north side, holds the national collection. Its quantity is humble compared with the Prado in Madrid and the Louvre in Paris, with only 2200 paintings, but its quality is unique and the national collection can boast of some of the greatest early renaissance Italian paintings in existence.

It began in 1824, when the government bought 38 paintings from the collection of John Julius Angerstein (a successful Lloyd's underwriter), including Sebastiano del Piombo's (c.1485–1547) vast *The Raising of Lazarus*, Hogarth's *Marriage à la Mode* and works by Raphael, Rembrandt and Van Dyck. To this the gallery's founder, Sir George Beaumont, added sixteen more paintings, among them Rubens's *Autumn Landscape with a View of Het Steen*, Canaletto's *Venice: the Stonemason's Yard* and four by Claude Lorraine. They were all hung in Angerstein's house at 100 Pall Mall until William Wilkins completed his National Gallery building in 1838. One of its first visitors was the young Queen Victoria. Thanks to the judgement and energy of the gallery's first director, Sir Charles Eastlake, the national collection rapidly expanded. It was Eastlake who built up the Italian collection, purchasing Titian's *Bacchus and Ariadne*, Rubens's *War and Peace*, Rembrandt's *Woman Bathing* and Jacopo Tintoretto's (1518–98) *St George and the Dragon*. He took risks, too, thinking nothing of bringing back to England Bronzino's (1503–72) *Allegory with Venus and Cupid*.

The nave and altar of St Martin in the Fields, much of it the work of Sir Arther Blomfield in 1887. In 1924 the first religious service ever to be broadcast was conducted in the nave.

Eastlake died in Italy, searching for more works to buy for the gallery. The collection expanded further after his death, the gallery acquiring Paolo Uccello's (*c.*1397–1475) *Battle of San Romano*, Piero della Francesca's (1420–92) *Baptism of Christ* and Meyndert Hobbema's (1638–1709) *The Avenue, Middelharnis*, from which grew the gallery's superb Dutch and Flemish collection. In the twentieth century the number of paintings has grown, but at a slower rate, reflecting Britain's declining affluence, the two most recent major works acquired being Leonardo da Vinci's (1452–1519) cartoon of *The Virgin and Child with Saint Anne and John the Baptist* and Titian's *Death of Actaeon*.

Around the corner from the National Gallery is the **NATIONAL PORTRAIT GALLERY**, founded in 1856, a visual *Who's Who* of British history. It is probably the easiest gallery in London to find what you want. Apart from the kings and queens of England and the medieval portraits on the stairs, the entire collection is hung chronologically, so you start at the top and simply work your way down. Virtually everybody in English history you'll ever want to stare at is here, including Robert Adam, Sir Francis Bacon, Blake, James

Gainsborough's Mr and Mrs Andrews *(1752) shows the couple on their land in Suffolk. The setting of the couple in a rural landscape, with well-tended fields reflects the fashionable enthusiasm for farming among the upper and middle classes at this period.*

Boswell, Capability Brown, Lord Chesterfield, Churchill, Charles Dickens, Benjamin Disraeli, John Evelyn, David Garrick, Graham Greene, Nell Gwynne, William Hogarth, Samuel Johnson, the Duke of Marlborough, William Morris, Nelson, the two Pitts, Turner, the Duke of Wellington, Cardinal Wolsey and Wren.

Outside the National Portrait Gallery, Charing Cross Road, lined with bookshops and cosmopolitan cafés, runs northwards, almost touching LEICESTER SQUARE on the latter's eastern side. Leicester Square is the least recognizable of London's early squares, enveloped by cinemas, amusement arcades and fast-food outlets. The land belonged to Robert Sidney, Second Earl of Leicester, who built Leicester House between 1631 and 1635. It was one of the biggest houses in London, and dominated the north side of the square, where the Empire Cinema now stands. The house was built on common grazing ground, and in exchange for the land the Earl provided the open space in front of the house as a public square. Houses were built on the other sides in the 1670s, 'for the good and benefit of the family, the advancement of their revenue, and the decency of the place before Leicester House'. Hogarth lived at number 30 in 1733–64 and it was here that he painted *Marriage à la Mode*, *The Rake's Progress* and *Industry and Idleness*.

Leicester House was demolished in 1791 and by the mid nineteenth century most of the private houses had gone the same way. The square was celebrated for its Turkish baths and its theatres and music halls, drawing in thousands every night from all over London. There were dozens in the square and its surrounding streets, the most famous, the Alhambra, built like a mosque with two minarets, was opened in 1858. The theatres were knocked down in the 1920s and 1930s and replaced by cinemas, and Leicester Square remained packed every night. But as the British cinema of the 1950s and 1960s declined, so Leicester Square declined. It is now a sleazy place.

North of Leicester Square fans out Soho, at the base of which is 'Chinatown', spreading into the side streets on either side of Gerrard Street and Lisle Street, its shops selling Cantonese food, checker boards, acupuncture needles and Chinese herbs. It merges with Soho proper at Shaftesbury Avenue, where the Chinese restaurants draw in the English theatre crowds.

Soho was first built on in the 1640s, and contained a dozen grand mansions, including Monmouth House, home of King Charles II's illegitimate son, the Duke of Monmouth (1649–85). Before that the area was known as Soho Fields. By the time Soho Square was laid out in the 1680s, the area was already known for its French Huguenot refugees. It was the Huguenots who first gave Soho its cosmopolitan character, which it still retains. By 1720 the London historian John Strype (1643–1737) was writing of 'abundance of French people, many whereof are voluntary exiles for their religion, live in these streets and houses, following honest trades'.

By the nineteenth century, when Karl Marx (1818–83) had lodgings here, Soho was the most overpopulated slum in London, with 327 inhabitants per acre, attracting the political refugees, artists, Bohemians and prostitutes for which it is famous. The prostitutes have stayed; the rest have fled – although they can be seen at night furtively returning to visit Ronnie Scott's Jazz Club. Soho was still cosmopolitan at the turn of the century. John Galsworthy (1867–1933), the popular novelist, described it in *The Forsyte Saga* as 'untidy, full of Greeks, Ishmaelites, cats, Italians, tomatoes, restaurants, organs, coloured stuffs, queer names, people looking out of upper windows'. Today the xenophobic Galsworthy would still wince at Soho. The Greeks and 'Ishmaelites' have left, but the Italians are still here, running delicatessens, coffee shops, restaurants and peep shows, alongside Maltese, Chinese, Vietnamese, Jamaicans, West Indians and Bengalis.

East from Soho and Leicester Square is Covent Garden. To get there you pass Great Newport Street where the Photographers' Gallery stands, and continue along Long Acre, where Thomas Chippendale had his furniture workshop. COVENT GARDEN is where Francis Russell, fourth Earl of Bedford, laid out London's first square, and Inigo Jones built the 'handsomest barn in England'. Jones, who had started his career as a carpenter at St Paul's churchyard, had visited Italy, and he planned Covent Garden like an Italian piazza with rows of three-storey houses and colonnades lining the north and east sides, 'fit for the habitation of gentlemen and men of ability'. Similar terraced houses on the south side replaced Jones's Bedford House after it was demolished in 1700. On the west side looms the majestic blind, Tuscan portico of his church, ST PAUL'S COVENT GARDEN, where Pepys saw 'an Italian puppet show', the first recorded Punch and Judy show in England, in 1662, and Dr Henry Higgins first encountered Eliza Dolittle in *My Fair Lady*.

St Paul's, which was completed in 1633, was the first church to be built in London since the Reformation, and the first classical church to be built in Britain since the Romans left. Its gigantic portico is its greatest oddity, since it marks the back rather than the front of the church. (The Anglican bishops insisted that the altar should face the east end.) To enter the church you must go into the side streets behind and come in through the delightful churchyard. There lie Grinling Gibbons, Peter Lely, the caricaturist Thomas Rowlandson (1756–1827), Ellen Terry (1848–1928) and the highwayman Claude Duval (d.1670), on whose stone is inscribed:

> *Here lies Du Vall: Reader, if male thou art*
> *Look to thy purse, if female to thy heart.*

You enter St Paul's and come in through the west screen, where a limewood wreath by Grinling Gibbons hangs. Above is the single west end gallery, added by Thomas Hardwick (1752–1829) in the 1790s after a fire. The interior of the church is a simple double cube. At the far end is Hardwick's altar with a classical screen on either side of it and a reredos of Corinthian columns and pediment. With so many theatres and opera houses in its parish, St Paul's is the actors', dancers' and street performers' church, and along the

St Paul's churchyard, Covent Garden. The modest door to the church is the main entrance. Inigo Jones, St Paul's architect, wanted the church to face west so that his giant portico facing Covent Garden would be the entrance, but William Laud, the episcopalian Bishop of London, would not have it, hence the almost domestic west door from the churchyard.

walls of the interior are plaques to Marie Lloyd (1870–1927), Ivor Novello (1893–1951), Margaret Rutherford (1892–1972), Boris Karloff (1887–1969), Gracie Fields (1898–1979), Stanley Holloway (1890–1982), Rachel Roberts (1927–80), Anna Neagle (1904–86), Kenneth More (1914–82), Sir Michael Redgrave (1908–85), Noel Coward (1899–73), Dennis Price (1915–73), Hattie Jacques (1922–80) and Charlie Chaplin (1889–1977).

The square remained fashionable through the seventeenth and eighteenth centuries. Shops and coffee houses sprang up. The painters Sir James Thornhill, Sir Godfrey Kneller, Sir Peter Lely and Samuel Scott lived here, and it was in the back parlour of the bookseller Thomas Davies's house that James Boswell met Samuel Johnson on 16 May 1763 in a chance meeting that Boswell had been planning for months.

The fruit, vegetable and flower market, which became synonymous with the name Covent Garden, as Paris's market became synonymous with the name Les Halles, first appeared in 1656 as a few temporary lean-to shacks against the garden wall of Bedford House. The market was small, almost discreet, and did not reach any great size until the nineteenth century. The neo-classical market building in the centre of the square was built by Charles Fowler in 1831. At its height it employed over a thousand porters and provided London with most of its fruit and vegetables. But the traffic congestion it created was too disruptive to be tolerated in the centre of a great city, so in the 1970s the market was moved out to Vauxhall, south of the river. The site was were then turned over to fashionable shops and restaurants, art galleries and minor museums, stall holders and street performers. Fowler's neo-classical marketplace and the surrounding Georgian streets have been retained, the tiny shops and stalls selling beads, bangles, books, brown rice and beauty treatments overflowing from Covent Garden into Shorts Gardens, Neal Street and the charming Neal's Yard. Like Eliza Dolittle, the face is the same, only the accent has changed.

A block to the east of Covent Garden is the Royal Opera House, and a block further on is the Theatre Royal, Drury Lane. The first ROYAL OPERA HOUSE opened in 1732, and here in 1773 Oliver Goldsmith's play, *She Stoops to Conquer* had its first night. Two years later Richard Sheridan's *The Rivals* had its première. The theatre burned down in 1805. Robert Smirke rebuilt it, modelling it on the Temple of Mineva in Athens, and it is in that theatre that Mozart's *Don Giovanni* (1817), Rossini's *Barber of Seville* (1818) and Mozart's *Marriage of Figaro* (1819) were first performed in England. It too burnt down. The present building was erected by E. M. Barry in 1858. It is now the home of the Royal Opera and Royal Ballet companies, and on the far side of Bow Street by the Magistrates' Court, opposite Barry's familiar six-column Corinthian portico, is a lovely life-size statue of a young ballerina by Enzo Plazzotta (1921–81).

The original Drury Lane Theatre, on the site of the Theatre Royal, was built in 1663, and it was here that Charles II first saw Nell Gwynne, appearing in John Dryden's (1631–1700) *Indian Queen*. The great Shakespearean actor David Garrick worked here as actor and manager from 1747 to 1775. Richard Sheridan took over as manager and commissioned Henry Holland to rebuild it in 1794. His Greek Revival theatre, which was called the loveliest in Europe, burned down in 1809. Sheridan watched the destruction sipping a glass of port. 'Surely a man may take a glass of wine by his own fireside?' he asked. Benjamin Wyatt (1775–1850) rebuilt it in 1812 and the grand portico was added in 1820. It still stands, late Georgian and elegant, in spite of its bulk, with a domed entrance, a Doric vestibule and cliff faces of brickwork on the side walls. It has had its glorious moments. The actor Edmund Kean (*c*.1789–1833) made his first appearance here in 1814, and the clown, Joseph Grimaldi (1779–1837), made his last in 1818. Diaghilev's (1872–1929) Ballet Russe performed here in 1913 and *My Fair Lady* had the first of its 2281 performances at the Theatre Royal in 1958.

Walk north from Covent Garden, up Neal Street and the top end of Shaftesbury Avenue, and on across New Oxford Street to Bloomsbury and the

The Greek Revival pediment of Robert Smirke's British Museum, opened on 19 April 1847.

BRITISH MUSEUM. The base of the British Museum's collection is the bequest of Sir Hans Sloane in 1753 of his library and natural history objects, his 'private cabinet of curiosities', as he called it. It was housed in Montagu House on the site of the present museum. Other collections were added, including George III's library and the collection of Greek vases, owned by Sir William Hamilton (1730–1803). When his wife Emma's lover, Nelson, won the Battle of the Nile in 1798, tons of Egyptian antiquities including the Rosetta Stone – all effectively loot – were brought over to the museum. In 1816 they were joined by the Elgin Marbles, the sculptures from the Panthenon in Athens, shipped to England by Thomas Bruce, Seventh Earl of Elgin (1766–1841). By now Montagu House was completely overcrowded, there was no order to the displays, not even labels on the exhibits. Marble statues elbowed against stuffed giraffes and Buddhas sat on top of collections of coins. Cobbett called it 'the old curiosity shop'. In 1824 Robert Smirke began the Athenian temple with its instantly-recognizable Ionic portico that replaced Montagu House and now holds the most comprehensive collection of antiquities in the world. It took twenty years to complete.

From first coming through the entrance it is a place to marvel in. Ahead is the old circular Reading Room of the British Library (now in the process of moving to Euston Road), surrounded by 27 miles of shelving, and covered by a 40-foot dome, beneath which Karl Marx, Thomas Carlyle and virtually every British writer and academic for nearly 150 years has sat in frustration waiting for books to arrive. To the left of the museum's main entrance, corridors lined with Middle Eastern antiquities lead to the Egyptian Sculpture Gallery holding the Rosetta Stone, and the Duveen Gallery holding the Elgin Marbles. To the right of the main entrance, rooms displaying rare and beautiful manuscripts and books, including the Magna Carta and the Lindisfarne Gospels lead to the King's Gallery of illuminated manuscripts, signatures and books. They include the Gutenberg Bible and a Shakespeare first folio. At the far end of the museum, beyond the old Reading Room, is the King Edward VII Gallery, containing the museum's priceless collection of Buddhas and of Chinese porcelain, bronze, ivory, terracotta and jade. Up the stairs, on the first floor, are Egyptian mummies, Anatolian tombs, medieval clocks, Greek vases, Roman coins, Viking treasure and a thousand other things.

Outside, three squares almost touch the British Museum: Bloomsbury Square, Russell Square and Bedford Square. BLOOMSBURY SQUARE, to the south-east of the museum, its big plane trees marking the beginning of Bloomsbury, was laid out by Thomas Wriothesley, fourth Earl of Southampton in the 1660s, who built his own town house, Southampton House, on the north side. It was a big development over open fields. John Evelyn, who came to dinner in Bloomsbury Square, called it 'a little town'. None of the houses now remain, but houses on the north side, built in 1800 when Southampton House was demolished, by a local builder employed by the

This relief from the central palace at Nimrud, the heart of the Assyrian empire, was carved in around 745–27 BC, and shows a scene from a siege.

Bedford Estate, James Burton, still stand, giving some idea of how the square must have once looked.

The earls of Southampton linked up with the dukes of Bedford in marriage and as the countryside north of Bloomsbury Square was built over in the eighteenth century, the new squares took on the names of the family: Bedford, Russell, Tavistock and Woburn. The squares of Bloomsbury were fashionable when they were built, but by the mid nineteenth century had degenerated into the merely respectable. Then, with the development of London University behind the British Museum in the early twentieth century, Bloomsbury attracted artists, writers and intellectuals, such as Lytton Strachey (1880–1932), Clive Bell (1881–1964), Virginia Woolf (1882–1941), E. M. Forster (1879–1970) and John Maynard Keynes (1883–1946) – the Bloomsbury Group, whose goal in life, 'the pleasures of human intercourse and the enjoyment of beautiful objects', places them alongside that equally exclusive Burlington Group.

RUSSELL SQUARE, north-east of the British Museum, its plane trees much thinned since the Great Storm of 1989, was begun in 1800. Today it is dominated by the University of London's Senate House, built in 1932, on the west side, and the terracotta fantasia of the Russell Hotel on the east side. A few of the original late Georgian houses survive on the south-west corner, built, like the ones on the north side of Bloomsbury Square, by James Burton.

BEDFORD SQUARE, laid out in 1775 just to the west of the British Museum, is still surrounded by its Georgian houses, and is one of the very few complete Georgian squares left in London. Early in the morning, or on a Sunday when the traffic is minimal, it presents one of the most beautiful Georgian vistas in London: four trim and uniform sides of grey London brick and a line of wrought iron balconies, the monotony broken by the central house on each side, stuccoed and pilastered, like a controlled flourish. It is the epitome of the London Georgian square, and the perfect place to end a walk that has taken you through a dozen of the finest squares in central London, and one and a half centuries of London's history.

Bedford Square, the last complete Georgian square in Bloomsbury, and one of the most beautiful squares in London. Right up until 1893 the square was closed off by gates and tradesmen were obliged to deliver to the residents in person.

6
The Regent's Canal

....

LIMEHOUSE *to* KENSAL GREEN

The River Thames is not the only waterway running through London. Across north London, forming an approximate bow from Limehouse Basin to Brentford, curves the Regent's Canal and its west London extension, the Paddington Branch of the Grand Junction Canal, now called the Grand Union Canal. The REGENT'S CANAL was built between 1813 and 1820, and its line marks the northern suburbs of London at that time. Some of the canal was cut across fields, but once the canal was in use the land was developed, the bricks and timbers brought in on barges, which explains the band of late Georgian and early Victorian terraces and squares alongside the canal in Hackney, Islington, Camden and Paddington. There are still builders' merchant stores along the canal bank in Islington and Camden.

Until the arrival of the railways, ships and flat-bottomed boats were the only vehicles available for transporting heavy goods. In the late eighteenth century England's river routes were supplemented by an intricate network of canals linking the newly-industrialized Midlands with the great cities and rivers of England. The first canal to reach London came in 1794, the Grand Junction Canal, linking the Oxford Canal in the Midlands to the River Thames at Brentford. In 1801 the owners of the canal cut a thirteen-mile extension from just above the Thames at Brentford to Paddington, a small village to the west of London. It was called the Paddington Branch. In 1802 a proposal was made to link the Paddington Branch to the River Thames at Limehouse, providing a direct link between Birmingham and the London Docks. The chief promoter of the scheme was none other that the Prince Regent's architect, John Nash, who was laying out Marylebone Park (later renamed Regent's Park). He was also one of the canal company's major shareholders, and he risked his own fortune on the project. The $8\frac{1}{2}$ mile section opened on 1 August 1820, with the Prince Regent sailing along the canal from Regent's Park to Limehouse in the City State Barge.

OPPOSITE *Sculpture in water, in Queen Mary's Gardens, encompassed by the Inner Circle, at the very centre of Regent's Park.*

145

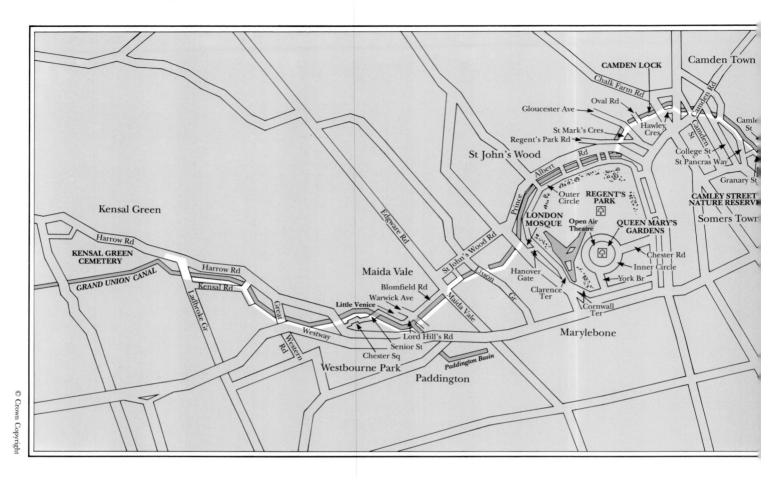

You can follow the entire length of the canal from Limehouse to Brentford along the towpath, though some may find the broken supermarket trolleys and empty beer cans along the far eastern stretches a little insalubrious, and the miles of 1930s housing estates and ketchup factories along the far western stretches a little boring. The central section, from Islington, through Camden Town and Regent's Park to Little Venice and to Kensal Green Cenetery beyond, is the most rewarding.

Unlike the Canal St Martin in Paris, the Regent's Canal has no literary associations. There has been no de Maupassant to record its pointless tragedies, though George Orwell (1903–50) did enjoy walking along the towpath. Nor has it been the subject of any great feature film, like Michel Carné's *Hotel du Nord* about Paris's canal. The only known film about the Regent's Canal is a 1924 silent documentary called *Barging Through London*.

Today, 35 years after the last horse-drawn barge passed through its locks, the canal still has its charms: the wild flowers that trekked into the city centre from the country along the towpath and railway lines; the locks which the East End kids use as diving platforms in the summer; the lock keeper's

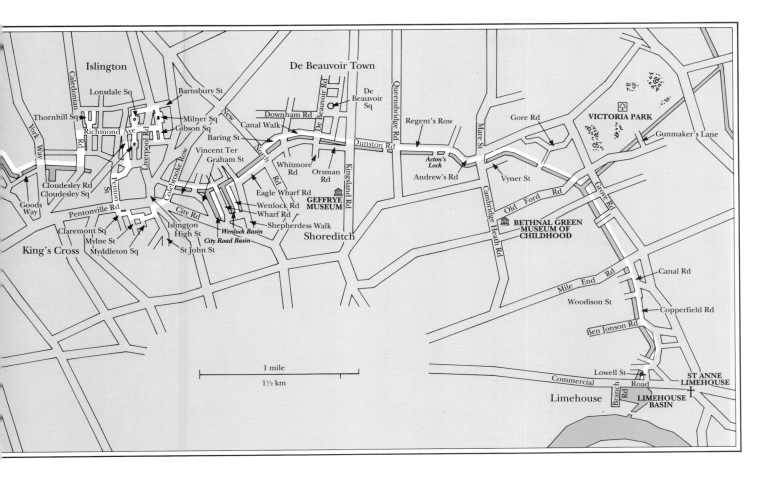

cottages that look like illustrations from Victorian children's books; and the fishermen sitting Buddha-like in anoraks by the water's edge.

The best place to start a walk along the canal is at the end of it, where it reaches the Thames at Limehouse Basin. The basin is overlooked by the tower of Hawksmoor's church of **ST ANNE LIMEHOUSE** (see p. 13), a monolith of faith topped by an eight-sided lantern.

Limehouse was an obvious place to end the canal, in the middle of the old docks, so goods made in Birmingham could be sent all the way to the London Docks by water. There were four acres of quays and wharfs working here once, unloading coal from the collieries on to the barges that took it all over the country. Then the Basin died, like so much else in the East End – blame the War, the withering of the Port of London, the slum clearance, the colonization from Dockland. Limehouse Basin was annexed by Dockland and due for redevelopment in the 1980s. Steel and glass and wine bars on the water's edge were to rise up around the industrial ruins. Then the recession of the early 1990s came. So the ruins have survived, and the purple fire-weed still flaunts itself on the soot-coloured brickwork.

From Limehouse Basin, lined by the archaeology of the nineteenth-century industrial age, the Regent's Canal takes leave of the Docks and goes north underneath the Commercial Road and the 1838 railway viaduct that now carries the trains of the Dockland Light Railway, then rises up a gentle flight of locks, each with its own lock keeper's cottage: Commercial Road Lock, Salmon Lane Lock, Johnson's Lock and Mile End Lock. It crosses the Mile End Road, turns gently to the west, and continues through a mixture of open space, industrial ruin and quiet domestic low-rise canalside estates, to Victoria Park in Hackney, where it is joined by the Hertford Union Canal, which links the Regent's Canal to the River Lea $1\frac{1}{4}$ miles away.

You cross the Hertford Union Canal on a cambered cast iron bridge built in 1830. On the right of the towpath stretches Victoria Park, once seen as the green jewel of East London, now but a shadow of its former self. The park was laid out in 1845 to be East London's Regent's Park by James Pennethorne, John Nash's adopted son and – some said at the time – the Prince Regent's illegitimate son, who also erected the arcade beside the boating lake. The extraordinary gothic drinking fountain that looks like a souvenir model of the Albert Memorial was designed by H. A. Darbishire and given to the park by the philanthropist Angela Burdett-Coutts (1814–1906). The park retains some of its glory, particularly in the early Victorian houses on its periphery, looking fool-hardy and plucky, surrounded by the tower blocks of Hackney. But it is unfair to associate Hackney merely with tower blocks. It contains dozens of Georgian and Victorian terraces and squares, wonderful warehouses which have been converted into studios, workshops and community centres; and it boasts more artists per acre than anywhere in Europe.

Here the towpath take on a rural charm with trees overhanging it, while on the far side, by Old Ford Bridge and Old Ford Lock, clusters of Victorian buildings overshadow the canal, and the terrace of the Royal Cricketers pub goes right down to the bank. At the far end of the Park you can see Pennethorne's formal entrance to Victoria Park on Bonner Hall Bridge, with its Regency wrought iron railings. As the canal leaves the park it curves, and beyond the curve, Mare Street, which is carried over the canal on a bridge, leads south to the Bethnal Green Museum of Childhood. Beneath the bridge, on the far side from the towpath, you can see the bricked-in arch that once led to the Mare Street coal basin, and which fed the gasworks at Mare Street, whose vast gasholders weigh so heavily on the skyline.

THE BETHNAL GREEN MUSEUM OF CHILDHOOD stands in the old Brompton Boilers, removed from South Kensington in 1872, and given a protective brick exterior. Inside you can appreciate both the collection and the extraordinary post-Modern-looking iron structure.

The French poet Charles Baudelaire (1821–67) once said that 'the toy is the child's first initiation into art', and the only criticism you can make of the Museum of Childhood, is that it turns toys into art – which is understandable considering it is a branch of the Victoria and Albert Museum (see p. 110). It is

OPPOSITE *St Anne, Limehouse: designed by Hawksmoor in the shape of a Greek cross, an exercise in exquisite brutality.*

a place of return, return to your own childhood and to those of your parents and grandparents. Here is the largest toy collection on display in the world. On the ground floor are 46 doll's houses, the oldest made in Nuremberg in 1673. In the flanking galleries are electric trains, model farms, barrel organs, wedding dresses, children's clothes, Indian, Chinese and Javanese puppets, lead soldiers and dolls galore, including the 39 dolls of the Powell family, collected between 1754 and 1912, and providing a unique record of children's clothing for 158 years.

The canal curves again, and straightens out at Acton's Lock, from where it continues in a straight line past Laburnum Basin, which once fed coal to the Laburnum Street Gasworks but now provides a basin for canoes. Just past the basin after Haggerston Road Bridge, Kingsland Road Bridge leads south to the Geffrye Museum. The **GEFFRYE MUSEUM** is a surprise. Set in one of the most impoverished districts in London, the museum occupies the central range of three ranges of almshouses, built with red brick in 1715 in an outdated Restoration style. It was financed from the bequest of Sir Robert Geffrye (1613–1704), Lord Mayor of London in 1685. The ranges form an large open court around three sides of a simple garden.

Inside, the museum is made up of a series of rooms linked by a single corridor stretching the entire length of the central range. After an introductory display of Georgian shop fronts, which succeeds in suggesting an eighteenth-century London street without the hint of a theme park, and includes a complete carpenter's shop, the rooms are furnished in different styles from the reigns of Elizabeth I to Elizabeth II.

The splendid carved oak chimneypiece in the Elizabethan Room came from a house in Stapleford, Essex. The door in the Stuart Room was in the Pewters' Company Hall before the Great Fire of London, and on the oak panelled walls is a most incongruous combination of portraits: Oliver Cromwell and two of Charles II's lovers, Barbara Villiers, Duchess of Cleveland, and Nell Gwynne. Some of the earliest English walnut furniture can be seen in the William and Mary Room, and next to it, in a room the size of a broom cupboard, stands the diarist John Evelyn's ebony cabinet, or 'Closet of Curiosities' as he called it, made for him in Paris in 1652. Then comes the almshouse's simple and unpretentious chapel, with its rare fixed pews looking like docks in court, and a 1930s Reading Room, where you can sit and read books and magazines on English art and furnishings.

Past the Reading Room the display continues. There is furniture made in the style of Thomas Chippendale and a spinet built by Herbert von Kamp in 1762 in the Early Georgian Room, and furniture by Thomas Hepplewhite (d.1786) and a piano made in Leipzig in the Late Georgian Room. The Regency Room is stark yet luxurious, classical yet English. The mid Victorian Room could only be English, while the equally English Art Nouveau Voysey Room shows that a revolutionary style created in Paris can go with bedroom slippers. At the end of the corridor and up the stairs the 1940s and 1950s

The frontage of the late Jacobean Geffrye Museum and its south wing, built in 1715 at the behest of Sir Robert Geffrye, in a late Jacobean style, long past the era when it was fashionable.

rooms show you everything that you or your parents tried to escape from.

Back on the towpath, a steel-plated footbridge with a cobble-stoned approach takes you across Kingsland Basin, opened in 1830 and now occupied by houseboats. On the other side of the basin you come to de Beauvoir Town, cut off from the canal by a thin grey line of concrete council flats. It is worth the diversion to wander through de Beauvoir Town. Its houses are still predominantly late Georgian and early Victorian, in late Classical, Italianate and (in de Beauvoir Town's heart, de Beauvoir Square) Jacobean style. All of these styles blend well, creating a little quarter of well-to-do, middle-class 'good taste' in the middle of the Inner City. On the other side of the canal, on the south side, is Hoxton, one of the most depressed quarters of inner London.

The towpath continues westwards to the industrial–ecclesiastical Kelaty's Oriental Carpet Warehouse by New North Road Bridge. It had originally been built as a power station for the Metropolitan Railway, then in 1919 it was converted into London's first film studio, where Alfred Hitchcock (1899–1980) started his cinema career. It was known as Islington Studios and its productions included Will Hay's *Oh Mr Porter!* (1937), Carol Reed's *Bank Holiday* (1938), Frank Launder and Sidney Gilliat's social realist documentary *Millions Like Us* (1943) and Hitchcock's own *The Lady Vanishes* (1939).

From New North Road the towpath rises up the slope at Sturt's Lock, and continues west beneath Wharf Road Bridge, built in 1830, to Wenlock Basin. Here silver-white swans, chimney-sweep-coloured coots, white-bibbed dippers, brown-speckled garganeys, rust-headed teals and red-and-yellow-beaked moorhens nest beneath cascades of weeping willows, and swim with their chicks beneath the bows of the red and green houseboats supporting little gardens growing out of flowerpots on their roofs. Parallel to it, and a little further on, lies City Road Basin, with quiet modern low-rise housing along one side, and a children's playground and boat club along the other.

The canal rises another step at City Road Lock, with its lock keeper's cottage and canalside builders' merchants, and continues under Frog Lane Bridge, which once led to an eighteenth-century inn, Frog Hall. Here you cross over the bridge, built in 1816, and join the towpath again on the other side where the canal enters a deep cut. This is Walter Sickert's 'hanging gardens of Islington'. On the right are the back gardens of the romantic gothic houses of Noel Road, built in the 1840s and still with their make-believe castellation; and on the left are the wooded canal banks below Vincent Terrace. 'It's just like Venice,' Sickert used to say.

Suddenly the Canal disappears into a 1000-foot long tunnel beneath Islington Hill. The tunnel is too narrow for a towpath and in the early days of the canal the horses used to be led above ground to rejoin it at the Caledonian Road, while the bargemen lay on their back and pushed their feet against the tunnel ceiling, propelling their barges along like men walking backwards. Then, in 1826 navvy-power was replaced by steam-power, and the barges were towed through the canal by a miniature steamboat that worked its way through the tunnel on a chain along the canal bed.

> The passage of this mode has a truly tartarean aspect (wrote Thomas Cromwell in his *Walks in Islington*). The smoke, the fire, and the noise of the engine, uniting with the black gloom of the arch, the blackness of the water, the crashing of the vessels against the sides of the tunnel and each other, and the lurid light that glimmers beyond each distant extremity, form an aggregate of the *infernalia* that must be witnessed to be adequately conceived.

Islington, which the Regent's Canal runs under, was made by the canal. Before that it had been a village beside the New River, an artificial waterway excavated between 1609 and 1613 to bring drinking water to London. A few years earlier Stow had written of Islington's dotty skyline: 'like Midsummer pageants, with towers, turrets and chimney pots'. Oliver Goldsmith used to head for it when he left the Temple and wanted a walk in the country. The late Georgians and early Victorians turned the village into a series of squares, with building materials brought by barge along the canal. It is still a place of squares: Claremont Square, Myddleton Square, Thornhill Square, Gibson Square, Cloudesley Square, Canonbury Square, Lonsdale Square and Milner Square. Each is outstanding in its own way: Claremont Square for its

Regency elegance, Myddleton Square for its combination of different-sized houses within a single unity, Thornhill Square for its sweeping curves and Victorian church, Gibson Square for its Regency dignity, Cloudesley Square for not being a square at all and having a church by Sir Charles Barry, Lonsdale Square for its gothic solidity, and Milner Square for being the only place in Britain where you can experience the French Mechanical style of architecture, which you will either love or hate.

The canal runs under the heart of Islington: the Angel, Camden Passage, the High Street, Barnsbury Road, the bottom of Liverpool Road and Chapel Market. West of Chapel Market it continues beneath the Barnsbury Estate, a village-like council estate of low-rise houses and twisting lanes, and re-emerges just to the east of the Caledonian Road, where a few clusters of late Georgian housing still survive between the canal and King's Cross Station.

On the other side of Caledonian Road, the south side of the canal is dominated by a heavy Victorian warehouse. Beside it is Battlebridge Basin, named after a battle between the army of Boadicea and the Roman legions under Suetonius Paulinus believed to have been fought there, but which turns out to have taken place about ten miles away. Battlebridge Basin was once infamous. It fed some of the most polluting of London's industries – tile yards, boneyards, glue factories and dustheaps – and was surrounded by the inevitable early nineteenth-century slums. Cynics called it 'Belle Isle'. Later Battlebridge Basin became the unloading place for tons of ice which was stored in deep wells beside the canal, imported from the Arctic by Carlo Gatti, the first ice-cream producer in Britain.

Beyond Battlebridge Basin, Maiden Lane Bridge carries York Way over the canal, and on the other side of it you come out of the bridge's shadow to witness one of the most spectacular views in London: an almost flat foreground of wasteland and railway yards, and beyond it, on the skyline, the giant canopy of King's Cross Station, the twin neo-gothic towers of Sir George Gilbert Scott's St Pancras Station Hotel (1878), the roof of the new British Library on Euston Road, the late 1960s British Telecom Tower and – as you walk further – the gasholders of the old Imperial Gas Company, built in 1860 and decorated with interlaced tracery and Tuscan columns.

The canal makes a sharp turn to the right at the gasworks and the canal bank on the far side of the towpath completely changes its character. In spring and summer there are waves of wild flowers: Indian balsam, bur-reed, yellow flag, flowering rushes, white waterlily, sneezewort and butterbur. They grow in the Camley Street Nature Reserve (entrance in Camley Street), a piece of railway waste until 1983, when it was lovingly turned into this water marsh, the scene enhanced by the fairytale Victorian lock keeper's cottage at St Pancras Lock and the little village of houseboats in St Pancras Basin, once a coal wharf for the old Midland Railway Company.

The oblique bridge on the other side of the West Midlands Railway bridge once led to the mansion of William Agar, one of the most notorious

Victorian cast-iron gas holders just to the south of Camley Street, photographed from the towpath.

Camden Square, one of the most delightful squares in Camden Town. V.K. Krishna Menon, the Indian politician, lived at number 57 between 1924 and 1947.

landlords in London. His land, which ran from the site of the present St Pancras Station to Camden Town, was open fields before the canal was cut. The canal brought industries and Agar, after squeezing thousands of pounds out of the canal company as compensation, turned the district into one of London's worst shanty towns. It was called Agartown, and it was a blot on London for 30 years until the St Pancras railway line swept it away.

You continue past St Pancras Way and 'Lawford's Brick and Tile Works', another of the canalside builders' merchants and one of the last to use wharf deliveries, and under Camden Road Bridge and Camden Street Bridge, where the far side of the canal is taken up by the ruins of the ABC Bakery, all Art Deco and Odeon-style, white and tatty. You turn a corner at Kentish Town Bridge and the TVAM studios come into view, housed in a converted brewery, and suggesting an Art Deco joke with eggcups on the roof instead of the conventional pineapples.

The canal rises in steps here, up through three more locks, Kentish Town Lock, Hawley Lock and Hampstead Road Lock, which most people call

CAMDEN LOCK, and which stands by a castellated lock keeper's cottage, now a British Waterways Board canal information centre.

On the right-hand side, by Camden Lock, is Camden Lock Market, sited on the old Dingwell's Timber Wharf, and crowded every Saturday with bead sellers, record sellers, macrobiotic food sellers, second-hand clothes sellers, Moroccan carpet sellers and mad ladies in the antique business. The timber wharf was rehabilitated in 1973. The cobblestones have stayed, so have the stables with their haylofts above them, which have been converted into shops, restaurants, wine bars and cafés, while the wharf's central buildings have been turned into a restaurant and discothèque.

Running beneath Camden Lock are a series of tunnels that stretch as far north as the Roundhouse, the magnificent engine house built by the railway engineer Robert Stephenson (1803–59) and now an arts centre, and south to Gilbey's Bonded Warehouse on the far side of the canal. They are known as the Camden Catacombs and were built for the Welsh pit ponies brought to London to shunt the railway wagons in the early days of steam trains. Used to the darkness of the coal mine, the ponies were housed in underground stables. A few of the tunnels are now used as storage space by British Rail; the majority are deserted, the haunt of rats, bats and the occasional derelict.

Camden Town, like Islington, was rural before the arrival of the canal. It was not even a village, it was farmland belonging to the Manor of Cantelowes, which held the land somce the Domesday Book, and it did not change its name until 1749 when the heiress of the estate married the Earl of Camden. In 1791 the first 1400 houses were built, and with the coming of the canal the entire district, from St Pancras to Highgate, was soon filled in with bricks and mortar. Though middle-class in its early days, Camden Town became a slum in the late nineteenth century, and remained a land of boarding houses and bedsits until the 1970s when the batteries of front door bells gave way to brass door knobs, the grey net curtains to screens of house plants and the rag trade sweat shops to television production company offices, though a few Irish and Cypriot patches survive.

On the other side of Camden Lock, the canal has retained its character: tatty, industrial, and with the paintwork peeling. But before continuing along the towpath, walk up to the top of the bowed iron footbridge at Camden Lock, and look back at the canal descending the stairs of Camden Lock, Hawley Lock and Kentish Town Lock. They are the last locks you will see for a long time. The canal has reached its highest point, 86 feet above Limehouse Basin, and flows lock-free all the way to the steep stairs down to river-level at Norwood and Hanwell Locks, just above the Thames at Brentford.

Return to the towpath and walk on westwards, past Gilbey's Art Deco 1937 bonded warehouse on the south side, looking like a beached ocean liner. An iron footbridge on the towpath takes you over the entrance of the covered basin of the Interchange Warehouse, built in 1905 like a palazzo in Venice and with a disused railway link through the Camden Catacombs to the

Euston main line. Two railway bridges designed by Robert Stephenson follow, and then all of a sudden you notice that the warehouses have disappeared and the gardens of Regency villas come right down to the water's edge. This is the frontier of Nash's London.

In the Middle Ages REGENT'S PARK had been part of the manor of Tyburn and belonged to the Nunnery of Barking. Henry VIII took the land over when the monasteries and religious houses were dissolved and turned it into an extension to his hunting grounds. Charles I mortgaged it for arms and ammunition in the Civil War and Parliament cut down a quarter of the ground's trees for the Navy and then sold the land off as three farms during the Protectorate. Charles II resold the leases, subsequent monarchs resold them again, and the land was still countryside in the 1800s. The leases were all due in 1811 and John Nash, the Prince Regent's architect, saw the opportunity of cutting a grand road on a north–south axis from the Prince Regent's palace, Carlton House, through Piccadilly and across Oxford Street to Marylebone, developing the site around a park, and creating in effect England's first garden city. He was already working on his Regent's Canal scheme and his original idea was to cut the canal right through this garden city; but potential residents objected; they feared that the language of the bargees would lower the tone of the neighbourhood.

His plan was to maintain the open space, called Marylebone Park, and to encircle it with grand terraces, combining urban architecture with a rural landscape. To the east, a three-quarter-mile branch of the canal led to a service area for tradesmen at the old Hay Market by Albany Street. (The branch, from Cumberland Basin, was filled in with rubble after World War II.) By 1823 virtually every site in the scheme had been let and Nash's garden city of magnificent neo-classical stuccoed and colonnaded terraces, Hanover Terrace, York Terrace, Chester Terrace and Cumberland Terrace, were taking shape. South of the park, by now renamed Regent's Park in honour of Nash's patron, the beautiful and symmetrical ranges of Portland Crescent led past Nash's elegant Church of All Souls to the new Regent's Street, which travellers compared to the rue de Rivoli as one of the most splendid streets in the world. Not everybody liked the scheme. Augustus Pugin wrote:

> Owing perhaps to the desire of abandoning the petty scale and character of ordinary houses, these buildings are designed in an air of pretension that they cannot support. On a cursory view, they present an idea of palaces, but more minute inspection shows these seemingly spacious edifices to be clusters of common-sized dwelling-houses.

The Regent's Canal first touches Regent's Park at Park Village East. It is worth leaving the towpath here, and if you cannot walk the entire circle of neo-classical terraces, you should at least wander around Park Village East and Park Village West, and admire the almost Athenian cottages Nash built in these make-believe neo-classical villages.

ABOVE *This bridge across the Regent's Canal amply demonstrates the Victorian exploitation of the versatility of cast and wrought iron.*

OPPOSITE *St Andrew's Place: part of Nash's Athenian garden city around Regent's Park.*

Beyond the bridges carrying Regent's Park Road and Prince Albert Road, the canal turns a corner at the Cumberland Basin, then runs in a straight line on the northern boundary of Regent's Park alongside the site of London Zoo, opened by the Zoological Society in 1828.

You can see the hawthorn, oak, ash, sycamore, elm and willow tops from the canal bank. The park itself is beautiful, laid out as a Victorian garden, which is confusing considering the park's name. Its flower displays in QUEEN MARY'S GARDENS are the most artistic in London, it contains an exquisite little-known Italianate garden lined with statuary beside St John's Lodge, and its enchanting open-air theatre performs plays by Shakespeare every afternoon and evening in summer, weather permitting. At the far western edge of the park the gilded minaret of the London Mosque calls the faithful to prayer.

At the end of the park, where the canal goes under Park Road Bridge, the canalside becomes residential again and makes a curve to the south to avoid Lord's Cricket Ground (which was built with spoil from the excavation of the canal). It crosses under Lisson Grove, passes another village of houseboats, then disappears into a tunnel by a house built on the canal bank with its front door on the top floor at street-level and the bedrooms on the bottom floor at canal-level. It is called 'The Upsidedown House'.

You can rejoin the canal by walking along St John's Wood Road, and down Aberdeen Place to Maida Vale, where it re-emerges at one of its most charming stretches, between Blomfield Road and Maida Avenue, flanked by Victorian villas, and overlooked by the tall and romantic Early English style Catholic Apostolic Church, designed by John Loughborough Pearson (1817–97) in 1891 but no longer in use. Lillie Langtry (1853–1929), Edward VII's mistress, and Joan Collins have lived here. You could be in a quiet district of Amsterdam. Pevsner called the stretch 'one of the most attractive Early Victorian tree and stucco landscapes in London'.

Maida Avenue ends at Warwick Avenue, where the canal comes into LITTLE VENICE, and the Regent's Canal meets the Grand Union Canal and its short branch leading south through an urban wasteland to Paddington, at Browning's Pool. It is an idyllic spot; there is a tree-covered island in the middle. The poet Robert Browning (1812–89) lived overlooking the island at 19 Warwick Crescent between 1862 and 1887, and it was there that he wrote *The Ring and the Book*. The island and the pool are now called after him. Both Browning and Byron compared the spot with Venice, but the term 'Little Venice' was not in use until the 1950s. It was invented by an estate agent.

The pool is surrounded on three sides by stuccoed Regency and early Victorian houses. On the fourth side is a motorway. Classical statuary belonging to a local garden-furniture business lines the canalbank. From Little Venice the towpath crosses the canal to the south side, and as you walk along it, the tall and narrow spire of George Edmund Street's St Mary Magdalen Paddington, built between 1868 and 1878 in a north German gothic style, pierces the sky from a mound made by excavated canal spoil.

OPPOSITE *Regent's Park from the boating lake, with Nash's Hanover Terrace behind.*

BELOW *Little Venice, where the Regent's Canal and the Grand Union Canal meet at a village of houseboats.*

The canal continues on, flanked by civilized housing estates, to the Harrow Road Bridge, where the housing estates briefly disappear and the Regent's Canal, M40 Motorway (the Westway) and the Paddington main rail line travel together for a quarter of a mile: three eras of transport side by side. They separate again at Carlton Bridge, built in 1870 and immediately recognizable by its intricate cast-iron balustrade.

Westbourne Park was not even a village before the coming of the canal. It was a farm in the Middle Ages, belonging to the Abbey of Westminster, and named after the stream that flowed through its fields. In the sixteenth century a grand house, Westbourne Park, was erected. It was rebuilt in 1740 by Isaac Ware (d.1766), a sucessful chimney sweep who became an architect. But with the coming first of the canal and then of the railway the rural isolation of Westbourne Park was brought to an end. Soon the fields were covered in new roads and houses from material brought by barge from along the canal.

In its early years the newly built-up Westbourne Park was a genteel place, for the middle class. Thomas Hardy (1840–1928), the novelist, lived at 16 Westbourne Villas from 1863 to 1867. But by the end of the century much of it had already degenerated into slums. It became a staging place for immigrants, first the Irish, then the West Indians, and then the Asians. By the 1960s it was attracting beatniks and hippies, who romanticized its poverty and racial mix. Rock stars like Van Morrison wrote songs about it and Virgin Records established their main office in an alley off Portobello Road.

In spite of the colonization in the last twenty years of middle-class owner-occupiers (often the same beatniks and hippies, but now a little balder), it has retained its cosmopolitan, multi-racial and 'alternative' character, and – in the cold council estates and crumbling bedsits and squats off Ladbroke Grove – its poverty. Reggae music beats out in the small hours from West Indian clubs, dope dealers hang around in All Saints' Road, and Berbers from Tangier (mostly waiters and washers-up) drink mint tea in the working class Moroccan café in Portobello Road. Portobello Road itself hosts the most hybrid market in London every Saturday, starting with stalls selling antiques at the Notting Hill end, and finishing at stalls selling transistor radio parts, books that no one wants, and second-hand records by Fats Domino at the Ladbroke Grove end. Its annual carnival on the August Bank Holiday weekend, the Notting Hill Carnival – a cascade of West Indian bands and dancers, with sightseers joining in the dancing and parties on every balcony – tells you far more about modern London than the Lord Mayor's Show.

The canal continues north-west from Carlton Bridge, with Ladbroke Grove running parallel on the south side, and Harrow Road running hard up against it on the north side. The canalside displays poverty and loneliness: Victorian bedsits in need of new paint, empty factories whose owners have gone bankrupt, second-hand clothes shops and laundrettes. A brick bridge takes you over Port-A-Bella Dock, built for refuse barges in 1894 and now restored. A few yards on, the canal crosses under Ladbroke Grove and you are confronted by a post-modern supermarket on one side and a rambling Victorian cemetery on the other.

The cemetery is **KENSAL GREEN CEMETERY**. It covers 56 acres, stretching along the canal in the shadow of the gasworks. It was opened in January 1833, the first of the seven 'hygienic' cemeteries laid out in London (before that corpses had to make do with the overcrowded London churchyards), and is the only one designed in a Greek Revival style. The Athenian entrance arch stands in a Doric semi-circle, and the gravelled walkways, 'of sufficient width for carriages', are lined by Ionic idiosyncrasies and free-thinking angels. There is a wonderfully arrogant centricity about it all, with Anglicans, who go unhindered to heaven, in the middle; 'Turks, Jews, Infidels, Heretics and unbaptized folk', who go elsewhere, in one corner; Nonconformists, who may become a social embarrassment in heaven, in another; and Catholics, in their own cemetery, St Mary's, half a mile further up the Harrow Road.

It is worth searching the ruins for the flying angels balanced on Mary Austen Gibson's Corinthian temple; the tomb of Major-General Sir William Casement, guarded by four Attila-the-Hun-lookalikes, the outrageously incongruous neo-gothic funeral cake home of the deceased members of the Ricketts family, the veiled angel on the tomb of Ann Gardner and the tomb of Francis Thompson (1859–1907), the priestly opium poet who wrote *The Hound of Heaven*, which has an inscription by Eric Gill (1882–1940).

Others you might come across as you wander through the cemetery are: Sidney Smith, the Canon of St Paul's who found Amen Corner a little too awkward (see p. 70); Sir Marc Isambard Brunel (1769–1849), his wife Sophia, and their son, Isambard Kingdom Brunel (1806–59); the cartoonist George Cruikshank (1792–1878, 'artist, designer, etcher, painter ... and ... for 30 years a total abstainer'; the novelists, William Thackeray, Wilkie Collins (1824–89) and Anthony Trollope (1815–82); Dickens's sister-in-law and the model for Little Nell, Mary Hogarth; the architect Decimus Burton; Augustus Frederick, Duke of Sussex (1773–1843) and Princess Sophie (1777–1848), both offspring of Geoge III; several members of the Ethiopian Imperial Family in exile; Emile Blondin (1824–79), the tightrope walker who crossed the Niagara Falls in 1859; and James Miranda Barry (d.1865), Inspector-General of the Army Medical Department, and the first woman military doctor, though she wasn't discovered to be a woman until she was stripped in preparation for her embalming after her death.

The canal continues west, through a London that becomes first suburban and then increasingly rural, becoming just another pretty canal. If you do continue you will be rewarded with the Glaxo Factory and Mother's Pride Bakery, the odd sensation of looking down on the North Circular Road from the canal's aqueduct and the rolling landscape of Sunbury Golf Course. You end up at Bull's Bridge, where you can either turn right for Birmingham, or left for Osterley Park, Brentford and the Thames.

Sarcophagus guarded by sphinx in Kensal Green Cemetery, the first of the 'hygienic' London cemeteries, and the only one in a predominantly Greek Revival style.

7

The View from the Heath

....

In the north of London, high on the east–west ridge of chalk overlooking the city, are two villages, Hampstead and Highgate. They are places of weatherboard houses, Regency cottages and narrow streets, and they have survived as villages because the steepness of the hills they stand on discouraged suburban development. The two villages stand about four miles from the centre of London, one on either side of Hampstead Heath. Fitz Stephen (d.*c*.1190), secretary to Thomas Becket and London's first guidebook writer, wrote of the Heath at the end of the twelfth century:

> On the north are corn fields, pastures and delightful meadows intermixed with pleasant streams, on which stand many a mill whose clack is happy to the ear. Beyond them an immense forest extends itself, beautied with woods and groves, and full of the lairs and coverts of beasts and game, stags, buck, boars and wild bulls.

Each village had its own ponds, Hampstead Ponds and Highgate Ponds, the two sources of the River Fleet (now beneath ground), which unite just above Camden Town Tube Station, and flow beneath Farringdon Street, joining the Thames at Blackfriars Bridge. The walk across the heath is one of the most beautiful in London.

> The walks across the fields from Highgate to Hampstead, with ponds on one side and Caen Wood on the other, used to be (and I hope is still, for I have not seen it for some years) one of the prettiest of England. *Poet's* (vulgarly called Millfield) *Lane* crossed it on the side next to Highgate, at the foot of a beautiful slope, which in June was covered with daisies and buttercups; and at the other end it descended charmingly into the Vale of Health, out of which rose the highest ground in Hampstead,

wrote the poet and radical James Leigh Hunt (1784–1859).

OPPOSITE *Highgate Cemetery: at rest, in a quiet but discerning neighbourhood, with interesting neighbours, and a good view of London to contemplate through the hereafter.*

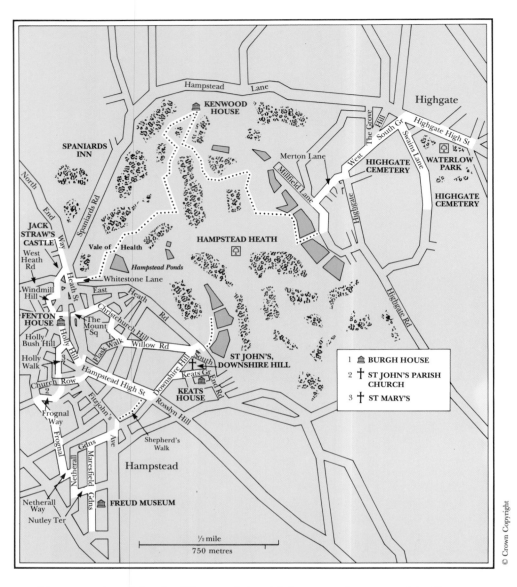

Hampstead, originally 'Hamstede', which means homestead in Saxon, was a manor and farm in the tenth century, owned by the Abbey of Westminster. William the Conqueror granted it to Ranulph Perrel, husband of Ingelrica, his discarded mistress, and it remained a manor and farm until the seventeenth century when a handful of grand houses were erected and squatters began building cottages on the edge of the Heath. In 1665 thousands of Londoners flocked to Hampstead Heath to escape the Great Plague. The judges of the Law Courts camped out in what is now called Judges' Walk on West Heath. They gave judgement under the trees and slept under canvas. A year later London burned down, and most of the forest was cut to rebuild it.

HAMPSTEAD WELLS were the making of Hampstead. They first became known in the 1680s, when buckets of healing water were sold by a local

woman, Dorothy Rippon, at a halfpenny a bucket. In 1698 Susanna Noel, mother of the Earl of Gainsborough, bequeathed the wells and six acres for the benefit of the poor of Hampstead. The spa became fashionable but the poor did not do very well out of it. An Assembly Room was built in Well Walk by the celebrated local physician, Dr Gibbons, who had done so much to advertise the medicinal value of the springs. Flask Walk, where you went to buy the spa water by the flask, was built up. So was Well Walk, which had a hundred lime trees laid out along it. A row of whitewashed cottages went up in Squire's Mount, and some larger houses in Heath Street. But by 1709 polite society had abandoned Hampstead. 'Its nearness to London brings so many loose women in vampt-up clothes to catch the City apprentices, that modest company are ashamed to appear here' (John Mackey: *Journey Through England* 1709). Hampstead still grew. In 1712 the first Hampstead Fair took place.

Holly Hill, Hampstead, winding up through the old village to the Heath.

Hampstead came back into vogue in the Regency era. First the Bohemians, and then fashionable society, flocked there for the bracing air. A new assembly room had been built in 1780 and a hamlet was growing up in the fold of two hills east of Whitestone Ponds, **THE VALE OF HEALTH**. Regency villas and cottages were being built east of Hampstead High Street on Downshire Hill and Willow Road, and west of Hampstead High Street in Holly Walk and Hampstead Grove. Today its population is the most intellectually sophisticated (some would say the most pretentious) in London.

The best place to start a walk through **HAMPSTEAD VILLAGE**, and across the Heath to Highgate Village, is from Hampstead Tube Station, where Hampstead High Street, Holly Hill, and Heath Street meet. The eighteenth-century houses with their modern shop fronts in Hampstead High Street run down Hampstead Hill and up Heath Street. There are boutiques and restaurants, and an awful lot of antique shops.

Holly Hill takes you up the steep slope to Holly Bush Hill, where a triangle of green opens up. It is a lovely spot. To the west the Georgian houses are raised on an embankment. To the north by Windmill Hill is a sedate line of late seventeenth- and early eighteenth-century houses, Volta House, Bolton House, Enfield House and **FENTON HOUSE**, which is the oldest, built in 1693, and accommodating the wonderful Benton–Fletcher collection of early keyboard instruments amid English, French and German eighteenth-century porcelain. Then to the east, standing at a slight angle to the rest, built of brick and weatherboarding and painted white, is Romney's House.

The painter, George Romney (1734–1802), came to Hampstead in 1797 at the end of his career, lonely, ill and still bitter in spite of his success. He bought a house and stables, demolished the stables, and built a studio and gallery, enclosing half the garden beneath a timber arcade. It was the first purpose-built studio in London, 'a singular house', according to one of his friends, 'the painting room and gallery have been nobly planned, but all domestic conveniences overlooked'. He stayed only two years, then went back to his wife in the Lake District and died five years later.

Walk south-west down the slope of Mount Vernon, to the corner house where the novelist Robert Louis Stevenson (1850–94) lived, then turn left into Holly Walk, a passage bordered by flowers and cottages, running down the steep slope towards the squat zinc spire and battlemented brick tower of St John's Hampstead. On the left-hand side is a group of petite Regency cottages, built between 1813 and 1816, with tiny lanes running off them, each lane lined with more cottages, some pink-washed, some green-washed, blue-washed, some red brick, and some white and weatherboarded, each with their own enchanting front garden.

Set in the middle of the range of cottages facing Holly Walk, is the Catholic church of **ST MARY'S**, with a stuccoed front and a Tuscan doorway. It sits in perfect proportion to the cottages around, and is one of the smallest Catholic churches in London. It is also one of the earliest, founded in 1816 by

Abbé Morel, a refugee from Revolutionary France, who lies in the church like a medieval saint or potentate, his effigy attended by angels. Where the cottages come to an end the lane opens up into an overgrown graveyard. It is an extension of the churchyard of St John's, at the bottom of Holly Walk, and its jewel is the Hammersley monument about half way down the lane, a very domestic-looking temple sheltering an angel about to fly off with a corpse.

ST JOHN'S CHURCH is Hampstead's parish church. It was built in 1745. Henry Flitcroft, architect of Woburn Abbey, offered his services free of charge but was politely refused. Its style is a strange mixture of baroque and gothic, and its graveyard, where the painter John Constable and the architect Norman Shaw are buried, tumbles down the hill like in an old print of the Apocalypse. Inside the church is a tunnel-vaulted roof supported on gigantic pillars and a three-sided gallery. There are box pews in the nave and a bust of the poet John Keats (1795–1821) to the right of the altar.

Outside the church, at a right angle to Holly Walk, runs Church Row, one of the prettiest streets in London. On the south side, built in stages to match the contours, is an early Georgian terrace, constructed in 1720 out of brown-red brick, and lightly diapered. The terrace forms a complete unity, though no two houses are exactly alike. On the north side is a delightful hotchpotch of Georgian and early Victorian town houses, the house in the middle weatherboarded, painted white and with an oversailing bay coming out into the street. Between them, running down the middle of Church Row, is a line of lime trees. The novelists H. G. Wells (1866–1946), Wilkie Collins and Compton Mackenzie (1883–1972), and the architect Sir George Gilbert Scott, lived here. So did Thackeray's daughter, Anne Ritchie, who described the row as 'an avenue of Dutch red-faced houses, leading demurely to the old church tower that stands guarding its graves in the flowery churchyard'.

From here a fascinating diversion will take you through Frognal and past the house of the children's illustrator Kate Greenaway (1846–1901) to the **FREUD MUSEUM**, the last home of Sigmund Freud (1856–1939), the founder of psychoanalysis. (Those who believe psychoanalysis is a waste of time and that you are far better off being busy, can walk straight along Church Row, across Heath Street and down Hampstead High Street to Downshire Hill.)

The way to Freud's house takes you from St John's Church down Frognal Way, a charming gravel lane dotted with Athenian and Gothic Regency cottages, and Maxwell Fry's 1935 Sun House, a pattern of glass and white horizontals, and one of the first truly modern buildings.

From Frognal Way you walk down Frognal to Kate Greenaway's house, built by Sir George Gilbert Scott to look like something out of one of her book illustrations. Apart from that childhood highlight the journey to Freud's house is not the most glittering of journeys. It is repetitive and monotonous, like a journey through analysis. Then you turn right and walk through Netherhall Way, Netherhall Gardens and the unfortunately named Nutley Terrace and reach the end of your journey at 20 Maresfield Gardens.

The white and gold interior of St John's church, Downshire Hill, intimate and pretty, a late Georgian exercise in light-weightedness, light-heartedness and simple lightness.

Sigmund Freud's former home is a house rather than a museum, but a house in mourning. You expect secular funeral music. Freud moved in on 27 September 1938, aged 83, suffering cancer of the jaw. He was a refugee from the Nazis, but had managed to bring with him from his home at Berggasse 19, Vienna, his favourite books, his collection of Greek, Roman, Oriental and Egyptian statues, a few pieces of Austria peasant furniture belonging to his daughter Anna, his Persian carpet and his couch.

His study and library on the ground floor were obsessively preserved by Anna Freud, exactly as they were when Freud died on 23 September 1939. Here are his antiquities, which he once confessed he was more addicted to than anything save cigars. The walls are lined with books – not the collection of a lifetime, but a selection in haste, the ones he chose to take with him: books on art, archaeology, history, philosophy, Judaism; novels by Dostoevsky, Flaubert and Anatole France; the plays of Shakespeare; a history of Hinduism. The study floor is covered by an enormous Persian carpet. There is a desk in the middle, and the couch against one wall. It is covered by a Kurdish rug of many colours – like Joseph's coat. It looks Jungian, but it is definately Freudian; and on it have lain 'Dora', 'Little Hans', 'The Rat Man', 'The Wolf Man' and all the others; and Freud sat in a green tub chair unseen behind them, listening – one hopes. Walking through the rooms, you constantly feel that you are in a house that people live in, the house of a Hampstead intellectual, frozen in time since the 1930s. And everywhere you feel the man's presence. On the staircase going up to Anna Freud's room are two portraits of him, one by Ferdinand Schmutzer, sketched in 1926, the other by Salvador Dali sketched in 1938. Freud liked the Schmutzer and wrote 'only now do I feel myself preserved for posterity'. Dali never showed Freud his drawing, for it so obviously conveyed Freud's imminent death.

From Freud's house you can walk up Maresfield Gardens, turn east, cross Fitzjohn's Avenue, cut through the narrow footpath of Shepherd's Walk and cross Hampstead High Street to Downshire Hill, one of Hampstead's prettiest Regency streets. It gets prettier the further you go along it, the villas decorated in stucco, and displaying intricate iron-worked balconies above front gardens boasting as many colours as Freud's Kurdish rug. Dante Gabriel Rossetti lived there in the early 1860s with his wife, the tragic and beautiful Elizabeth Siddal.

About half way down stands **ST JOHN'S CHURCH**, built in 1818 and set in a garden enclosed by ornamental iron railings. Sparse and classical, with a modest portico held up by two pillars and a domed cupola on top, it stands in a perfect setting, on the corner where Keats Grove meets Downshire Hill. A minute's walk down Keats Grove, past the late eighteenth- and early nineteenth-century cottages, takes you to **KEATS HOUSE**.

John Keats (1795–1821) began writing poetry while training to be a surgeon at Guy's Hospital, and sent a poem called *Solitude* to Leigh Hunt, who lived in Hampstead. Hunt published it in his magazine *The Examiner*. They met in October 1816 at Hunt's white-painted cottage in the Vale of Health. Keats was twenty years old. The next year he dropped out of medical school to concentrate on his poetry and went to Hunt's cottage to tell him. Shelley was there and the two men met for the first time. That night Shelley returned home to be told that his wife Harriet Westbrook had drowned herself in the Serpentine (see p. 109).

Return to Downshire Hill and continue east as it opens up to the Heath; and at the end of Downshire Hill it is worth the short excursion across Heath Road to see Hampstead Ponds and the backs of the rambling early Victorian houses of South Hill Park behind them. Then make your way up Willow Road to Well Walk. In the early eighteenth century, when Hampstead Spa was at the height of fashion, there was an Assembly Room and a Pump Room

in Well Walk, and two rows of lime trees leading to the Heath. Today the only memory of it all is the Victorian fountain between Church Hill and the Heath, and the name of the street.

Keats moved to Hampstead in the spring of 1817 with his brother Tom, who was developing tuberculosis. They took lodgings at No 1 Well Walk, the home of the local postman. There he wrote the first book of *Endymion*, finishing the poem at Burford Bridge, where he went for peace and quiet, and to get away from the Hampstead Scene.

He was famous, and dined with Mr William Wordsworth. But when he ventured to disagree with the great man Mrs Wordsworth informed him, 'Mr Wordsworth is never interrupted.' He met Coleridge too.

> A loose, slack, not well-dressed youth met Mr Green and myself in a lane near Highgate. Mr Green knew him and spoke. It was Keats! He was introduced to me and stayed a minute or so. After he had left us a little way, he came back and said 'Let me carry away the memory, Coleridge, of having pressed your hand!' 'There is death in that hand,' I said to Green, when Keats was gone.

He became friendly with Charles Wentworth Dilke and Charles Armitage Brown, who occupied the white semi-detached cottage, then called Wentworth Place. On 1 December 1818 Keats's brother Tom died and Keats moved into Wentworth Place, sharing the eastern half with Brown. The western half had been let to a Mrs Brawne, a widow with three children, and in the summer of 1819 Keats became engaged to Fanny, the eldest daughter.

The next year was his most fertile. *To Psyche, On Indolence, On Melancholy* and *Ode to a Grecian Urn* were composed there, and *Ode to a Nightingale* was written under a plum tree in the garden. But Coleridge had been right. Racked by consumption, Keats left for Italy in September 1820, and died there in Rome, aged 25, on 23 February 1821. 'I weep for Adonis – he is dead,' Shelley wrote.

In 1826 the painter John Constable moved into number 40 Well Walk. Constable loved the Heath, where he did 'a great deal of skying'. Before Well Walk he had lived all over Hampstead: at 2 Lower Terrace, Hook's Cottage near Fenton House, and 25 Downshire Hill. He stayed at 40 Well Walk, 'a comfortable little house', for the rest of his life. His youngest son was born in it and his wife died in it, leaving the poor man to look after seven children. He died on 31 March 1837, and was buried in St John's Churchyard.

Overlooking Well Walk from New End Square is **BURGH HOUSE**. It was built in 1703 in the reign of Queen Anne, and in the 1720s it was the home of Dr William Gibbons, the spa's physician, to whom we owe the wrought iron gates that bear his initials. Though now an arts centre and local history museum, enough of it survives to get some idea of its Queen Anne interior. The oak staircase is original to the house, but the exquisite wood panelling in the Music Room came from the old Assembly Room on Well Walk.

ABOVE *Well Walk: here in the eighteenth century, when Hampstead was famous as a spa, stood the Hampstead Assembly Room and the Hampstead Pump Room. The street was the most fashionable in Hampstead.*

OPPOSTIE *Keats House, Keats Grove. John Keats lived in the house from the death of his brother Tom in December 1818 until his departure for Italy in September 1820, and it was in the garden that he wrote* Ode to a Nightingale.

From Burgh House walk up New End Square into the labyrinth of lanes and passages at the top of Christchurch Hill, and get lost amongst the Georgian and Victorian terraces, cottages and villas in Squire's Mount, Elm Row, Cannon Place, New End Square and Hampstead Square, all huddled beneath the Victorian spire of Christchurch.

Cross Heath Street and go through an alley into Mount Square, not a square at all, more a small and intimate *place*; then cross over Hampstead Grove and make your way to Admiral's Walk, which was originally the carriage drive to Admiral's House. The house, which Constable painted, stands on the skyline as white as a canvas sail, and more like a ship-of-the-line than a house in Hampstead. It was built in the early eighteenth century and given its nautical superstructure by the eccentric Admiral Matthew Burton (1715–95) who is rare amongst admirals for having been captured by Moorish pirates without any clothes on and sold into slavery. He was eventually ransomed and he used to fire salutes from a couple of cannon he kept in the garden every time Britain scored a naval victory. A century later, between 1854 and 1864, the Admiral's House was the home of the architect Sir George Gilbert Scott. Its neighbour, Grove Lodge, also painted white, is a little older, and was the home of the novelist John Galsworthy from 1918 until his death in 1933.

A little further on, Lower Terrace and Windmill Hill (which runs beside Judge's Walk) take you on to Hampstead Heath at London's highest point, 433 feet above sea level, and marked by a flagpole beside Whitestone Pond.

HAMPSTEAD HEATH was forest and farmland in the Middle Ages, but it was already attracting intellectuals in Elizabethan times. John Gerard, the herbalist, made countless journeys there. He found heather and gorse 'upon Hampstead Heath near London, where all sorts do grow, except that of the wild flowers, and that which beareth berries'. There were orchids at North End and Highgate, and 'cotton grass groweth upon bogs and such like moorish places, and is to be seen upon the bogs in Hampstead Heath'. In the 1690s and 1700s the Hampstead Water Company dammed the River Fleet and excavated Hampstead Ponds and Highgate Ponds as reservoirs for London's growing population. Then, once Hampstead Spa became fashionable, the Heath was transformed from a wilderness to a place of recreation.

John Soame, a local doctor, who had something of an interest in the matter, waxed lyrical in the Heath's praise:

> Hampstead Heath, being chiefly sand and gravel, is always dry and pleasant, unless it be in excessive and long rains; yet in a few days time of dry weather, you may walk very well, the water soon runneth off. This Heath also is famous for the vast number of useful plants that grow all over it . . . . The Apothecaries Company very seldom miss coming to Hampstead every Spring, and found a greater variety of curious and useful plants, near and about Hampstead, than in any other place.

But before starting the walk across Hampstead Heath to Highgate, walk north from Whitestone Ponds past the weatherboarded Jack Straw's Castle, one of London's most famous pubs, first mentioned 1713, and standing at a gathering place of the peasants who were revolting against the poll tax in 1381. The brown early eighteenth-century house on the other side of the road was the home of the Quaker abolitionist Samuel Hoare, and amongst those who visited the house were Elizabeth Fry and William Wilberforce. Beyond Jack Straw's Castle take the path through the woods towards one of the most enchanting follies in London: a romantic ruin high on a hill, the terrace punctuated by neo-classical statuary, and everything overgrown with roses and creepers, built by the millionaire, Lord Leverhulme (see p. 102) – but visit it in the daytime; at night the woods become an insalubrious place.

Return to Jack Straw's Castle and Whitestone Pond, and cross North End Way. Below you the slope descends to a cluster of eighteenth- and nineteenth-century cottages beside a pond, almost hidden in the fold between two hills,

Kenwood Park in Hampstead Heath, where the heath's roughness is progressively mellowed towards the house.

the Vale of Health. In spite of its name it was a malarial swamp in the eighteenth century, its only inhabitant Samuel Hatch, an harness-maker. Gradually, as squatters moved in, the single cottage became a hamlet, then the squatters were bought out by middle-class romantics like Leigh Hunt, and the hamlet turned into a village. Its minuscule lanes and weatherboarded cottages are a delight, and it has been the home, not only of Leigh Hunt (who took a room in 1816 after his release from prison for libelling the Prince Regent), but also of D. H. Lawrence (1885–1930), Edgar Wallace (1875–1932) and Compton Mackenzie (1883–1972).

From the Vale of Health walk north-east, roughly parallel to Spaniards Road, through woods where oaks, beech, ash, hazel and birch grow. People who like pubs should head towards the Spaniards Inn – all wood panelling and low beams – though since the land to the south of the inn is enclosed, you have to make your appoach to the inn along the Spaniards Road. Others can just wander in a vague north-easterly direction through the heathlands, and amongst trees, bracken and gorse. Gradually the heathland changes into parkland. There are glimpses of statuary. You see a Barbara Hepworth (1903–75) here and a Henry Moore there. You walk on and find yourself in an English garden. Then you see ahead, looking down on its own lake spanned by the facade of a bridge, Adam's Kenwood, white and stuccoed, and perfectly balanced with the library on one side and the orangery on the other, standing out on a rolling khaki landscape of trees, grass and people in Barbour coats exercising their dogs.

Robert Adam, who gave **KENWOOD HOUSE** its glory, described the view in his *Works in Architecture*:

> A great body of water covers the bottom, and serves to go round a large natural wood and tall trees rising one above another upon the side of a hill. Over the vale, through which the water flows, there is a noble view let into the house and terrace, of the City of London, Greenwich Hospital, the River Thames, the ships passing up and down, with an extensive prospect, but clear and distinct, on both sides of the river. To the north-east, and west of the house and terrace, the mountainous villages of Highgate and Hampstead form delightful objects.

The core of the house is Restoration. In 1754 it came into the hands of William Murray, Earl of Mansfield (1705–93), who commissioned his fellow Scotsman Robert Adam to transform it. The library that he created is the most exquisite Adam interior in London. Today the house holds the Iveagh Bequest of predominantly seventeenth-century Dutch and eighteenth-century English paintings. You enter into the hall, beneath a ceiling painting by Antonio Zucchi of Bacchus, god of wine, and Ceres, goddess of agriculture. A door to the left leads to the Adam neo-classical extension of library and ante-chamber, which you enter through a colonnade. The library is spectacular, 'a room for receiving company', as Adam called it, oblong, with

bookshelves at each end. One wall is taken up by windows looking down at Kenwood Lake, the other by mirrors, reflecting the view, and the 'company'. There are classical screens at both ends, and mythological panel paintings on the walls and ceiling by Zucchi.

North of the ante-chamber is the dining room lobby, full of pastoral paintings by Boucher, while in the dining room itself, a self-portrait of Rembrandt gazes contendedly across the room at Jan Vermeer the Elder's (1628–91) serene seventeenth-century *Guitar Player*. In Lord Mansfield's dressing room are paintings by Reynolds, Gainsborough and Joseph Wright of Derby, and in the breakfast room are William van der Velde the Younger's *Sea Scene*, Claude de Jongh's 1630s panorama of Old London Bridge and Albert Cuyp's study of Dordrecht. Further on, in the housekeeper's room, are two views of Rome by Panini (*c.* 1692–1765/8) and two views of the Grand Canal, Venice, by Francesco Guardi (1712–93). The final three rooms of the collection are the restrained climax, displaying some of the finest eighteenth-century English painting in England. In the Orangery are four enormous Gainsboroughs: *Mary, Countess of Howe*, *Lady Brisco*, *Two Shepherd Boys with Dogs* and *Foxhunt*. The Green Room is hung with Reynolds, Romney, Gainsborough and Lawrence, and in the Music Room, standing out in its simplicity amongst Sir Joshua Reynolds's beauties, is George Romney's exquisite *The Spinstress*.

Leave Kenwood House and walk down the slope and along the west side of Kenwood Lake, where classical concerts are held on Saturday evenings in the summer and the slopes of Kenwood are packed with music-loving picnickers; then on through South Wood to Highgate Ponds, the five ponds strung out like beads and formed by the damming of the River Fleet. It is an enchanting walk of trees, bracken, grass, grey squirrels and water, becoming progressively less cultivated. Cross one of the dams between the lower ponds and walk up Millfield Lane to Merton Lane. The rather ordinary heathside houses in the two lanes mark the beginning of Highgate Village.

Claude de Jongh painted this view of Old London Bridge some 36 years before it burned down in the Great Fire. One of a number of Dutch and Flemish artists who worked in England before the Commonwealth, he shows here the shops which lined both sides of the bridge.

Highgate has been a village on the Great North Road since the Middle Ages and was lined with taverns. Though never as glamorous as Hampstead, like the latter it remained a village right up until the middle of the nineteenth century. It is quieter, a trifle more *petit-bourgeois*, and though Coleridge lived at 3, The Grove after kicking his opium habit, the only poet Highgate has produced is John Betjeman.

Highgate West Hill, which Merton Lane leads into, is steep; and the houses are uninteresting until you turn the corner at the top of the hill and see before you one of the most lovely Georgian views in London. At a small green, beside an eighteenth-century pub, the Flask, the street fans out into three, with The Grove running north, and Highgate West Hill and South Grove branching off to the north-east. Lined up along the north-west side of The Grove, behind a line of trees, are perfect late seventeenth-century and early eighteenth-century brick terraced houses. More such eighteenth-century houses line Highgate West Hill. The most southern of the three streets, South Grove, is the most charming. It takes you past early Georgian houses, late Georgian cottages and two churches to Pond Square, where there had once been a pond and a ducking stool for witches. Now there is only a village green, but it is a green surrounded by a beautiful mixture of the fronts and backs of Georgian houses and cottages, some weatherboarded, some pink-washed, some white, some red brick. At the end of Pond Square, running south down the hill, is Highgate High Street, still very much a 'coachy' place of Georgian inns, like the Gate House Tavern, built on the site of the 1386 gate house to the Bishop of London's park. Along the street Queen Anne and early Georgian houses hide behind their modern shopfronts.

Down the hill, Highgate High Street becomes Highgate Hill. On the east side of the road, on The Bank, are the early seventeenth-century Cromwell House and the early eighteenth-century Lyndale House and Ireton House. On the west side you walk down towards Lauderdale House and Waterlow Park past the site of the cottage where the poet Andrew Marvell (1621–78) lived in the 1670s. Marvell's neighbour was the appalling Earl of Lauderdale of Ham House (see p. 25), Charles II's powerful minister. Marvell, an ardent republican, intensely disliked him, saying that he 'deserves a halter rather than a garter'. The cottage was demolished in 1868. Below the cottage is the entrance to Waterlow Park and Lauderdale's own suburban retreat, Lauderdale House. The oldest parts of the house are late Elizabethan, but it was so remodelled in the eighteenth century that you wouldn't guess. John Ireton, brother of the Cromwellian general, Henry Ireton, acquired the house after the Civil War and Lauderdale took it over after the Restoration. The story that Charles II's mistress Nell Gwynne lived there and, despairing that the king would ever confer a title on their son, threatened to throw him out of the window, provoking the royal cry 'Save the Earl of Burford', may not be strictly accurate but deserves to be true. It is the kind of thing that you re-member long after you leave.

The Grove, Highgate: built in the 1680s and one of Highgate's most picturesque streets.

But before you do leave Highgate, make your way down to the bottom of Waterlow Park, by Swain's Lane, where **HIGHGATE CEMETERY** lies spread out on either side of the lane. Highgate Cemetery is not the oldest of London's Victorian cemeteries. Kensal Green (see p. 161) is the oldest. But it is the most romantic, the most gothic and, standing on a hill overlooking London, the most perfectly sited.

It was opened in 1839, designed by the architect Stephen Geary. His aim was to attract the new Victorian bourgeoisie, people who wanted to leave their mark on the world. He built them a celebration of death, with graves and mausoleums rising up the hillside to culminate in the 'Egyptian Avenue' cut into the slope, leading to the vault-lined 'Circle of Lebanon' a catacomb encircling a gigantic cedar tree.

Highgate had no difficulty attracting its clientèle, and soon Highgate's own inhabitants, who had complained that the cemetery would lower the value of their houses, were applying to the London Cemetery Company for keys to walk amid the graves and glades. The cemetery was so successful that an extension was laid out on the east side of Swain's Lane, next to Waterlow Park, linked by a tunnel and hydraulic lift. The east side is more ordered and it contains the graves of William Friese-Greene (1855–1921), the inventor of cinematography, George Eliot and Karl Marx, whose monument is probably still the most visited in the cemetery.

The true Victorians can be found in the more obviously romantic western cemetery, to which guided tours are provided by the Friends of Highgate Cemetery, who manage this wooded burial ground. John Galsworthy, whose parents were buried in Highgate, describes one such Victorian interment.

> From that high and sacred field, where thousands of the upper middle class lay in their last sleep, the eyes of the Forsytes travelled across the flocks of graves. There, spreading in the distance, lay London with no sun over it, mourning the loss of its daughter, mourning with this family, so dear, the loss of her who was mother and guardian. A hundred thousand spires and houses, blurred in the great grey web of property, lay there like prostrate worshippers before the grave of this, the oldest Forsyte of them all.
> (*The Forsyte Saga*)

In Highgate Cemetery, like Westminster Abbey, there may be a touch of snobbery in its choice amongst some of its 166,700 inhabitants, giving them the conceit of thinking they are lying next to people much more interesting than they were ever likely to meet in their lifetime. Buried with them are the scientist Michael Faraday (1791–1867), the cricketer Frederick Lillywhite (1792–1850), the feminist writer Radclyffe Hall (1886–1943) and her lover Mabel Batten, Charles Dickens's long-suffering wife Catherine Dickens (1815–70), the balloonist Charles Green (see pp. 34 and 106), Rossetti's wife Elizabeth Siddal and his sister Christina, the diarist Henry Crabb Robinson, the authors Herbert Spencer (d. 1903) and Mrs Henry Wood (d. 1887), the father of the London Fire Brigade Sir Eyre Massey Shaw (1830–1908), the Chinese scholar and poet Arthur Waley (1889–1966), the inventors of the Chubb lock and Hovis bread, and Jacob Bronowski (d. 1974).

You look out from the 'City of the Dead' on the top of Highgate Hill at an enormous London spread out before you. It is a *living* city. You can see Canary Wharf, the Tower of London, the Natwest Tower, St Paul's, St Pancras Station, Big Ben and The Telecom Tower; between them are a dozen tower blocks and a hundred church spires and towers by Wren, Hawksmoor, Gibbs, Smirke, Nash, Wyatt, Barry, Pugin, Scott, Street, Butterfield and Waterhouse; and all around are hundreds of thousands of slate roofs, each protecting a private world, but together giving London life, and creating one of the world's great cities.

OPPOSITE *The Egyptian Avenue, Highgate Cemetery, paying its own tribute to the tombs of the pharoahs in the Valley of the Kings.*

Appendices

....

CHRONOLOGY OF EVENTS   KINGS AND QUEENS
ARTISTS AND PATRONS   OPENING TIMES

CHRONOLOGY OF EVENTS

BC

55–54	Julius Caesar twice invades Britain

AD

43	Claudius invades Britain and builds fort and settlement of Londinium on Thames.
61	Boadicea defeats Romans and sacks Londinium.
597	Arrival of Augustine's mission; St Paul's Cathedral founded.
644	Plague ravages London.
851	London pillaged by Danes
1014	First London bridge built.
1049	Westminster Abbey begun.
1066	Norman invasion; Battle of Hastings.
1078	White Tower built.
1079	City of London granted first charter.
1097	Westminster Hall completed.
1086	St Paul's burned in city fire.
1123	Foundation of St Bartholomew's hospital
1136	Bridge destroyed in city fire.
1176	Old London Bridge begun.
1185	Knights Templar build New Temple by river.
1191	First Lord Mayor of London elected.
1209	London Bridge completed
1214	King John's charter (Magna Carta).
1265	First parliament held in Westminster Abbey Chapter house.
1290	Expulsion of Jews by Edward I.
1314	Old St Paul's completed.
1327	Incorporation of first city trade guilds.
1347	Merchant Taylors established.
1348–58	Black Death sweeps through London, killing one third of population.
1371	Charterhouse inaugurated.
1382	City damaged in Peasants' Revolt.
1411–16	Guildhall built.
1476	Caxton sets up first printing press in Westminster.
1483	Murder of princes in the Tower.
1509	Dean Colet founds St Paul's School.
1530	St James's Palace built.
1561	Foundation of Westminster School.
1568	Royal Exchange founded.
1587	Rose Theatre built.
1588	Queen Elizabeth rallies troops at Tilbury; Spanish Armada defeated.
1599	Shakespeare's Globe Theatre built at Southwark.
1605	Gunpowder Plot to blow up Parliament discovered.
1619–22	Banqueting Hall built in Whitehall.
1635	Leicester Square laid out.
1649	Charles I beheaded outside Banqueting House.
1650	Jews permitted by Cromwell to return to London.
1660	Restoration of Monarchy under Charles II.
1661	Covent Garden market opened.
1665	The Great Plague.
1666	The Great Fire.
1671	Drury Lane Theatre opened.
1675	Wren begins to rebuilt St Paul's.
1676	Royal Observatory opened at Greenwich.
1677	First street lamps introduced.
1682	Chelsea Royal Hospital founded.
1684	St James's Square laid out.
1694	Foundation of Bank of England.
1695	Grosvenor Square laid out.
1697	St Paul's opened.
1698	Whitehall Palace destroyed by fire.
	Berkeley Square laid out.

1703	Buckingham House built.	**1858**	Thames befouled in Great Stink.	**1936**	Crystal Palace destroyed by fire.
1724	Guy's Hospital founded.		Present Royal Opera House opened.	**1937**	Coronation of King George VI and Queen Elizabeth.
1730	Serpentine formed in Hyde Park.	**1860**	Trams begin running in London.	**1939–45**	Second World War.
1739–40	The Great Frost.	**1863**	First underground trains arrive.	**1940–41**	London hit by enemy air raids, causing extensive damage and casualties.
1740	London Hospital instituted.	**1870**	Thames Embankment inaugurated.	**1944–45**	London damage by V1 flying bombs and V2 rockets.
1755	First Trooping the Colour.	**1871**	Royal Albert Hall opened.	**1946**	Opening of Heathrow Airport.
1762	Buckingham Palace becomes royal residence.	**1872**	Albert Memorial completed.	**1948**	London hosts Olympic Games.
1768	Royal Academy founded.	**1878**	First electric lighting on London streets.	**1951**	Festival of Britain on the South Bank.
1771	Apsley House built.	**1879**	First London telephone exchange opened.		Royal Festival Hall opened.
1773	Stock exchange founded.	**1884**	Brompton Oratory completed.	**1953**	Coronation of Queen Elizabeth II.
1775	Bedford Square laid out.	**1888**	London County Council established.	**1973**	Opening of new Stock Exchange.
1809	Gas lighting introduced in Pall Mall.	**1894**	Tower Bridge opened.	**1974**	Covent Garden fruit and vegetable market moves south of Thames.
1812	Regent's Park laid out.	**1897**	First omnibus runs from Victoria to Charing Cross.	**1976**	National Theatre opened on South Bank.
1824	National Gallery founded.		Tate Gallery opened.	**1982**	Barbican Centre opened.
1828	Zoological Gardens opened.		Queen Victoria's Diamond Jubilee.	**1984**	Thames Barrier, to prevent possible flooding, inaugurated.
1829	Metropolitan Police Force established by Peel.	**1901**	Death of Queen Victoria.	**1986**	Greater London Council abolished.
1829–41	Trafalgar Square laid out.	**1909**	Port of London Authority set up.	**1989**	Rose Theatre uncovered.
1834	Houses of Parliament gutted by fire.	**1914–18**	First World War.		
1836	London University founded. London's first railway (London Bridge to Deptford) opened.	**1924–25**	British Empire Exhibition, Wembley.		
1840	Penny postage introduced.	**1926**	General Strike paralyzes London.		
1847	British Museum opened.	**1936**	BBC inaugurates television service from Alexandra Palace.		
1851	Marble Arch (built 1827) moved to present Hyde Park site				
	Great Exhibition in Hyde Park.				
1857	Victoria and Albert Museum moved to South Kensington.				

KINGS AND QUEENS

Aethelstan	924–39
Edmund I	939–46
Edred	946–55
Edwy	955–7
Edgar	959–75
Edward the Martyr	978
Aethelred II	978–1016
Canute	1016–35
Harold I	1037–40
Hardicanute	1040–2
Edward the Confessor	1042–66
Harold II	1066
William I	1066–87
William II	1087–1100
Henry I	1100–35
Stephen	1135–54
Henry II	1154–89
Richard I	1189–99
John	1199–1216
Henry III	1216–72
Edward I	1272–1307
Edward II	1307–27
Edward III	1327–77
Richard II	1377–99
Henry IV	1399–1413
Henry V	1413–22
Henry VI	1422–61 & 1470–1
Edward IV	1461–70 & 1471–83
Edward V (never crowned)	1483
Richard III	1483–5
Henry VII	1485–1509
Henry VIII	1509–47
Edward VI	1547–53
Mary I	1553–8
Elizabeth I	1558–1603
James I	1603–25
Charles I	1625–49
Charles II	1660–85
James II	1685–8
William III and	1689–1702
Mary II	1689–94
Anne	1702–14
George I	1714–27
George II	1727–60
George III	1760–1820
George IV	1820–30
William IV	1830–7
Victoria	1837–1901
Edward VII	1901–10
George V	1910–36
Edward VIII (never crowned)	1936
George VI	1936–52
Elizabeth II	1952–

ARTISTS AND PATRONS

Names of churches, public buildings, monuments, squares, parks, etc., are those with which the artists and patrons are most closely associated.

Adam, Robert (1728–92), architect: Syon House; Apsley House; St James's Square; Portman Square; Fitzroy Square; Portland Place; Adelphi; Theatre Royal, Drury Lane; Chelsea Royal Hospital; Westminster Abbey; and Kenwood House.

Albert, Prince (1819–61), consort of Queen Victoria: Great Exhibition.

Anne, Queen (1702–14): St James's Palace; Kensington Palace; Kensington Gardens; Buckingham House; Queen Anne's Gate; St Mary-le-Strand and other remaining '50 New Churches'.

Archer, Thomas (1668–1743), architect: St John, Smith Square; and St Paul, Deptford.

Barry, Sir Charles (1795–1860), architect: Houses of Parliament; Parliament Square; Trafalgar Square; Treasury; Pall Mall; Bridgewater House; Royal College of Surgeons; and Lancaster House.

Blake, William (1757–1827), artist and poet: Tate Gallery; and Victoria and Albert Museum.

Blomfield, Sir Arthur (1829–99), architect: Southwark Cathedral; Royal College of Music; Royal Courts of Justice; St Mark, North Audley Street; St Paul, Clapham; St Peter, Eaton Square; and St James, Clerkenwell.

Brown, Lancelot 'Capability' (1716–83), landscape gardener: Syon Park; Hampton Court; and Royal Botanic Gardens, Kew.

Brunel, Isambard Kingdom (1806–59), civil engineer: Paddington Station; and Burrell's Wharf.

Burlington, Richard Boyle, Third Earl of (1695–1753), architect and patron of Kent, Rysbrack, Campbell, Handel, Pope, Swift: Burlington House; and Chiswick House.

Burne-Jones, Sir Edward (1833–98), painter: Holy Trinity, Sloane Street; All Saints, Putney; and Tate Gallery.

Burton, Decimus (1800–81), architect: Athenaeum; Pall Mall; Hyde Park Corner; Regent's Park; and Royal Botanic Gardens, Kew.

Campbell, Colen (1676–1729), architect: Burlington House; Kensington Palace; Greenwich Hospital; and Marble Hill House.

Canaletto (Giovanni Antonio Canal) (1697–1768). painter: Ranelagh Gardens; River Thames; Sir John Soane's Museum; National Maritime Museum; and National Gallery.

Chambers, Sir William (1723–96), architect: Somerset House; Albany; Marlborough House; and Royal Botanic Gardens, Kew.

Charles I (1625–49), patron of Van Dyck, Inigo Jones: Hyde Park; Somerset House; Pretty Palace, Greenwich; Covent Garden; Hampton Court; Richmond Palace; Westminster Hall; and Banqueting House.

Charles II (1660–85), patron of Wren, Gibbons, Hawksmoor: St Paul, Covent Garden; Royal Opera House; Theatre Royal, Drury Lane; St James's Park; Royal Observatory, Greenwich; Hampton Court gardens; Greenwich Hospital; and Chelsea Royal Hospital.

Constable, John (1776–1837), painter: Hampstead; Victoria and Albert Museum; National Gallery; Tate Gallery; and Courtauld Institute Galleries.

Cranmer, Thomas (1489–1556), archbishop: Guildhall; and Tower of London.

Dyck, Sir Anthony van (1599–1641), painter: National Gallery; and Wallace Collection.

Elizabeth I (1558–1603): Somerset House; Middle Temple Hall; Charterhouse; Tower of London; Deptford; Westminster Abbey; Westminster School; Richmond Palace; amd Victoria and Albert Museum.

Flaxman, John (1755–1826), sculptor: St Paul's Cathedral; Westminster Abbey; Royal Opera House; St Giles-in-the-Fields; Christ Church, Spitalfields; and University College, London.

Flitcroft, Henry (1697–1769), architect: Chatham House; and St Giles-in-the-Fields.

Gainsborough, Thomas (1727–88), painter: Buckingham Palace; Kenwood House; National Gallery; Royal Academy; and Tate Gallery.

Gibbons, Grinling (1648–1721), sculptor and woodcarver: Hampton Court; St Paul's Cathedral; Chelsea Royal Hospital; Marlborough House; Kensington Palace; St James's Piccadilly; St Clement, Danes; St Margaret, Lothbury; St Paul, Covent Garden; St Mary Abchurch; St Mary, Aldermary; St Margaret Pattens; St Nicholas, Deptford; Cock Tavern, Fleet Street; and Victoria and Albert Museum.

Gibbs, James (1682–1754), architect: St Martin-in-the-Fields; St Clement, Danes; St Mary-le-Strand; St Peter, Vere Street; Orleans House; and St Batholomew's Hospital.

Gill, Eric (1882–1940), sculptor, engraver and typographer: Broadcasting House.

Guinness, Edward Cecil, First Earl of Iveagh (1847–1927), philanthropist: Kenwood House.

Hardwick, Philip (1792–1870), architect, son of Thomas: Euston Station; Wellington Barracks; St Bartholomew the Less; New Hall, Lincoln's Inn; and Goldsmith's Hall.

Hardwick, Thomas (1752–1829), architect: St Paul, Covent Garden; St Marylebone Parish Church; St John's Wood Church; St Barlolomew's Hospital; St Bartholomew the Less; and St Barnabas, King Square.

Hawksmoor, Nicholas (1661–1736), architect: associate of Wren; Westminster Abbey; St Paul's Cathedral; St James's Palace; Kensington Palace; St Anne, Limehouse; St Mary Woolnoth; St Michael Cornhill; St George, Bloomsbury; St Alfege, Greenwich; Greenwich Hospital; Chelsea Royal Hospital; Christchurch, Spitalfields; St George-in-the-East; St George the Martyr; St Bartholomew's Hospital; St Andrew-by-the-Wardrobe; and St Lawrence, Jewry.

Henry VIII (1509–47): Hampton Court; Whitehall Palace (wine cellar); St James's Palace; St James's Park; Hyde Park; Tower of London; Bridewell Palace; Greenwich Palace; and Richmond Palace.

Hogarth, William (1697–1764), painter and engraver: Hogarth's House; St Bartholomew's Hospital; Hunterian Museum of Medicine; Tate Gallery; National Portrait Gallery; Sir John Soane's Museum; Kenwood House; Lincoln's Inn; Thomas Coram Foundation; and National Gallery.

Holbein, Hans the Younger (1497/8–1543), painter: Whitehall Palace; St James's Palace; Hampton Court; Crosby Hall; Royal College of Surgeons; and National Gallery.

Hunt, William Holman (1827–1910), painter: St Paul's Cathedral; and Tate Gallery.

James, John (1672–1746), architect: Greenwich Hospital; St Paul's Cathedral; Westminster Abbey; St George, Hanover Square; and St Mary, Twickenham.

Jones, Inigo (1573–1652), painter and architect: Banqueting House, Whitehall; Queen's Chapel, Marlborough House; Old St Paul's, St Paul, Covent Garden; Queen's House, Greenwich; and Lindsay House, Lincoln's Inn Fields.

Kent, William (1685–1748), painter and architect: Horse Guards; St James's Palace; Kensington Palace; Chiswick House; Hampton Court; Royal Botanic Gardens, Kew; Clermont Club, Berkeley Square; and St George, Hanover Square.

Kneller, Sir Godfrey (1649–1723), painter: Hampton Court; Marble Hill House; Kensington Palace; Westminster Abbey; and National Portrait Gallery.

Landseer, Sir Edwin (1802–73), painter and sculptor: Trafalgar Square; St George, Hanover Square; Tate Gallery; National Portrait Gallery; and Kenwood House.

Lawrence, Sir Thomas (1769–1830), painter: Royal Academy; Kenwood House; Sir John Soane's Museum; National Gallery, Wallace Collection, Tate Gallery; and Victoria and Albert Museum.

Leighton, Frederick, Lord (1830–96), painter and sculptor: Royal Academy; Leighton House; and Tate Gallery.

Lely, Sir Peter (1618–80), painter: Guildhall; Hampton Court; Ham House; and Kensington Palace.

Lutyens, Sir Edwin (1869–1944), architect: Whitehall, Cenotaph; British Medical Association; Newcastle House, Lincoln's Inn Fields; Midland Bank; and Lutyens House.

Martin ('Mad') John (1789–1854), painter: Tate Gallery.

Millais, Sir John Everett (1829–96), painter: Royal Academy; and Tate Gallery.

Moore, Henry (1898–1986), sculptor: St Stephen Walbrook; St Paul's Cathedral; Kensington Gardens; Kenwood; Battersea Park; New Scotland Yard; Embankment; and Tate Gallery.

Nash, John (1752–1835), architect: Regent Street; Piccadilly; Regent's Park; Park Crescent; Park Square; Sussex House; Chester Terrace; Carlton House Terrace; Trafalgar Square; Buckingham Palace; Royal Mews; Clarence House; Marble Arch; All Souls, Langham Place; Ulster Place; and Haymarket Theatre.

Paxton, Sir Joseph (1801–65), architect: Crystal Palace; Royal Botanic Gardens, Kew; and Chiswick House.

Pennethorne, Sir James (1801–71), architect: Buckingham Palace; Marlborough House, Museum of Mankind; Public Record Office; and Somerset House.

Pugin, Augustus Welby Northmore (1812–52), architect: Houses of Parliament; Southwark Cathedral; and Church of the Immaculate Conception.

Reynolds, Sir Joshua (1723–92), painter: Royal Academy; Apsley House; Ham House; Marble Hill House; Hunterian Museum of Medicine; Victoria and Albert Museum; National Gallery; Wallace Collection; and Kenwood House.

Romney, George (1734–1802), painter: Victoria and Albert Museum; and Kenwood House.

Rossetti, Dante Gabriel (1828–82), painter and poet: Victoria and Albert Museum; Tate Gallery; and National Gallery.

Rubens, Sir Peter Paul (1577–1640), painter: Banqueting House; National Gallery; and Wallace Collection.

Scott, Sir George Gilbert (1811–78), architect: Albert Memorial; Foreign Office; St Pancras Station; Lincoln's Inn; Westminster Abbey; St Margaret's Westminster; and St Michael Cornhill.

Scott, Sir Giles Gilbert (1880–1960), architect, grandson of George: Houses of Parliament; Bankside Power Station; Waterloo Bridge; Guildhall; and Royal Geographical Society.

Shaw, Richard Norman (1831–1912), architect: Bedford Park, Chiswick; Chelsea Embankment; and Royal Geographical Society.

Smirke, Sir Robert (1781–1867), architect: British Museum; Inner Temple; Somerset House; Custom House; and Royal Opera House.

Soane, Sir John (1753–1837), architect and collector: Sir John Soane's Museum; Bank of England; Chelsea Royal Hospital; Treasury; Westminster Hall; and St Pancras Parish Church.

Street, George Edmund (1824–81), architect: Royal Courts of Justice; and St James the Less, Westminster.

Stubbs, George (1724–1806), painter and etcher: Lincoln's Inn Fields; Tate Gallery; and National Gallery.

Thornhill, Sit James (1675–1734), painter: Greenwich Hospital; Hampton Court; St Paul's Cathedral; and Westminster Abbey.

Turner, Joseph Mallord William (1775–1851), painter: Tate Gallery; Sir John Soane's Museum; and National Gallery.

Walpole, Horace (1717–97), collector, writer and connoisseur: Strawberry Hill; and Lincoln's Inn.

Watts, George Frederick (1817–1904), painter and sculptor: Postman's Park; St Botolph, Aldersgate; Lincoln's Inn; Kensington Gardens; and St James the Less.

Webb, Sir Aston (1849–1930), architect: Buckingham Palace; The Mall; Victoria and Albert Museum; and St Bartholomew the Great.

Webb, John (1611–72), architect, pupil of Wren: Whitehall Palace; and Greenwich Palace.

William III (1689–1702) and **Mary** (1689–94): Hampton Court; Kensington Palace; Chelsea Royal Hospital; Greenwich Hospital; and Chapel Royal.

Wren, Christopher (1632–1723), architect, mathematician and astonomer: Hampton Court, Marlborough House; St James's Palace; Kensington Palace; Chelsea Royal Hospital; Monument; Tower of London; Greenwich Hospital; St Paul's Cathedral; St Stephen Walbrook; St Peter Cornhill; St Michael Cornhill; St Mary Abchurch; St Magnus the Martyr; St Dunstan-in-the-East; St Olave, Jewry; St Edmund the King; St Margaret Pattens; St Vedast; St Mary-le-Bow; St Margaret, Lothbury; St Lawrence, Jewry; St Anne and St Agnes; St Bride, Fleet Street; St Martin-within-Ludgate; St Clement, Danes; Lincoln's Inn Church; St Andrew's, Holborn; St James's Piccadilly; St Mary Aldermary; St James Garlickhythe; and St Andrew-by-the-Wardrobe.

Wyatt, Benjamin (1775–1850), architect: Duke of York's Column; Lancaster House; White's Club; Apsley House; and Drury Lane Theatre.

Wyatt, James (1746–1813), architect: Banqueting House; Westminster Abbey; and Royal Military Academy.

OPENING TIMES

Most churches in central London are open from 10.00 until 4.00 or 5.00, but they may be open only for services on Sundays. Cemeteries are liable to be closed to visitors during services. Hours of opening can be shorter during the winter. The royal parks are generally open from 9.00 until sunset. Most museums and public buildings are closed on Bank Holidays and Sunday mornings.

Apsley House, see Museum, Wellington.
Banqueting House, Whitehall, Tuesday to Saturday 10.00–5.30; Sunday 2.00–5.30.
Bethnal Green Museum of Childhood, see under Museums.
British Library, see under Museum, British.
British Museum, see under Museums.
Carlyle's House, Cheyne Row, Wednesday to Saturday 11.00–5.00; Sunday 2.00–5.00
Central Criminal Court, during legal terms, Old Bailey, Monday to Friday 10.30–1.00 and 2.00–6.00.
Chelsea Physic Garden, Swan Walk, mid-April to mid-October, Wednesday and Sunday 2.00–5.00.
Chelsea Royal Hospital, Royal Hospital Road, Monday to Saturday 10.00–12.00 and 2.00–4.00; April to September Sunday 2.00–4.00.
Chiswick House, Burlington Lane, Chiswick, April to September daily 9.30–6.30; October to March Monday to Saturday 9.30–4.00.
Courtauld Institute Galleries, see under Galleries.
Dickens's House, Doughty Street, Monday to Saturday 9.30–5.00.
Dr Johnson's House May to September Monday to Saturday 11.00–5.30, October to April 11.00–5.00.
Freud Museum, see under Museums
Galleries
   Courtauld Institute, Somerset House, Strand, Monday to Saturday 10.00–6.00.

Hayward, South Bank, during exhibitions, Monday to Wednesday 10.00–8.00; Thursday to Saturday 10.00–6.00; Sunday 12.00–6.00.
National, Trafalgar Square, Monday to Saturday 10.00–6.00; Sunday 2.00–6.00; June to August Wednesdays until 8.00.
National Portrait, St Martin's Place, Monday to Friday 10.00–5.00; Saturday 10.00–6.00, Sunday 2.00–6.00.
Queen's, Buckingham Palace Road, Tuesday to Saturday 10.30–5.00; Sunday 2.00–5.00.
Serpentine, Kensington Gardens, Summer 10.00–6.00; Winter 10.00–4.00.
Tate Millbank, Monday to Saturday 10.00–5.50; Sunday 2.00–5.50.
Geffrye Museum, see under Museums
Geological Museum, see under Museums
Gray's Inn, see under Inns of Court
Guildhall, Gresham Street, Monday to Saturday 10.00–5.00; May to September Sunday 10.00–5.00.
Ham House, Ham Street, Richmond, Tuesday to Sunday 11.00–5.00.
Hampton Court Palace, Hampton Court Road, Hampton, April to September daily 9.30–6.00; October to March daily 9.30–4.00.
Hayward Gallery, see under Galleries
Highgate Cemetery
   East: April to September 10.00–5.00, October to March 10.00–4.00 (unless otherwise

indicated to the London Tourist Board, tel. 071 730 3488)
   West: By guided tour only: April to September 12.00, 2.00 and 4.00; October to March 12.00, 2.00 and 3.00. October to March 10.00–3.00.
Houses of Parliament Visitors may attend debates when Parliament is sitting (mid-October to July except for recesses at Christmas and Easter):
   Commons Monday to Thursday from 4.15, Friday from 11.00
   Lords Monday to Wednesday from 2.30, Thursday from 3.00 and Friday from 11.00
Inner Temple, see under Inns of Court
Inns of Court
   Grays Inn Gardens May to July Monday to Friday 12.00–2.00; August to September Monday to Friday 9.30–2.00.
   Middle Temple Hall Monday to Saturday 10.00–noon, 3.00–4.30.
   Inner Temple Hall Monday to Friday 10.00–11.30, 2.30–4.00.
   Lincoln's Inn Garden Monday to Friday 9.30–5.00.
Keats House, Well Walk, Monday to Friday 2.00–6.00, Saturday 10.00–5.00, Sunday 2.00–5.00.
Kensington Palace, Kensington Gardens, Monday to Saturday 9.00–5.00, Sunday 1.00–5.00.
Kenwood House, Hampstead Heath, April to September daily 10.00–6.00; October, February and March 10.00–5.00; November to January 10.00–4.00.
Kew Palace, Royal Botanic Gardens, Kew, April to September daily 11.00–5.30.
Law Courts, see under Royal Courts of Justice
Lincoln's Inn, see under Inns of Court
Marble Hill House, Richmond Road, Twickenham, closed Fridays; February to October 10.00–5.00; November to January 10.00–4.00
Middle Temple, see under Inns of Court

Museums:

Bethnal Green Museum of Childhood, Cambridge Heath Road, Monday to Thursday and Saturday 10.00–6.00; Sunday 2.30–6.00.

British, Great Russell Street, Monday to Saturday, 10.00–5.00; Sunday 2.30–6.00.

Freud, Maresfield Gardens, Wednesday to Sunday, 12.00–5.00.

Geffrye, Kingsland Road, Tuesday to Saturday 10.00–5.00; Sunday 2.00–5.00.

Geological, Exhibition Road, Monday to Saturday, 10.00–5.00; Sunday 1.00–6.00.

of London, London Wall, Tuesday to Saturday, 10.00–6.00; Sunday 2.00–6.00.

of Mankind, Burlington Gardens, Monday to Saturday, 10.00–5.00; Sunday 2.30–6.00.

National Maritime, Romney Road, late March to late October Monday to Saturday 10.00–6.00, Sunday 2.00–6.00; late October to late March Monday to Saturday 10.00–5.00; Sunday 2.00–5.00.

Natural History, Cromwell Road, Monday to Saturday 10.00–6.00; Sunday 1.00–6.00

Science, Exhibition Road, Monday to Saturday 10.00–6.00; Sunday 1.00–6.00.

Sir John Soane's, Lincoln's Inn Fields, Tuesday to Saturday 10.00–5.00.

Victoria and Albert, Cromwell Road, Monday to Saturday 10.00–5.50; Sunday 2.30–5.50.

Wellington Museum, Apsley House, Piccadilly, Tuesday to Sunday 11.00–4.50.

National Gallery, see under Galleries.

National Maritime Museum, see under Museums.

National Portrait Gallery, see under Galleries.

Natural History Museum, see under Museums.

Old Bailey, see Central Criminal Court.

Old Royal Observatory, Greenwich, Greenwich Park, April to October Monday to Saturday 10.00–6.00, Sunday 2.00–6.00; November to March Monday to Saturday 10.00–5.00, Sunday 2.00–5.00.

Royal Botanic Gardens, Kew, Kew Green, February daily 9.30–5.00; March, September to October 9.30–6.00; April to August Monday to Saturday 9.30–6.30, Sunday and Bank Holidays 9.30–8.00; November to January 9.30–4.00.

Royal Courts of Justice, Strand, during legal terms Monday to Friday 10.30–1.00 and 2.00–4.00.

Public Records Office, Chancery Lane, Monday to Friday 9.30–4.45.

Queen's Gallery, see under Galleries.

Royal Academy of Arts, Burlington House, Piccadilly, daily 10.00–6.00.

Royal Mews, Wednesday and Thursday 2.00–4.00.

St Paul's Cathedral, daily 8.00–6.00.

Science Museum, see under Museums

Serpentine Gallery, see under Galleries

Sir John Soane's Museum, see under Museums

Southwark Cathedral, Borough High Street, daily 8.30–6.00.

Syon House, Syon Lane, Easter to October Sunday to Thursday 12.00–5.00.

Tate Gallery, see under Galleries

Tower of London, March to October Monday to Saturday 9.30–5.00, Sunday 2.00–5.00; November to February Monday to Saturday 9.30–4.00.

Victoria and Albert Museum, see under Museums

Wallace Collection, Hertford House, Portman Square, Monday to Saturday 10.00–5.00, Sunday 2.00–5.00.

Wellington Museum, see under Museums

Westminster Abbey, Broad Sanctuary, Monday, Tuesday and Thursday to Saturday 8.00–6.00; Wednesdays 8.00–7.45; Sunday between services.

Glossary of Terms

....

Apse Projecting part of church, usually semicircular and vaulted, at end of choir, aisles or nave.

Baroque Artistic and architectural style prevalent in the seventeenth and eighteenth centuries, characterized by exaggerated windows, columns, mouldings, etc., in a desire to break up the surface of the wall.

Caryatid Draped female figure used to support an ENTABLATURE.

Catacomb Subterranean cemetery with galleries and recesses for tombs.

Column Cylindrical or tapering pillar, usually consisting of a base, shaft and capital, supporting an ENTABLATURE, or standing alone as a monument.

Composite Order Roman order of architecture, combining CORINTHIAN and IONIC features.

Corinthian Order The lightest most slender and most ornate of the Greek architectural orders, featuring a fluted column and an upturned bell-shaped capital adorned with acanthus leaves.

Doric Order Oldest of Greek architectural orders, with a fluted, baseless shaft and a moulded capital.

Entablature Flat architectural member supported on a colonnade, on which the roof rests.

Gothic Architectural style widespread in western Europe from the late twelfth to early sixteenth century, notable for the use of pointed arches, rib vaults and flying buttresses.

Greek cross Cross with upright and transverse arms of equal length, intersecing at mid-point.

Ionic Order Light, graceful Greek architectural order with slender proportions and spiral volutes on the corners of the capitals.

Latin cross Cross with long upright and shorter transverse arms, interesting above mid-point.

Pilaster Square or rectangular pillar projecting from a wall. Like COLUMNS, pilasters appear in all the architectural orders and carry entablatures. Because they are attached to the wall, they have little practical architectural function.

Renaissance Italian revival of classically inspired art, which took root in the fourteenth century and spread to the rest of western Europe; European style of art and architecture characteristic of this period, conventionally distinguished as Early, High and Late Renaissance.

Rococo Ornate, often fanciful, style of decoration and architecture originating in France, prevalent in the eighteenth century.

Romanesque Style of architecture and painting, prevalent in Italy and western Europe from the tenth to the thirteenth centuries, featuring round arches, barrel and groin vaults, decorative arcades and profuse carved ornament.

Stucco Very fine plaster used for decoration of walls, ceilings, etc.

Tuscan Order Roman architectural order, simple and plain in style.

Further Reading

....

Barker, Felix *Highgate Cemetery, Victorian Valhalla*

Betjeman, John, *Betjeman's London*

—— *The City of London Churches*

Davies, Hunter *A Walk Around London's Parks*, 1983

Ebel, Suzanne and Impey, Doreen *London's Riverside*, 1975

Essex-Lopresti, Dr *Exploring the Regent's Canal*

Jones, Edward and Woodward, Christopher *The Architecture of London*

Pevsner, Nikolaus *London (The City and Westminster)*

——*London (excluding the City and Westminster)*

Rasmussen, Steen Eiler *London, A Unique City*

Rouse, A. L. *The Tower of London*

Saunder, Ann *The Art and Architecture of London*, 1984

Service, Alastair *The Architects of London*

The Time Out Guide to London

Weinred, Ben and Hibbert, Christopher (eds) *The London Encyclopedia*, 1983.

Index

....

References to illustrations appear in italics, after the text references.